Gael Turnbull (1928-2004) was born in Edinburgh, but grew up in Jarrow and in Blackpool, before emigrating to Winnipeg at the outbreak of the war with his father and mother, respectively a Scottish Baptist Minister and an American of Swedish descent. He returned to England in 1944 to complete his schooling and then to study Natural Sciences at Cambridge University. After rejoining his family in North America, he studied for an MD at the University of Pennsylvania and then, in 1952, became a GP and anaesthetist at Iroquois Falls Hospital in northern Ontario as well as providing medical assistance at logging camps in the area. There followed a short stay in London (1955-56), and a position as anaethetist at Ronkswood Hospital in Worcester until 1958, followed by a similar position at the Ventura County hospital in California. He returned to Worcester in 1964, to avoid the possibility of being sent to Vietnam as a medical orderly. He was to work as a general practitioner and anaesthetist until his retirement in 1989, whereupon he returned to live in Edinburgh.

An independent figure, he was central to the early transatlantic poetic contacts which were to have a transforming effect on many poets in Britain in the 1950s and 1960s. Frequently collected and anthologised, his own poetry was deeply personal and owed little to any particular school, although it is fair to say that his admiration for the work of William Carlos Williams, another poet-doctor, never left him and was an early driving force behind the discovery, and the maturing, of his own poetic voice.

D1232622

Also by Gael Turnbull

Trio (Contact Press, Montreal, 1954)
The Knot in the Wood & fifteen other poems (Revision Press, London, 1955)
Bjarni Spike-Helgi's Son and other poems (Origin Press, Ashland, Mass., 1956)
A Libation (The Poet, Glasgow, 1957)
With Hey, Ho . . . (Migrant Press, Ventura & Worcester, 1961)
To You, I Write (Migrant Press, 1963)
A Very Particular Hill (Wild Hawthorn Press, Edinburgh, 1963)
Twenty Words, Twenty Days (Migrant Press, Birmingham, 1966)
Briefly (Tarasque Press, Nottingham, 1967)
A Trampoline (Cape Goliard Press, London, 1968)
I, Maksoud (Exeter Books N° 19, Exeter, 1969)
Scantlings (Cape Goliard Press, 1970)
Finger Cymbals (Satis, Edinburgh, 1971)
A Random Sapling (Pig Press, Newcastle-upon-Tyne, 1974)
Wulstan (Blue Tunnel, Bradford, 1975)
Residues: Down the Sluice of Time (Grosseteste Press, Pensnett, 1976)
Thronging the Heart (Aggie Weston's, Belper, 1976)
What Makes the Weeds Grow Tall (Five Seasons Press, Hereford, 1978)
If a Glance Could Be Enough (Satis, 1978)
Rain in Wales (Satis, 1981)
Nine Intersections (Circle Press, London, 1982)
Traces (Circle Press, 1983)
A Gathering of Poems 1950-1980 (Anvil Press Poetry, London, 1983)
From the Language of the Heart (Mariscat Press, Glasgow, 1983,
                              Gnomon Press, Frankfort, KY, 1985)
Circus (Five Seasons Press, 1984)
A Year and a Day (Mariscat Press, 1985)
Spaces (Satis, 1986)
Coelacanth (Coelacanth Press, Dublin, 1986)
A Winter Journey (Pig Press, Durham, 1987)
As From a Fleece (Circle Press, 1990)
While Breath Persist (The Porcupine's Quill, Erin, Ontario, 1992)
To the Tune of Annie Laurie (Akros Publications, Kirkcaldy, 1995)
For Whose Delight (Mariscat Press, 1995)
A Rattle of Scree (Akros Publications, 1997)
Transmutations (Shoestring Press, Nottingham, 1997)
Etruscan Reader 1 (with Helen Macdonald and Nicholas Johnson)
          (Etruscan Books, Buckfastleigh, 1997)
Traces (Objectif Press, London, 1998)
Amorous Greetings (Vennel Press, Staines, 1998)
More Amorous Greetings (Longhouse, Green River, VT, 1999)
Might a Shape of Words (Mariscat Press, 2000)
Dividings (Mariscat Press, Edinburgh, 2004)

GAEL TURNBULL

There are Words
Collected Poems

Shearsman Books
in association with
Mariscat Press

Published in the United Kingdom in 2006 by
Shearsman Books Ltd
58 Velwell Road
Exeter EX4 4LD

in association with Mariscat Press, 10 Bell Place, Edinburgh EH3 5HT.

ISBN-10   0-907562-89-2

ISBN-13   978-0-907562-89-4

Acknowledgements
Previously uncollected poems were originally published in the following journals, pamphlets and anthologies: *The Canadian Forum, Chapman, CIV/n, Le coin de table, Combustion, Construction, Critical Survey, The Dark Horse, Essence Press, The Glasgow Magazine, Hummingbird, Meanjin, Montemora, New Writing Scotland, Oasis, Object Permanence, Painted Spoken, Palantir, The Paper, Penniless Press, The Poet, Poetry Review, Poetry Salzburg Review, The Red Wheelbarrow, The Scotsman, Shearsman, Zed₂O; Making Connections: A Festschrift for Matt Simpson*, 1996; *News for the Ear: A Homage to Roy Fisher* (ed. Robinson & Sheppard, Stride, 2000); *'Unknown is Best': A Celebration of Edwin Morgan at Eighty* (Mariscat Press & The Scottish Poetry Library, 2000); *The Storey's Story* (ed. Glass, 2004); *The Hand That Sees: Poems for the Quincentenary of the Royal College of Surgeons of Edinburgh* (ed. Conn, 2005). Most of the remaining poems were previously collected in the publications listed opposite the title page.

Thanks also to Aggie Weston's, Akros Publications, Anvil Press Poetry, Blue Tunnel, Cape Goliard, Circle Press, Coelacanth Press, Contact Press, Essence Press, Etruscan Books, Five Seasons Press, Gnomon Press, Grosseteste Review, Longhouse, Mariscat Press, Objectif Press, Origin, Pig Press, The Poet, The Porcupine's Quill, Revision Press, Satis, Shoestring Press, Tarasque Press, Vennel Press and Wild Hawthorn Press for supporting the author throughout his writing career.

The publisher gratefully acknowledges financial assistance from
Arts Council England.

Contents

Trio (1954)

Lines for a Bookmark   23
Try Again   23
To the Point for Once   24
Post-Mortem   25
Socrates   26
Lumber Camp Railway   27
Nansen and Johansen   29
Twentieth Century   30
Citizen   31
Aspects   31
Love Poem 1   32
Love Poem 2   33
Inscription for a Mirror   34
Counsel   34
Lines for a Cynic   35
Ballade   35
A Landscape and a Kind of Man   36
Epitaph   37
In a strange city   37
Industrial Valley   39
Nightpiece, Pittsburgh   39
Excavation   40
May   41
A Poem is a Pearl   41
A Song   42

The Knot in the Wood (1955)

Thanks   43
Enough   43
If you couldn't laugh   44
The dog next door   44
The Moon   45
In Memory of George Orwell   45
Boys in the Street   46
Dawn over the City   46
The Sensualist   47
He may wander far   47
The Drunk   48

A Dying Man 48
The Mistake 49
And what if 49
The Words 50
If He Sings It 50

Bjarni, Spike-Helgi's Son & other poems (1956)
Bjarni Spike-Helgi's Son 51
Gunnar, from his burial mound 54
Valgard, called the guileful, to his son Mord 55
Thorir of Garth, and Asdis, Grettir's mother 56
Gudrun, old and blind, to Bolli, her son 59
The Author, to Bjarni Herjulfsson 62
An Irish Monk on Lindisfarne, about 650 AD 63
A Painting of Beatrice Sforza 66
Suzanne Bloch in a Billiard Room 67

A Libation (1957)
A Libation 68
A Fish-hook 69
Black Spruce, Northern Ontario 70
You Said I Should 71

Early Poem collected in *A Gathering of Poems 1950-1980* (1983)
The Suicide 72

Uncollected (1949-1960)
Derelict, City Morgue 73
June Nineteenth – Rosenbergs executed – Riots in East Berlin 74
The Octopus Ride 75
A Portrait 76
The Sun 77
The Look 78
A scar closes a wound 79
An Apology 80
A Chorus (of sorts) for Tess 81
For Gaston 82

With Hey, Ho . . . (1961)
Conundrum Blues 83
One in a Multitude 83

Driving (A Litany)   84
Two Tunes (for Roy)   85
A Round   86
Spiritual Researches   87
Well . . . (for Ian)   87
Now That April's Here   88

To You I Write (1963)
The Wind   89
And what I thought   89
A Beast   90
They have taken   91
A Letter, of Sorts   92
Perhaps if I begin   98
A Voice, Voices, Speaking   104
Is there anything left   107
All right   109
Don't Know Blues   110
I'm sorry   111
She'll come   112
How far?   112
To think here   113
A Well Known Road   113
I would speak of him   114
So the heart   115
Yes, sunshine   115
A Breath of Autumn   116
For an Anniversary   117
He and She   117
I look into   118
You and I   120
To be shaken   121

A Very Particular Hill (1963)
A Hill   122
La Sainte Face (a painting by Rouault)   124
At Mareta   125
The Mind Turns   127
A Western   128
At the Mineshaft of a Ghost Town in S. California   129
Death Valley   130
George Fox, from his Journals   131

Twenty Words, Twenty Days (1966)   133

Briefly (1967)
    Briefly   153
    Done speaking   153
    However   154
    Simply   154
    Be So   155
    The ever-presence   155
    Make some   155
    A song   156
    Where   156
    Not piecework   156
    Thighs gripping   157
    Two Jibes   157
    A blindfold   158
    Rightly   158
    Didn't ask   158

A Trampoline (1968)
    One word   159
    Homage to Jean Follain   160
    Sunday Afternoon   161
    The Priests of Paris   162
    "Les Toits"   163
    Victoria Regina Imperatrix   164
    Thoughts on the 183rd Birthday of J.M.W. Turner 165
    Six Fancies
        A Fragment of Truth   166
        Learning to Breathe   167
        A Wild Joy   168
        An Accident   169
        No Instructions   169
        The scratching sound   170
    A Case   171
    The Sierra Nevada   173
    For a Friend   174
    An Actress   175
    A kite   176
    By Auction in a Marquee in the Grounds   177

I, Maksoud (1969)

I, Maksoud   179
A sea-stone   179
For a Jazz Pianist   180
Riel   181
John Bunyan: of Grace   182
Hommage a Cythera   183
After Catullus   184
A Song   185
Walls   186

Scantlings (1970)

It's dark   193
Seven Snapshots, Northern Ontario   195
Six Country Pieces   197
In the silence   199
Maria   199
A Girl   199
Inventory   200
Cigolando   200
For Us: An Invocation and a Processional   201

Uncollected (1961-1970)

A Sea Story   204

Finger Cymbals (1974)

Five/Four Time   206
At Witley Court   207
A Meagre Song   208
Dandelion Seeds   209
Lake   211
Amber Toad   213
For a Chinese Flute   215
There is no Why   216
Where the Wind Blows   217
Mid February, Snow on the Wind   218

A Random Sapling (1974)

A random sapling   219
A Regret   219
Went to Hell   220

How Could I Not 220
A textured mist 221
Happiest 221

Residues (1976) 222

If a Glance Could Be Enough (1978)
Knarsdale 246
There's more 247
The Borders Revisited 248
Could it be 249
You're right 249
It's been 250
The Last Fool: Berkeley Churchyard 251
Watching a Burning House at Night 251
Aurora 252
If a Glance Could Be Enough 253

A Gathering of Poems 1950-1980 (1983)
A Lamb 256
Edge of Air 257
Waves on the Shingle 258
It is there 259
Witley Court Revisited 260
A Reflecting Telescope 261
Never 262
The small change 263
Remake 263
Keeping 264
I am the Scythe 264
Scarcely I speak 265

Uncollected (1971-1980)
Time is 272
You are 273
Town and City 274
Some Resonances and Speculations 275

Rain in Wales (1981)
Babylon 280
Ballad 281

Daft about   282
Everyone was there   283
How I Did My Bit for Peace   284
The Galvanised Dustman   285
You and I   286
Rain in Wales   287
What Makes the Weeds Grow Tall   288
Wulstan   290

From the Language of the Heart (1983-5)
A blind musician   292
As kelp   292
Love is   293
The dissipations   293
The Unwavering Sun   294
The seeking   294
It Can Happen   295
It was   295
No   296
As the wind   297
And I Think it Yours   298
A Birth   299
The Ruin   300
First loves   300
It is not   301
How much hurt   301
If I take a stone   302
Even the Sun   303
These rings   304
A Winter Wedding   304
Your Hands, Their Touch   305

Spaces (1986)
Beginnings   306
Coal Mine   306
A Wedding Ring   307
The Fodder   307
New Year   308
What may be   308
For Shari   309
From the Sanskrit   309

Spaces   310
A Marriage   310
Edinburgh   311
A stye   311
Butterfly   312
Accounts   312
A Last Poem   313

from A Winter Journey (1987)
It is late afternoon and already dark   314
A wind from the north   315
Into the chasm   316
Hour of the Wolf   317
A child lets go of its mother's hand   318

Uncollected Poems (1981-1990)
Wherever   319
A Tight-Rope Act   319
A Trapeze Act   320
A Sun Dial   321
Garioch Dead   321
Staples   322
Homage to Jean Tinguely   323
Great Aunt   324
Even One Day   325
The Elements   326
The Platitudes   327
A Place Called Gefryn   328
Something So Singular   329
A Riddle for Jill   330

While Breath Persist (1992)
A Racing Walker   331
A Clown   331
The Slater   332
As from a Kiln   333
At MacDiarmid's Grave   333
On the Somme   334
Almost Lost Poem   334
Takings   334
By the Tweed   335

A Voltige Act   335
Mornese   336
Homage to Cid Corman   336
Yes (1)   337
Yes (2)   337
Homage to Edwin Morgan   338
Beneath   338
All the Blue: From the Director's Book of Josiah Spode   339
To Tell Us   341

To the Tune of Annie Laurie (1995)
To the Tune of Annie Laurie   342
One Hundred Years On   343
Information   344
'The Gates of Eden'   345
The Scotch Asphodel (Tofieldia palustris)   346
"A Handkerchief with a Moral Purpose . . . "   346
Calvinism   346
Either way (after Bridget Riley)   347
Tea leaves   347
Sky Lights   347
T'time in the Caucasus   348
A Dictionary   348
Dark Ages carving of a creature . . .   348
Poetics (Genesis I, v.3)   349
The Parthenon   349
No Answer   349
Edinburgh   350
Morningside Road   350
With Thanks and Homage to That Critic   351
The Poetry Reading Poem   352
Going South   352

For Whose Delight (1995)
For Whose Delight   353
Nowhere   354
The Daughter of Alasdair Ruadh   354
Comic Relief   355
Buzzard   356
A Cairn   357
Perhaps   357

A Cat   358
There are words   359
A Poem Containing   360
Though we must have coals (1813)   361
When I Write to You: The Diapason Closing   364
Impellings   366

A Rattle of Scree (1997)
Also   384
Bass Rock   384
Not Sand   384
Gone   385
National Trust   385
After   386
Wreaths   386
An Òran (The Song)   387
Near Sloc Dubh, South Uist   387
When I Said   388
In Memoriam Norman MacCaig   388
Definitions   389
For You, Once Enemy   389
Whin   390
December Leaves   391
To all the Gods   392
Lifetimes   393

Etruscan Reader 1 (1997)
A Good Warfare   394
Erskine of Linlathen   395
The Real News   396
The Ballad of Rillington Place   397

Transmutations (1997)
There is   399
"Why is   399
Burning juniper   399
They are everywhere   400
Not only   400
A very ingenious mechanism   400
A sparrow   401
It's a stubborn beast   401
This fear   401

Estuaries   401
As a stone skittering   402
Started . . .   402
This craving   402
Surprised in a mirror   403
As recently as   403
Clutter   403
At the university   404
"Did you really   404
The inscription states   404
Last curtain down   405
Just as I discover   405
Lappings of day   405
A long beat   405
An idiot child   406
Heard once   406
For months, determined   406
When I said   407
While looking   407
In the corner of   407
He hears that   408
Anywhere they can be found   408
An old man sitting   409

Might a Shape of Words, & other transmutations (2000)

Might a shape   410
The sea   410
'It's because   410
Scarcely   411
Always so sure   411
The pitch of a voice   411
Wandering onto a beach   412
Deciding   412
Perhaps   412
A young mother   413
A boy is amazed   413
She said   413
It was as if   414
A man wakes   414
Every evening   414
'It's best we don't   415

Reading another man's 415
Going to school 415
Checking 416
Taken severely ill 416
A woman goes 417
A man stands waving 417
After many years 418
A woman has 418
Many years 418
Awakening 416
Somewhere between 419
Awakening 419
A man stops 420
You won't find the name 421
He had rehearsed 421

Uncollected Transmutations (1995-2003)

At least once 421
An evening of conversation 421
In my dream 421
My clothes fit. 422
A bird 422
He explained 422
Searching through 422
As it happened 423
He was someone 423
The only name 423
Walking 424
He had desired her 424
Home again 424
Standing here 425
The worst 425
Unimaginable 425
A spirited lady 425
The girls 426
If you ask 426
Retarded 426
When I pointed out 427
A snowstorm 427
At certain moments 427
Wandering into 428
He wishes 428

Leaving himself   428
He reported   429
A memoir   429
Remarking   430
It can happen   430
You can still see it there   430

Uncollected (1990-1999)
The Kid   431
William McTaggart   431
A Bit Part: from Chekhov   432
This Rigmarole of Going On   433
85th Birthday Greetings
          in Terms of a Public Monument   434
Nothing   434
For André Breton One Hundred Years from his Birth   435
Islands   436
The Words   438
A Perception of Ferns   439
The Nicing   440
A letter from   441
Or So We Are Told   442
A Little Kindling for John Christie   443
We celebrate   443
All Those Good Fellows   444
Sureties   445

Uncollected Texturalist Poems
Refractories / The efficiency of . . .   447
A Lady of Pleasure, The Netherbow,
          Seventeen Hundred and Something   448
Better than was   449
From the Equator to the Pole: A Figure for the Earth   450
Herein described   451
Though I Have Met with Hardship   453
Jeffrey to Cockburn 28 June 1832   454
Do not be deterred   455
How in Sundry Sorts They Were Shattered   456
In Reference to our Being   457
James Young Simpson: If it is our mission . . .   458
from lazy blue flowers   459

Transits: A Triptych (unfinished draft, 2004)   460

Uncollected (2000-2004)
   The going   468
   For an Old Friend, Beyond the Grave   469
   National Poetry Day   469
   Observed at N.E. Corner of Bank Street and Royal Mile   470
   The Great Grand-Daughter of Sine Reisedeach
                  Reports to her Cousin in Australia   471
   Five Resonances / Echoes from Apollinaire   472
   These Transits / All That's Given / What's Here   474
   Since   475
   Not to Forget   476
   Do you . . .   477
   Into Harbour   478

Some Afterwords by the Author   479

Author's Notes to the poems   482

Editorial Notes   485

Index of Titles   491

Introduction

Sorting out the papers of someone close who has recently died arouses, as might easily be imagined, a mixture of emotions – great loss and sadness, but also the pleasure of happy memories and, in my case, a voyage of discovery. Gael had lived over two-thirds of his life before we met, so I had not shared his early writing and publishing, nor the literary friendships which were so important to him, although he had, of course, talked about them. Since his death I have catalogued over a thousand books from his poetry library, ranging from small fragile booklets from the fifties and sixties to the glossier publications of today's up-and-coming young poets. Among them was the book given to him by William Carlos Williams, whom Gael greatly admired, to commemorate their only meeting. By then an old man, Williams had written in it, in a shaky hand, and tucked into it was a letter from his wife Freda, saying how much they had enjoyed the visit. Even in the week he died, a letter arrived for Gael from a little-known young poet whose work he had just discovered, and whom he had visited a couple of weeks before. It was truly a life-long passion.

A few lines in a diary from 1966 sum up how Gael felt about poetry: 'my real work is that of finding some way to write a few poems – all else is incidental'. That does not mean that he did not wholeheartedly fulfil his roles as a family man, doctor and friend, but writing was of immense importance to him from the age of about fifteen and continued to be so until he died. He kept commonplace books throughout his life and wrote to poets whose work he enjoyed, often long before their poetry was recognised by others, establishing life long friendships. He was a keen correspondent and kept all the letters he received, from poets as diverse as Basil Bunting and Ian Hamilton Finlay, Cid Corman and Robert Creeley, amongst many others. He sent new poems to friends for their comments and had a remarkable ability to be honest about the work of others without offending them.

It has been my enjoyable task to gather up Gael's poems from the wide variety of magazines and pamphlets stashed in his study, for this volume. There were mimeographed sheets stapled together, like *Contact* and *Combustion*, published in Toronto in the 1950s. In one a Gael Turnbull poem is sandwiched between poems by Allen Ginsberg and Jack Kerouac. There were piles of Scottish publications containing his recent work, and there was everything in between. Having published a little magazine himself, he believed in encouraging others. I am happy that his letters, papers and most of his poetry library are now housed in a Special Collection in the National Library of Scotland.

I have also been in a position to check the various published versions of his work, so that the latest revision is the one which appears here. Gael often referred to himself as a 're-arranger of words' and sometimes he went on re-arranging them long after a poem was published, if he wasn't entirely happy with it. He was always exploring new forms, sometimes going back to an earlier idea which he had put in his 'compost heap' having been unable to find the right way to use it at the time.

Gael's wish was that his poetry should speak for itself – he saw no need for his photograph on a cover or a biographical note, although he agreed to go along with the convention. He used to say that poetry should be published anonymously so that the poem could be judged for itself and not the name associated with it. That is not how the world works, but I hope, as he would, that these collected poems will indeed speak for themselves.

Jill Turnbull
March, 2006

Publisher's Note

There are two obvious ways to approach the compilation of a *Collected Poems* such as this: order the poems chronologically, or place them in the context of their original publication, thus making a 'Collected Books'. Dates for Gael Turnbull's poems are often impossible to ascertain and, in any event, as Jill Turnbull observes in her Introduction, Gael was an inveterate reviser of his own work, which tends to distort the chronology. In view of this, we opted for a 'Collected Books' approach, but with one major difference: the most recent revised version of each poem would be used, albeit placed in the order of its original publication. Where the original text has been replaced by a later revision, sources have been given in the Notes at the end of the book. We have thus outlined Gael Turnbull's publishing career through a large number of small-press publications and a few more substantial volumes. The few exclusions from this survey are: (a) private publications – small editions of the author's own work, intended largely for circulation amongst friends; (b) the late *Amorous Greetings* chapbooks which, although delightful, seem more at home in their original environment; (c) translations, including *Dividings*, which was published posthumously and was still in print at the time this *Collected* was published; and (d) one significant volume – *A Winter Journey* (1987) – which has been excluded in accordance with the author's wishes, although six poems from that volume have been preserved: one which had already appeared in a previous collection, and five which the author subsequently collected in *While Breath Persist* and *Etruscan Reader 1*. The prose journal *A Year and a Day* (1985) was also considered to lie outside the natural bounds of this compilation.

Uncollected poems have been assigned to the decade of their composition, in so far as this could be safely ascertained, and have been placed after the last publication from that decade: thus the uncollected poems from the 1950s appear after *A Libation*. Approximately 70-80 pages of uncollected work have been left out of the final volume, where we felt that the poems did not merit inclusion in a major retrospective such as this, or where their function (performance pieces, for instance, or occasional poems) seemed to make them unsuited to the book. It remains possible that some of this work will see the light of day in other forms. The spelling in poems that originally appeared in North American publications has been anglicised for this edition; obvious spelling errors in the original editions have also been corrected.

The contents of this volume have been assembled with the advice of Jill Turnbull – who was able to provide photocopies, typescripts and obscure publications, as well as variants of many of the poems – and of Hamish Whyte at Mariscat Press, who published several collections of the author's work and knew the author well. It needs also to be said that some of the poems included here had been intended by the author for a volume called *Time is a Fisherman*, a large Selected Poems that had been scheduled for publication in 2005 by Etruscan Books. Letters to, and notes for, Nicholas Johnson – Etruscan's publisher – have helped clarify several issues in the compilation of this much larger volume.

Tony Frazer
March, 2006

Lines for a Bookmark

You who read . . .
May you seek
As you look;
May you keep
What you need;
May you care
What you choose;
And know here
In this book
Something strange,
Something sure,
That will change
You and be yours.

Try Again

"Poetry New York" it said
On the mail box and ahead
Up three half-lit flights I groped
To the farthest door and hoped
That in New York at last I'd found
Poetry; but at the sound
Of each knock I gave, there came
Echoes only back, the same
Appropriately hollow rhyme
Answering me every time.

To the Point for Once

I made one cry of terror
That day upon the lake
And it had an earnest sound,
When I was no longer able
And thought that I must drown.
O that was an honest shout
When the dark came up beneath me
And I saw the light go out:
O I loved the sunshine dearly
When the water bubbled close about my mouth.

Post-Mortem

Death is easy and without regret,
Laid out here on a marble table.
The limbs relaxed in a formal pattern
And the eyeballs upward in a vulgar stare.

Here lie the tools and the map of the battle,
The ditches dug, the abandoned weapons –
After the confusion and bewildered exile,
Ridiculously drowning in a single tear.

Here were trumpets, and a penny whistle.
A cathedral organ with the stops full out
The drum of boredom, and the foolish giggle,
The weeping lover, and the coward's shout.

Her world contracted in simple stages:
Friends, then family; several, then one;
A home, then house; a room, then walls;
And a last yellow curtain to obscure the sun.

Between two sheets she measured her body,
A desperate journey in the sweat of her bed,
Exploring the kingdom that she took for granted,
Memorising sorrow while the nurses chattered.

Time became a zig-zag on a hidden chart,
Framing each gesture as she tried to explain,
Making weary debate in a hospital bed
Without a jury on recurrent questions
Of the doctor's hope and the body's clamour.

Death is simple and the ultimate joke,
Like a faded wise-crack in that gaping mouth
That swallows all answers. Oh, death is the clown
That covers our face with our photograph.

Socrates

His stubborn decision
to drink the poison
may have shown the extent
of his intellect
but is not my notion
of what is human
and shows the defect
of disinterest

and though his attempt
to be quite detached
may have helped the logic
and been heroic,
it shows contempt
for the man attacked
and takes most of the point
from the argument.

Lumber Camp Railway

Coming down on the rail-car out of that country
That nobody wants except when it's frozen
(Where distance is not the places you go through
But only how long it takes to get there,
And the railway schedule is more important
And about as dependable as the sunshine)
We huddle together in a twilit box
That scuttles like a spider down a thread
(Or a run-away coffin in a haunted cemetery),
Our buttocks numb from jolting and boredom,
Smelling of cigarettes, woodsmoke and underwear,
Talking about alcohol, stupidity and accidents,
In French or English, confused by the rattle.

Travelling like that, I remember one day,
A fox ran out in front on the track
And everyone shouted and hoped we would hit it –
Little black feet like a pomeranian
Triangular face, bronze body, and tail
Like a thistle-down balloon floating gently behind him.
As the engine came on, he could not decide . . .
This side? . . . That side? . . . ridiculously frightened,
Swerving for his life in a flutter of snow.
Jerking his body in spasms of effort,
Then gone in the ditch. An Indian told me:
"The market is low. Fox are hardly worth trapping."

Coming down we belong to nothing about us,
Least of all, the forest (that endures us only
As the ocean endures the impertinent ship)
The arrogant, endless democracy of trees –
Snow-covered spruce, like rugged old kings
With long white hair and moth-eaten beards:
Jackpine, like scarecrows; birch like policemen;

And alders sprouting like nervous children –
Trees, trees, trees, like an unabridged dictionary,
Or crowds from all the city streets of the world
Observing perpetual Armistice Day,
Silent, at attention, waiting for judgement.

Then (like an island with peaks and clouds)
We see the roofs and smoke of the town,
And can hardly remember how long we were gone.
Hours or weeks? The days have slid together
Into the same anonymous blur with the trees.
The rail-car brings us in, like a faithful comet
That has wandered beyond the ring of the planets.
Compelled by the same sure gravity of need,
Back to the fuel oil, and solar comforts of home.

Nansen and Johansen

(86° 14' North, on April 7, 1895)

Daily they toiled across the dunes of snow,
Northward and northward on that twilit sea,
Knowing before they started that their goal
Was but the day of their own turning back,
Expecting only labour and retreat
And lukewarm sweat beneath their frozen clothes,
With only one same flat of empty sky
Above their bent and rime-encrusted heads –
With only one same kind of ice
Before, behind, beneath,
To cover up the darkness of the Arctic Sea.

At night they halted, fed their dogs,
Melted a scoop of snow to drink,
Ate, spoke, and slept; and counted up
How far they might have come that day,
How many miles.

But they did not know that, as they marched
So strictly north, beneath the ice
The ocean moved them southward, just as fast –

And measured by the stars they had not moved at all.

Twentieth Century

It will come. It always has.
And the survivors are the exception.

The midnight departure – the infestation by sirens –
the ebony truncheons – the jagged lights –
the fumbled packing by candle-glow –
the huddled bodies – the standing like cattle –
the nervous tension in the swollen bladder –
the animal faces in uniform, shouting –
the radio gibbering hatred –
the far-off grumble of explosions –
the neighbour weeping – the habit of precaution
and fear, fear, fear in the empty stomach –
and finally
the quivering silence after the accurate volley.

It will all come. Perhaps later.
But sometime. It always has.
And we who escape it for a lifetime
are museum curiosities, pupae in convents,
the lucky permanent children.

Citizen

Leaning back in his chair
Smoking after dinner,
Complaining about taxes,
People and the weather,
He hasn't got the slightest
Reason to consider
That the starving coolie
And the opium vendor
Both subscribe to the club
Of which he's a member.

Aspects

Naked by night
We both must bow
To the same need
As bull and cow,

And clothed by day
We both must go
Into the fields
To reap and sow.

Love Poem 1

I walk away
but cannot really leave you –

    cobwebs tangled in the meadow grass,
    your hair still sets confusion where I look –

        (and all the day
          whatever else I do)

I walk away
but cannot really leave you –

    a moist furrow where the ploughman walks,
    your body still exhales its warmth about me –

    strands of ivy green upon a winter tree,
    your hands still twine themselves about me –

    phrases by a cello that the mind has swallowed,
    your movements still unfurl their touch within me –

    disappearing moths in every shadow,
    the softness of your mouth moves just beyond me –

and though I thrust away all these my senses,
the very gap betrays me back to you –

        (and all the day,
          whatever else I do).

Love Poem 2

You believe in happiness:
To you, happiness is natural –
Like a distant view of evergreens
On a Californian mountain,
Somewhere you set out for
And wake up at in the morning;
(Not without discomfort
And frustration on the journey,
And arguments at breakfast
And insect-bites at night-fall) –
Not something you take lightly,
But can depend on for the future.

I'm suspicious of happiness:
To me, it's an exception –
Like a gleam of sunshine drowning
Behind a Hebridean island
And astonishing the twilight
With gold and magic castles,
That is seen but for an evening;
(And with all the next week . . . ashes
And clouds hiding the ocean
And rain soaked through my jacket) –
Not something that I trust,
But am thankful for in passing.

Inscription for a Mirror

Oh my earnest friend,
to think of all the silly
opinions you defend
and that you would be rid of
if you made an end
to your pious rule
of always contradicting
every apparent fool.

Counsel

(For Some Contemporaries)

Don't rupture yourselves
Tilting against windmills.
They'll fall despite you
If the timber is that rotten.

Better, dig some foundations,
And lay by some fuel,
And study Boethius –
For the ice age is coming.

Lines for a Cynic

A lofty stare. A fat behind.
These guard the opinions of mankind.

"I am hungry." "I have dined."
These summarise the human mind.

Ballade

Oh, yes, I am a nice boy.
   I have charm.
I exude a little joy.
   I do no harm.

Oh, yes, people like me.
   I am a success.
I smile politely.
   I cause no distress.

Oh, yes, you may be confident
   I won't intrude.
No nasty arguments,
   I won't be rude.

Always sympathetic,
   I won't offend.
So understanding,
   Such a dear friend!

A Landscape and a Kind of Man

I say "My Country" but there is not much
That I can hold for certain as my own,
That is that country and none other, such
As always will persist in me –

Only an area upon a map,
Convenient as a place from which to measure;
Only some words that I more often use;
Only some peculiarities I treasure
And that I seek in men and poetry;
Only some assumptions that I did not choose,
Responses inside which I'm trapped,
Some fragments and some gestures such as these;
Only some habits and some history.

Only a landscape that I find
Is a congenial pattern to my eyes,
And that I cannot help but see
Whenever I cast back my mind –
The chequered shadows and the angled lines
Of puckered streets and beetle roofs
In some brick-infested town
Where only the damp cobbles shine,
And slate and soot and sameness blend,
And smoke and cloud have no sure start or end,
Crowded upon the margin of a garrulous sea –

Only the names of some recorded men
Whose kindred I would he – such as Grocyn who,
After he had been teaching
What he had supposed he knew,
In public and before half London,
Admitted he was wrong and tried to start again.

Epitaph

Watching the movements of the eyes about him,
He tried to anticipate – not understand.
He lived by a contrivance of approximations.
'PERHAPS' was the mistake he made when be began.

In a strange city

In a strange city
The roofs are darker,
The streets narrower
The corners farther,
And my legs are brooms
(With toes of pebble)
Sweeping a multiplying
Harlequin pattern
Of necessary furrows
On capsized mountains
Of desiccated sidewalks;
And everywhere about me –
Children burst
Into feet and echoes
Like flags or goblins:
The eyes of the women
Are suspended, electric,
Heavy with silence
Like the fingers of the air
In the gap before the thunder:
And men demand answers
And turn away their shoulders
Into caves full of furniture,
Machinery or ledgers,

Like tortoises in beehives
With axes in each cupboard.

Thus I walk, I talk,
In a strange city –
So much, so many,
To encounter, to remember.
But that is not the end.
The city alters
And change is the strangest
In that once strange city –
Roofs are lifted,
Streets grow wider,
Corners come together,
Sidewalks are ploughed,
Children furled,
A woman brings me rain,
Cupboards fill with bread,
And my name is planted;
And I begin to populate
With common-place and habit
The soon familiar city.

Industrial Valley
(Northern England)

In those dour ingrown cities –
Where the smoke rises daily from factory millstones
To autograph the air, and the chain-gang houses
Are patient, and bricks are the only flowers
In those fungus valleys of prodigious iron –
Under the tombstones, the dead are mixing
Their bones with the gravel, while the living chisel
Coal from the rock and thatch their dwellings
With slate from the quarries; and the wives of habit,
Sodden with children, kneel on the doorsteps
Scrubbing the sidewalks; and down blocked-off alleys
The pneumatic drills are laughing as they bite
For they know that their logic
More than refutes the arrogant concrete.

Nightpiece, Pittsburgh

The houses sulk behind the leaves
That drip and snivel in consumptive gloom.
A drunken streetcar whinnies as it sways
And splashes through the puddles out of sight;
The echoes dissipate upon the stones.
Your eyelids gather dew like tufts of grass,
And through each melting lens you see
The streetlamps bubble into foam
And sprays of anvil-hammered sparks.
Three dooms fall slow, like corpses, from a clock –
Its yellow face hung like a cut-out moon
Above the neon froth and hunchback roofs.
The clouds turn, restless on the bed of hills.
The city mutters earthquakes in its sleep.

Excavation

They are digging up the street
Where I used to walk
Going for the milk.

They have put up a sign
Warning me to stop
Lest I fall into a pit.

The familiar surface
Of geometric concrete
Has given up its secret.

Such a burden of entrails!
Such confusion of moisture!
So long hidden and now laid bare

I had not thought,
Going for the bread,
That the daily journey hid

Such a mountain-depth of darkness
Buried silent underneath
The gossip and the sunshine of the street.

May

I sing
With my eyes
To the void
To delight
With the sky
In my mouth
And the blue
For my cry.

A Poem is a Pearl

The mind is an oyster;
And poetry is its habit
Of accretion upon strangeness
Explored within the mouth
And measured by contagion,
Haphazard as the sand
That grows by irritation
Within the tightened shell
That sucks upon the ocean,
As public and as hidden
And vain as is a woman
That knows herself by others
And leans upon their eyes,
As subtle as the flavour
Of names upon a journey,
As deliberate as mirrors
That cast the sun away
Yet alter with the gazer,
As restless as the tongue,
And personal as spittle.

41

A Song

I have set my heart so high
that no song ever may,
rising on the longest day,
reach to where
I look down upon the sky

I have set my heart so far
that no eyes ever can,
searching with the widest scan,
find out where
I am near behind some star

I have set my heart so wild
that no one ever shall,
given the impossible,
know just where
I am still like a child

> *– but my heart there*
> *is air, uncertain air.*

Thanks

Thanks and praise for
the knot in the wood

across the grain
making the carpenter curse

where a branch sprang out
carrying sap to each leaf.

Enough

for Robert Cooper

Very well then, admit
that it was largely at random.

Of course, there are certain traits,
and such.

Go at it as hard as you like
with the sharpest axe,
and it only splits
into smaller and smaller fragments.

Dishonest
to even try,
to even want to explain.

If you couldn't laugh

If you couldn't laugh or something,
you'd go crazy.

The neighbours yell at each other
and that helps.

My father prays, and the children
try anything once.

The sun beats on a pod until
it bursts.

The dog next door

The dog next door
is chained to the wall.

He lays in the dust
and whines.

The children throw rocks
and steal his bone.

Then he barks in fury
and wags his tail.

Their insults at least
are some relief.

The Moon

I have hated the moon
because she's a thief

and pitied her
because she is cold
and must scavenge for light

and envied the knack
of her imperial manner.

In Memory of George Orwell

Let's drink our tea out of a saucer
and weigh Bonaparte against Robespierre.

Let's admit that Lear got what he asked for –
if not what he wanted, what he asked for.

Let's toast a great English tradition:
to protect horses and dogs, before children.

Let's plant at least one apple tree,
a Cox's Orange Pippin, preferably.

Boys in the Street

They are too intent to smile.
Gently, with accustomed guile,
they twist their words beneath his skin
(who fights a rising flood within)
to erode, by their corrosive art,
the brim of his distended heart.
And, if you should ask them why,
"For the hell of it. To make him cry."

Dawn over the City

A silent chisel cracks the night
And golden splinters litter every height.
Each curtained window slowly grows more bright.
The clouds are branded, and the roofs are paved with light.

The Sensualist

For I have tasted kelp upon the breeze
far from the sea

and heard the clamour of men's words
long underground

and felt the pulsing of her breast
through a shut door

and seen my footprints in that earth
I have not trod.

He may wander far

He may wander far
but there'll come a time, no farther

when he finds that mountain source
beyond which he need not go

with ferns and running water,
with a buttress overhead –

let the horsemen harry the cities,
let the wind howl, let it rage!

The Drunk

for Irving Layton

I have stayed up all night,
I have gobbled my meals,
I have burned my lips, smoking.
I have muttered, "But, but . . .",
I have gone to the office
with different coloured socks
and my fly buttons open,

I have heard voices above the traffic –
skalds reciting before King Olaf –

and
I haven't touched a drop for months.

A Dying Man

I must, I must ask,
"Is there anything you want?"

afraid of his answer
for there's nothing to be given,

ashamed of my question
knowing he knows,

forgiven by a lie,
his merciful "No".

The Mistake

I have lived with my overcoat on
and my bags packed, ready
for any catastrophe –

But the secret police haven't arrived
and the house hasn't burned.
Worse, nothing happens . . .

And the stars dazzle the sky
above me and smile
in secret.

And what if

And what if he looks
silly? A child
on a wooden horse.

And what if he has
shut his eyes? A race
with only one entry.

And what if he is
lost? The reins
over the rump.

I wish him joy
and a turbulent ride.

The Words

I have pondered the words
of what were best spat out, being poison.
And have blurted not my heart, that concourse,
but slogans.

A woman with too many children
while rain drums on the window panes
lives in babble and loves
in silence.

If He Sings It

Not the degradations
of a metronome

or the mere contriving
of better mousetraps

but an architecture of
pauses

and evidence
like a footprint.

Bjarni Spike-Helgi's Son

The man who bred me,
breeds me yet.

That father whom I scarcely knew
but as an overbearing ox
who begrudged even the sky
above his neighbour's head,
who stirred mean quarrels,
killed and then was killed –

while I went in peace,
well loved by all who knew me,

wishing no part
with what I was already part.

★

We all went to the court, and I named Geitir as my father's slayer,
    and Geitir named himself and asked for atonement, not ashamed,
    but as a just man who wished a just outcome.

And the atonement was paid, one hundred of silver according to the
    law, and another thirty for the ambush.

And we swore oaths together, in the sight of all men, to keep our
    trust.

★

It was my mother brought them –

she
who bleeds in secret

and gives birth in blood,
gave me my blood,
binds us
by blood –

in a shut room,
snow over the windows,
the hearth stoked, incandescent –

reproach
thrust upon me,
a bundle of torn clothes,
twisted together concealing
something like charred pitch
caked in the weave,
something dark,
his,
my father's . . .

*

O Geitir, I have kept my trust.
Although you fell beneath my axe,
I did not strike,
and not at you.

Your head upon my knee.
Your question
(I will always hear,
though you never spoke),
"Who killed me?"

Whom you killed,
killed you,
killed me.

★

That night I walked alone.

No man saw the face I hid.

In night I walk.

No man sees the man I hide.

Gunnar, from his burial mound

My bones are under the turf,
here where men came and still come.

A thousand years ago,
here where the meadow is green,
I breathed this air and was glad.

A feud began. I don't know how.
I hated them. They hated me.
And all I did, I would do again
though I foreknew what would come of it.

There happened a chance to escape.
I had one friend and he urged me to go.
But when I stood there on the shore by the ship,
I could not.

I looked back
and saw the land that I knew
and the paths I had trod with my feet
and the walls I had built with my hands
and the sheep I had marked on the fells
and the hay here in the meadow
ready to mow,
for me to mow.

Did they think I would quit?

Though they took my breath,
I kept what I loved.

Valgard, called the guileful, to his son Mord

Listen carefully. Do as I tell you. It is very simple. You will talk. On
both sides of everything. They will be glad to believe slander. They
will do it for us. They will kill each other. And Njal.

That beardless ninny. He gives help in the courts. He dispenses
wisdom. His sons boast. My name is slighted. Our family is
trodden under.

Let him take counsel now. Let him help himself if he can.

I honour the old gods. You wear a cross and honour nothing. But you
fear me. You will do as I tell you. You are not good for much. But
every man has some talent. You can tell lies and sound plausible.

I am sick. I shall soon be gone. But in a dream I have breathed the
smoke. I have heard the crackle of dry timber. I have seen charcoal
mixed with blood. I have foreknown my vengeance.

I will rest in my cairn satisfied. You will live to be old. You will see
Njal and his sons burned in their house. You will swagger, a little.
You will have fame, of a sort.

It will have been your talk. It will have been other men's deeds. It will
have been my will.

You will wonder what went wrong. You will grind your teeth. You
will chew your fingernails. You will envy me. You will even envy
Njal.

Thorir of Garth, and Asdis, Grettir's mother

A: You, you, you –
how can you smile?

Th: It's pleasant in the sun.

A: How can you walk about
in the sight of other men
having contrived his death
who was the only man in Iceland
while he lived?

Th: True, he had big arms,
bigger than most.

A: Not merely size.
When the gangrene reached his groin,
when he could not stand,
could scarcely lift a finger,
it still took a dozen men to make an end,
and after
they could not free the sword out of his grip.

Th: He was a troll.

A: He rid the land of many monsters.
Poor farmers bless him to this day.

Th: Who but a troll could have done that?

A: Trolls love the dark,
and he hated the night, oh, desperately,
so that he could not live alone.

Th: Then he was cursed!
A Christian does not fear the dark.

A: He had seen awful things that haunted him,
eyes, blood-shot bursting eyes.

Th: The eyes of all the men he'd killed?

A: He killed no man unless provoked.

Th: Often and easily provoked.

A: And you provoked the courts to outlaw him,
unfairly,
when he was not here,
when he could not plead his case.

Th: I did not choose the quarrel.
I had done nothing,
no harm to him at all,
when he burned my sons, all three,
that night in Norway,
burned them as they slept,
helpless and unconfessed.

A: It was an accident.

Th: He killed a man in church
in the presence of the king.
He killed a friend as easily
for a bit of fish.
All accidents?

A: He was unlucky.

Th: Cunning enough
to live for all those years an outlaw.

A: Weren't nineteen years sufficient?

Th: Twenty years is the sentence on an outlaw,
that's the law.

A: And what did the law accomplish for you?

Th: Retribution. Mine.

A: Never yours.
Another man destroyed him
by trickery and witchcraft
for the sake of a reward you promised
and never paid.

Th: Would I pay a heathen
who had used sorcery?

A: Great fame in that!

Th: Will men think less of me
because I sought lawful vengeance?
They were my only sons.

A: He was my son.

(in *Grettir's Saga* there is no mention of a meeting
between Thorir and Asdis, but it is quite possible
that they might have met)

Gudrun, old and blind, to Bolli, her son

Whom did I love the best? whom did I
    love? did I love?

What was the worst I did? did I do
    the worst? what was the worst?

Who thinks of love? or thinks for the best?
    the best of love? or the worst of
    thought?

Do we say what we know? do we know what
    we love? do we love what we think?
    do we think what we do?

    ★

A bridal coif –
woven with gold,
gift of a queen,
beyond compare –
he gave to her,
not me. The shame
burns. And burnt, then,
destroying. All
a secret gone
to ashes, now.

    ★

I spun yarn for twelve ells of homespun
    while Kjartan died. That woman his
    wife did not laugh in bed that night.

I was heavy with you when they killed your
    father, yet I smiled as they wiped their spears
    on my scarf.

*

I did not show my tears when Thorkel drowned,
    though his ghost stood clear before me, the
    water trickling from his sodden clothes.

*

The lava flows beneath the fell.
The flowering turf rests on volcanic ash.
Sometimes I sing. Sometimes I mourn.
I did the things I did because . . .

*

. . . so many things. I saw and took and
    kept and had so much.

So many times. So many fights. So many
    names. Thord, Thorvald, Eldgrim,
    Kotkell, Grima, all the rest. So
    many dead.

So much. So far away. So long ago. Now
    I must grope to get a bit of bread,
    so near, so small.

*

It was all foretold of me
when I was young,
in a dream I had
before it all began.

Now all is told
and all that dream is done.
I woke then
and remembered all.
Now I remember all
before I sleep.

The Author, to Bjarni Herjulfsson

You don't say much for yourself, scarcely
    enough for a poem,

        "I was driven off course by a storm.
        I saw land
        but it wasn't where I was going."

I have to do the talking, to try to corner you with
    questions.

        "Why should I have gone ashore?
        Why should I go there again?
        Why do you want to know?"

Then perhaps the history books are right to give Leif
    Ericson all the glory?

        "I don't know what his plans were.
        Ask him, yourself.
        I manage my own affairs."

But you ought to make some sort of protest or give us
    a word of explanation.

        "I must be off.
        I have an appointment.
        I've told you all I know."

An Irish Monk on Lindisfarne, about 650 AD

A hesitation of the tide
betrays this island, daily.

On Iona, at dusk
(ago, how long ago?)
often (did it happen?)
I saw the Lord walking
in the surf amidst the gulls,
calling, "Come. Have joy in Me."

Yes, with these eyes.

Now, on strange rocks
(faintly through the wall)
echoing, the same sea roars.

Detail is my toil.
In chapel, verse by verse –
in the kitchen, loaf by loaf –
with my pen, word by word –

by imitation,
illumination.

The patience of the bricklayer
is assumed in the dream of the architect.

*

On the road coming, five days travel, a Pict woman (big mouth and
    small bones) gave me shelter, and laughed (part scorn, part pity) at
    my journey. "What do you hope for, even if you get there, that you
    couldn't have had twice over in Ireland?"

Then I told her of the darkness amongst the barbarians, and of the
great light in the monasteries at home, and she replied, "Will they
thank you for that, you so young and naive, and why should you
go, you out of so many?"

I said that I heard a voice calling, and she said, "So men dream, are
unsatisfied, wear their legs out with walking, and you scarcely a
boy out of school."

So she laughed, and I leaned my head on my hands, feeling the
thickness of dust in each palm.

Then she told me there was not another of her race left in that valley,
not one, nothing left. "And all in three generations. Once even
Rome feared us. Now my children are mongrels. And my husband
has left me. No matter. Or great matter. I am still a Pict."

Then she fed me, put herbs on my feet, wished me well, and I blessed
her but she said, "Save that for yourself; you will need it, when
your heart turns rancid, and your joints begin to stiffen on the
foreign roads. Remember me, when you come, returning."

So she mocked; and sometimes, even now, ten years later, I hear it as I
waken (receding in a dream), that laughter, broad, without malice.

★

Returning,
 in the mind, still there,
home:
– devout green hills
– intimate peat smoke
– a cow-bell beseeching
– warm fleece in my bed
– fresh water, fresh, a brook

Here:
– rain clouds like beggars' rags
– stench of burned weed
– fret of the chain-mail sea
– hard knees on cold stone
– dry saliva, salt fish

The gulls cry:
– believe
– achieve

The bells reply:
– some
– some

At the lowest ebb
you can leave dryshod
this fitful island.

A Painting of Beatrice Sforza

Her straight neck
is looped with diamonds.
Her hair is knit
with a golden ribbon.

Her profile is clear
against a turquoise sky.
Her gaze is afar
and it does not weary.

Her lips are set.
She appears in her calm
as obvious and secret
as a peak on the horizon.

Suzanne Bloch in a Billiard Room

A woman's voice (the grit-rub
of dust on a gramophone record)
singing of love (the crack
and rebound of billiard-balls) the vibration
of taut strings, plucked ("Huh? What's that?
A guitar?") the words ancient and foreign.
My voice, "It's a lute. And the song . ." ("Hey!
Want a paper?" a newsboy, "Who's winning?")

and the song
not just of that room:
a chanson in archaic French, "Il me suffit" –
the break of each phrase: a surprise,
the notes contrapuntal, almost discordant –

by texture, multiple
as the situation

and singular
as its gathering
of contending parts.

A Libation

Dug out of the earth, with charcoal stains and wicker marks.

Or china, on an embroidered cloth, with tea leaves at the bottom and lipstick on the rim.

Or tin, rusted, in an empty house.

Or white, with milk, invisible, frozen in snow.

Or afloat in the wake of a ship.

Or fluctuant under the thumb of a potter.

Perhaps in mid-air at a seance.

A cup without handle or bottom or sides, drinking my fancy that empties itself like a cup.

Evening, thirst, and a cup of water.

My heart in the cup of her hand.

A Fish-hook

You have put a fish-hook in my chest behind the breast-bone,

and one barb is around my gullet, and one around my wind-pipe, and
the third is embedded in the root of the aorta.

There is a cord attached, of tantalum-hardened steel, marvellously
supple,

and the least movement you make, that cord tightens, the tip of each
barb jerks deeper, the blood eddies around the metal.

You have the other end of that cord, you have hidden it, inside your
skull or at the base of your spine,

and though your hands are empty, you are winding it in,

and my mouth is dry as I flounder towards you.

Black Spruce, Northern Ontario

Standing out there in the snow and the silence, it seems easy to slight them.

Not only are there too many but they all look nearly the same and seem quite content to be shoulder to shoulder

as if making a ritual observance, perhaps to the sky, though that's way beyond them,

and too rigid in their stance to be altogether convincing, like a theatre crowd while the national anthem is playing.

Even considered singly there's a certain priggishness, as they discard their lower branches, as if to get as far away as possible from the muskeg in which they are rooted.

Cut down, they aren't good for much except paper-pulp or firewood – you can't really build anything with them –

yet seeing one lying on the ground, the white core exposed, I'm not so confident,

as I see the stump rings woven so tightly, so thin in places as to be almost uncountable, each of them an all too brief summer in the making.

You Said I Should

You said that I should write a villanelle.
Just as a gene perpetuates its flaws,
the pattern has been set. So what the hell

is there to do but do the thing as well
as can be done, despite Mendelian laws?
You said that I should write a villanelle,

but didn't say on what. It's terrible
the way this rattles on without a pause.
The pattern has been set. So what the hell

or heaven or earth or anything! I tell
you, now the thing has got me in its claws.
You said that I should write a villanelle

and so at last I have, as incredible
as Charlie Fisher's 'Ode to Santa Claus'.
The pattern has been set. So what the hell,

I'd best explain, before you sue for libel,
you're not to blame for this, merely because
you said that I should write a villanelle.
The pattern has been set. So what? Oh, hell . . .

The Suicide

I have waved a cardboard sword.
I have given a penny to a beggar,
I have put out my tongue at a policeman
when I thought that no one was looking.
I have burned the toast for spite,
I have chased dandelion seeds

because I could not be certain,
because I could not be certain –

I have dreamed of snow capped mountains,
I have dreamed of seven league boots,
I have dreamed –

I have put my head in the oven.

Derelict, City Morgue

Like fruit that some migrating bird has found
And pecked to satisfy a casual need,
Spewing the rancid core upon the ground
(Scarce pausing in its transit from the deed),
So is the still warm body of this man
Intruded on the officials of the town
Who must conclude for him as best they can
And have the causes legally set down.
He did not ask them questions while alive
Nor seek the help of doctors or police.
Without an income, how did he survive?
With such a stubborn pulse, why should it cease?
They rummage through his pockets and his heart.
Both are empty. And were from the start.

June Nineteenth – Rosenbergs executed – Riots in East Berlin

I hear their footsteps
(First a man, then his wife)
Down metallic corridors,
And the sound of doors closing,
And a silence, and later
The whisper of a doctor.

I hear crowds shouting
Defiance against soldiers,
And the clatter of rocks,
And the roar of a machine-gun,
And a man on the sidewalk
Coughing up blood.

Those footsteps, that coughing,
Shudder in my mind
("The garden needs rain.
The rhubarb is shrivelled,")
As I greet a neighbour
On the way to the post-office.

A letter from a friend:
"Have you a faith worth dying for?"
("At this time of the year
Forest fires are most dangerous.")
I count my pulse in the sunshine,
And have no answer.

The Octopus Ride

The couples scream as the spokes revolve and the swivel chairs go
    up and down, and you'd think that something would snap, some
    bolt fly loose.

But the belts and chains are guaranteed, and everyone knows that it
    must be safe, and wish that they too had nerve enough to enjoy
    the scare.

But my daughter is bored as we watch, and wants to go for an ice
    cream cone. She thinks it's just pretend, she can't understand

that it really is an octopus, and we go on it because we hope that
    there'll be a mistake, and the creature escape the command of
    the man with the switch, and hurl us like cannon balls over the
    dovecote roofs of the little town.

A Portrait

She's had every kind of x-ray and blood test
and been examined by innumerable doctors without any
definite findings except that she doesn't eat and
has shrunk to skin and bones and looks seventy-five
at forty-eight.

Now she lies under a patchwork quilt in an upstairs
room and tells me in a whining voice about her
mother who died twenty years ago.

"Nothing's ever been the same since. I can't help
crying whenever I think of her. I know it sounds
silly but really I can't."

And I know that she's utterly serious and probably
quite right and there's nothing I can do about it
except to come occasionally to listen

while her damn pekinese yaps at me from under the
bed and she wipes away her tears with pieces of
lavatory paper, dropping each piece into the
waste paper basket as she tears off another . . .
from roll after inexhaustible roll.

The Sun

To really understand, first, you have to empty your mind, and make
    sure that you know what it isn't –

that it isn't an over-ripe tomato, or a celestial egg, or a blood spot on
    the eyeball of a Jotun, or anything else equally likely.

After which, you must go indoors and draw all the curtains and stare
    at it through a pinhole until you can't stare any longer,

and then you close your eyes, to see it in the dark, throbbing under
    your eyelids,

but even this fades, or seems to fade.

You'll give up in disgust, and think that you'll never know

until one morning your wife will look at you and say,
    "What's the matter? Aren't you well?",

and you'll take the bus to work and grumble about the weather as
    you always do, but inside you'll be different, you'll be happy, just
    to know, at last,

to know that one flicker of light has lodged behind your eyes and
    begun to sprout,

and you'll study yourself in the mirror and keep feeling your
    forehead, waiting for the first mark to appear,

and berate yourself for a fool not to have realised
    from the beginning.

The Look

It can happen to any child at birth. The midwife or even an attendant can make the sign over it. Usually it happens by accident, as the gesture appears innocent.

If the child survives the first week, it will have the look. The parents may take it to all sorts of doctors or priests, or they may pretend to ignore it. Either way, it makes no difference.

People who have the look, you feel their gaze touching you on the street. Without turning around, you know when one walks behind you. This is a great trial for women, to feel strange eyes like feathers beneath their clothes examining their skin.

It is a problem too, for those who have the look, to conceal it. It is possible by keeping the eyelids half closed and the attention focused on some inanimate object to modulate the strength of the look. But even in sleep, it will keep others in the same room awake.

Two people both possessing the look can fight without movement and without noise. It is terrible to see them as they regard each other with their eyes mercilessly and fully open.

The combat may last several hours and neither moves from his place until it is finished. The police do not interfere and often a considerable crowd will gather to watch.

The first indication is a slight injection of the eyeball, and then the surface becomes dulled and the eyes begin to flicker slightly horizontally and circularly. By this time the loser has begun to tremble, and it is fearful to see how he wishes to break off the engagement but cannot do so. Finally the eyes turn black and shrivel up, like burnt raisins.

He no longer has the look. The spectators gather around to congratulate him on his cure. They lead him away by the hand. It is quite permanent.

A scar closes a wound

A scar closes a wound by proliferation from the cut edges to fill the
   gap, and then contracts, sometimes distorting the surface but
   often stronger than the original tissue.

So music may act, so a song might . . .

Which is a conjunction of words made at random, though not to be
   disowned, that draws on out beyond the initial fancy:

the wounds of music being silence – an incision between each note
   and then a greater laceration when the melody has ended.

The cicatrisation goes on progressively after, shrinking into strength,
   marking the struck ear.

An Apology

Because I don't suppose you hear,
I talk like this –

because I don't know where it goes,
I start at once –

because I don't quite understand,
I tell you why –

because I can't make out the words,
I write it down –

because I haven't got a tune,
I sing somehow.

A Chorus (of sorts) for Tess

A woman's voice, thin, uncertain, in a minor key,
Singing foreign words: a male voice asking,
"What's that? A guitar? A zither?": the vibrations
Of an instrument five hundred years dead, to accompany her:
The snick of dust on the record: the crack
And rebound of billiard balls, double or single:
My own voice, embarrassed, explaining, "It's a lute.
They played it themselves at the courts.
They sang songs like that to one another in the evenings.":
A news-boy, soprano and eager, "Want a paper?
I can't hear . . . Oh, you have one! Who's winning?"

Seven sounds: each changing: each different:
Three human: three mechanic: and the song
Not altogether either and not just of that room –
A chanson in archaic French, 'Il me suffit',
In a contrapuntal style that has gone out of fashion,
The notes of the lute not harmonic with the notes of the song
But polyphonic, intersecting, sometimes discordant,
Each in its own sequence, always in company,
The sum more than each, and not just by agreement.

The formal complaint of the song, the blunt questions,
The deliberate sonorous plucking, the grit-rub, the canons,
My answers, the heedless oblique interruption,
Are each, as they vary, adherent
To each other by need or by conflict
In that room for a moment – then parted.

And I'm asked, in dead earnest, "Are we disturbing you?
That's unusual music. Can I buy it in Pittsburgh?"

For Gaston

I never met you before,
before I met you today,
and today becomes tomorrow,
and tomorrow becomes forever –

with both feet off the ground at each stride,
your eyes following invisible sparrows,
your arms and hands moving like pennants
above a battlement of words –

in a nest of a room in a forest of houses,
woven with books and paintings and letters,
with an egg at the centre that trembles, ready to burst –
a globule of blue the sky laid at your feet.

It will hatch, who knows when? perhaps today,
and even you don't know what will come out
but whatever it is, it will have wings and a throat
and will soar over the chimneys singing as it goes

and the neighbours will stand in the street
obstructing the traffic
with the joint in the oven and the bath water running
to listen.

(1957)

Conundrum Blues

I said, let me see you, boy.
If I say, let me see you,
then, boy, I mean I don't want to see you –
I mean, jump, boy.

I said, do you hear me, boy?
If I say, do you hear me,
then, boy, I mean I don't want to hear you –
I mean, jump, boy.

I said, you tell me, boy.
If I say, you tell me,
then, boy, I mean I don't want to have to tell you –
I mean, jump, boy.

I said, jump, boy.
If I say, jump,
then, boy, I do mean jump –
and I mean jump, boy.

One in a Multitude

This young man says
He wants to write
Some day, and has
Both every right
And chance, and does
Not write, despite.

Driving (A Litany)

go at it –
  and the road curving ahead, with hedges and trees
  on each side, and a view of green hills with a
  church tower beyond –
nothing else –
  but a few half-timber cottages with television
  aerials, and a castle tump in a field with cows –
go at it –
  the car making no sound other than the sound it
  has made which becomes no more of a sound than
  the sound of my breath –
nothing else –
  between the last cup of coffee and the next cigarette,
  between Caxton Gibbet and Grafton Flyford –
go at it –
  surely it can't be much farther, surely we took the
  wrong turn at the fork, surely we've passed it, but
  surely –
nothing else –
  Caution, major road ahead. Caution, slippery when
  wet. Caution, concealed entry. Caution, it is
  forbidden to drive on this road when it is under
  more than three feet of water –
go at it –
  the speedometer is broken, the odometer is broken,
  the petrol guage registers empty –
nothing else –
  if you've got to , if you can, if there's nothing
  else but to drive –
go at it –
  and the road curving ahead, with etc. etc.

Two Tunes (for Roy)

(1)

It's the wrong room
in the wrong house;
I'm not even sure if it's the
        right street
    (What a thing to do . . .)

It's the wrong time
of the wrong day;
I'm not even sure if it's the
        right year
    (It couldn't happen to you . . .)

It's the wrong nut
for the wrong screw;
I'm not even sure if it's the
        right machine
    (And that's nothing new . . .)

It's the wrong word
on the wrong note;
I'm not even sure if it's the
        right tune
    (I suppose it's true . . .)

(2)

You haven't hear this song before,
so come in and say Hullo and shut the door.
    (That's the sort we are . . .)

You can't imagine how it's going to go.
You won't even know if you're supposed
                          to know.
       (That's the sort we are . . .)

Ring the door-bell and somebody'll come.
Keep on ringing if you want some fun.
       (That's the sort we are . . .)

If you think this song is such an awful
                          bore,
then you can go when you like – but shut
                          the door.
       (That's the sort we are . . .)

A Round

He starts to write a poem, "I . . ."
       but that is all, however hard he try.
              The stars are brilliant in the midnight sky.
He starts to write a poem "I . . ."
       and needs a handkerchief as time goes by.
              The wind comes cold out of the midnight sky.
And time goes by and only God knows why
       he starts to write a poem "I . . ."
              and that is all, however hard he try . . .

Spiritual Researches

Let us titrate
the soul of a potato –

O taxable courage!
O bonded verity! –

the assessment of proof
by inspiration.

Well . . . (for Ian)

It was a nice day.
I'm glad you came.
Don't go. All the same,
It may pour tomorrow,
Even if you stay.

Now That April's Here

It's raining on the brussels sprouts.
The fire is smoking in the grate.
Macmillan says he has no doubts.
Will Oxford beat the Cambridge eight?

Some bright intervals tomorrow.
Sixpence on a football pool.
Seven percent if you want to borrow.
Charles is settling down at school.

Put the Great back in Great Britain.
Write a letter to *The Times.*
Lots of fun with Billy Butlin.
It's a poem if it rhymes.

(1957)

The Wind

I dreamt I stood before a tree.
The tree was rooted in the earth.
The earth was firm beneath my feet.
My feet were hidden by the dark.
The dark was lit by many stars.
The stars were mingled with the leaves.
The leaves were restless as they sang.
They sang the changes of the wind.
The wind came ever from the sky.

And what I thought

And what I thought I had, I lacked;
and what seemed sure proved full of gaps,
with fragments only partly mapped;
and what I said, I would retract;
but in each word my mouth was trapped.

A Beast

It fell upon me out of the sky.
  I heard the beating of its wings.
It seized me by the shoulders.
  Its claws tore my skin.
It relieved itself down my spine.
  I vomited at the stench.
It put its beak into my mouth.
  My words became a babble.
It laid an egg inside my skull.
  I opened my eyes. I began to see.

They have taken

They have taken my father
  and chained him to a wall.
They have taken my mother
  and set her to pick thorns.
They have taken my sister
  and bred her to a beast.
They have taken my brother
  and cut one little cord in his heart.

My father fought his utmost
  until he crippled himself.
My mother toiled patiently
  until her fingers were barbed.
My sister fed her milk
  to raise up scorpions.
My brother forgot
  how to laugh or to weep.

My father studies his bondage –
  he has made that his life.
My mother clings to her pain –
  she has that much to grasp.
My sister loves her brood –
  she loves them, alas she does.
My brother grins and feels nothing –
  nothing at all, nothing.

A Letter, of Sorts

Dear M–, and "dear",
beginning, is
a word we use
to say: "I start
to write to you . . ."
but ending with
that word is not
to end but let
something begin.

I write it here
and for you, dear . . .

*

To write to you is to write to Post Office Box 1492 :
the number of a voyage . . . of a continent . . .

Looking for you is like opening a file-folder,
whereupon all sorts of pieces fall out –

scraps of conversation, snippets of photographs,
and a cloud of moments like dust obscuring my eyes.

"Pooh . . . it's all got to come from inside your head. Nowhere else.
You know that as well as I do. What else?"

*

    Perhaps the most convenient way to start would be to grab
whatever was most accessible, for example your wrist, and proceed
from there to realise your body in its bulk, a woman's body, no longer
young, not fat but big, which was young once,

and married when you were only fourteen, *"still wet behind the ears"* until your husband died three years later, two months after the divorce, *"before I even really understood what it was all about . . ."*

Or did you invent that? But you didn't invent the painting that you showed me, done by a local painter, of yourself naked, your massive thighs and buttocks green (a particularly verdant green, a most eyecatching and imperative green) which it gave you great satisfaction to show me . . .

*

Your third floor room. The dark climb past many shut doors. The incense clinging to the furniture. The manuscript sheets stacked on the table. The drawings pinned to the wall. The plants on the windowsill. The stale food. The fresh food. And something odd you have bought for the occasion, perhaps a coconut or a package of china tea. Your underwear hung up to dry on a string between the doorhinge and a nail in the wall.

*

Or at one o'clock in the morning. We were sitting on the curb at an intersection. The shadows of the insects flickered on the road, from the street-lamp above us. You were chuckling about the man on the tram we had just left, who had stared at you. *"He didn't know what to make of me! Did you see how he tried to pretend I wasn't there? But he couldn't be sure. Poor booby, he couldn't figure me out at all!"*

*

Or those –

the publisher who stole your manuscript and who you believed was waiting for you to die so that he could make his fortune –

the children you taught at school for a year and sent on a journey with Marco Polo to China, who painted and described it to you as they went, everything in minute detail and full colour, down to the Khan's favourite bathtub –

the art student you discovered had genius if only you could save it, whom you mothered and would have given your eyes for –

the brother you were convinced was plotting your destruction, in alliance with a small army of fellow conspirators across the country –

the eminent critic who wrote to you, "How did you manage to create all that by yourself? But I doubt if anyone can go beyond Finnegans Wake." –

the doctor at the mental hospital against whom you railed, yet didn't blame. *"After all he was only doing the best he knew how."* –

and myself whom you bombard with almost indecipherable postcards, describing where you have been and whom you have met and why the world is upside down.

*

But to admit it: that I can't stand you for more than an hour or two: that conversation in the usual sense is almost impossible. What's more, you know it, and even delight in making it worse, because I try to pretend that it's otherwise . . .

*

Then I hear your voice like a priestess in a Delphic temple,
your laugh like a three year old at the circus,
your step like Boadicea inspecting her troops before battle.
I see your eyes like a hunted doe,
your smile like a grandmother with twenty grandchildren around her,
your hands moving like birds at work on a nest in the midst of a
storm.

*

94

You too once wrote a letter. A letter to Christopher, to the patron of travellers. In a narrow room, with the door and window shut, at the height of summer, with heat like creepers choking the air. Strange smells came through the floor from the restaurant below. Trams rattled in the street. Neighbours muttered. Girls giggled in the lobby. Dark men leered on the stairs.

You saw it coming and you wrote a jungle letter. Coming in the distance, not so far away. A black leopard padding through the streets. *"O Christopher, hear me answer me."* The black leopard coming to swallow the sun. Its breath was heavy against the door. The paper was damp with your sweat. A shadow covered the window. The lamp had gone out. The ink had dried up. You couldn't even read what you were writing any more.

*

The midnight sky flickers pink
above the blast furnaces.

The moon throws grotesque shadows
over the cobblestones.

A puddle shimmers. A window rattles.
A cat disappears. A train wails.

The blood labours in the foundry
of the metropolis of your heart.

*

We were sitting in a cafeteria. I was embarrassed. People stared. Your voice was too loud. Your hat (my God what a hat) was a bumble-bee stuck on the end of a wire. You devised it yourself. It swayed as you talked. Explaining something, in answer to a query of mine. On and on. I responded, "Yes, of course . . .'", but was lost.

You smiled. At me, or just because of the hat? My coffee was finished, yours cold. Your cake crumbs littered the table. I wanted to go home, but I couldn't. You'd not finished, not yet. You went on, you went on. "Oh you wouldn't believe all the things I've seen Petty minds spiteful mean . . . They put me in the booby hatch Yes they did But you're too young . . . Oh the things . . . the things . . ."

★

One day we spoke

and walked together.

The sun was shining.

You spoke of . . . but

now I forget

or am not sure.

It makes no difference.

The sun will shine.

You will walk slowly

on the pavements

of a far-off city,

walking more slowly

as you grow older.

The sun is shining

and you laugh

at the strips of paper

blown from a sign.

The colours mingle

as they fall.

★

In Oklahoma there had been air and space and a great wind through your bones. As a child in Oklahoma, they had said, "You shall be a dancer. Or a singer", because you were so light, because your voice was so clear.

★

I have been sad

for your sake, at times.

"Not worth a hill of beans."

I know.

Perhaps if I begin

I.

Perhaps if I begin here this evening and go onward hopefully towards
   whatever kind of statement you might lead me into,

gradually it should become obvious where we are going as I go with
   you turning your back on me and striding off down a side street

with only one poorly functioning street lamp that appals me even as
   I am grateful for the light shining on the segment of the pavement
   that belongs to it alone now that you are gone,

as I go forward more slowly intending to follow, which accounts not so
   much for the gap between us as for the sensation of movement, the
   very knowledge of distance,

which is your gift to me to squander now this evening just as I begin
   . . . perhaps.

II.

I have thought about you a great deal which does not mean that I have
   thought of you but rather that my thought has been around you and
   not upon you

which may or may not be a tribute to you or to my thought but is one
   token of the activity which you exact.

Of course; when somebody else reads this they will speculate on what
   they call your real personality as if you had any such reality that was
   not the sum of a progression of expectant distortions

and the multiplication of all that I reluctantly acknowledge.

III.

In polite company when I am bored with the others or disgusted with my own pretensions then I sometimes invoke your name as a talisman

not because I believe that you are exempt from delusion or even tedium

but because in you they are so exemplified that I am instantly aware of the dimensions of the contamination and healed of the disease by the very enormity of the symptoms.

IV.

I believe in a very ordinary sense that your life has been a failure, and in a very extraordinary sense that you have succeeded.

I believe in a very happy sense that you knew what you were doing, and in a very sorry sense that you didn't know where it would lead you.

I believe in a very subtle sense that I will never come to an end with you, and in a very coarse sense that I finished with you long ago.

I believe in a very devout sense all that I believe, and in a very practical sense that I will never be sure.

V.

You told me a tale of your life: a tale that told about you: all the living that happened to you as you told it.

But not to be had, though I had it so often. Not to be fixed, though the details were lavish.

You said that you wept. Is it possible? That you laughed. Is anything possible, then?

VI.

There are things I will not say, because I am not sure that I can say them, because I dare not fail in trying to say them, because I think that you already know them.

I am told that in a certain species of spiders, the female consumes the male. Does he know this beforehand, and if he does, does it matter, and if it matters, is it to him a necessary fulfilment?

If I have failed you, it can't be helped. A child must tear his mother, to be born. Does he fail her in that? And if she cannot heal herself, who is to blame?

Sometimes when someone asks, "Do you believe in God?", I will reply, trying to joke, "Yes, I believe in Her."

VII.

These are not shadow battles –
though often battles, and of shadows.

These are not for you to read –
though to be read, and for you.

These are not meant as puzzles –
though when puzzling, they are meant.

These are not about you, really –
though about you, and real.

VIII.

It's clear that I've been going at random for a long time now.

You are standing at the top of a flight of stairs with a light bulb behind you.

The dazzle becomes the moon becomes a clock face becomes a signet ring.

I offer you a sheet of white paper with my name and yours written on opposite sides.

You laugh and it tears down the middle and a star falls out of the sky.

IX.

Where did it all go wrong? Did it go wrong at all?

Such "going" is wrong, perhaps. But where did that wrong begin?

Was there a place and a time, too far back to be traced, for the mistake that cannot be found, if it was a mistake?

Not even the weaver knows, if anyone knows, how it will look when the cloth is unrolled, if anyone looks for such – if anyone weaves.

X.

And they who read this will think it absurd that I should sit here writing this, all of it, as though it was of great importance,

as though the nature of importance is and as though they are, at all, to be thought of in the same way as I think of you, whom I could not have chosen and of whom I do choose to write.

I have tried to justify this, to justify you, to justify myself. I have said
to myself, "She isn't, this isn't what it seems, is not what they think
it is, not what they think she is, not that, no . . ."

but you are and this is what it seems and what you seem to be, what
you are to me – whatever they think and whatever I am.

XI.

Do you remember, do you, the things I remember, all the things,

or if not all, some of the things, some of the time, a few things, just
a few,

or even one or two, do you? or only one, one thing that I do?

I won't forget, though I forget much, most things, most of the time,
forgetting

as you forget, as you must, as it is all forgotten, so much

going into remembrance, as it does, all that is done, all that is, and all
this. Do you?

XII.

Going to work in the morning, I will walk beside a wall, beyond which
are trees and beyond that – I don't know.

Silly enough – to think of what I won't be able to see, even tomorrow,
if it comes.

A fragrance of blossoms comes sometimes through the leaves above
the stones, as I walk to work – as I must.

102

That's all – something hidden behind a wall, there on the other side, and I've never opened the door.

XIII.

Beyond a certain point, beyond this, perhaps even before, they who read this will have begun to smile knowingly to themselves, to point out the obvious.

Obviously this is a warm summer evening. A breeze blows in the garden. I've nothing else to do at the moment.

What are you doing? I miss you. The litter on this table is indescribable.

As far as it will go, and beyond any certain point, I love you – as far as it is obvious, which is far enough.

XIV.

Write to me, won't you, when I don't write, when I want you to write, as you often wrote.

I can't any more. There's a finish, somehow. I must end it here, if I can –

this stringing out words, on and on, who knows to whom, perhaps you after all. It's a habit like others perhaps, which is still quite a lot –

so if I send you a postcard, a picture of something, of anything bright, a painting of Venice, a snapshot of Hampton, a handful of daffodils,

if I do, will that do, will that be enough, without any more words?

A Voice, Voices, Speaking

I.

How can I tell you
what is in my heart?
My heart can't tell,
and that is more
than anything told.
All I can tell
is that in my heart
there are things to be told
to you.

II.

This is about as much good
as if I was
just muttering to myself.
I'll make myself heard
if I have to yell
until my teeth shake loose.
I'll break the windows
and rattle the pans.
I'll write it down
every blooming word
and shove it in your face.
I'll even stand on my head
and weep real tears.
Sooner or later
you've got to admit
I'm talking and
you hear me.

III.

I can't think why you don't reply
except that perhaps you could not say it –
in which case, I cannot think.

If it should have come to what cannot be thought,
then I cannot speak –
certainly not to you, except to ask.

I have to ask – though not of you,
who could not answer,
unless there was, after all, nothing to be answered.

To ask is the only possible answer to silence.
I can't think of a better –
except silence itself, which cannot be spoken.

IV.

It doesn't matter,
that is to most of us.
Even to me, to whom it matters,
most of the time, it doesn't.
What does it matter?
As if all this could matter, to you.
When something does matter,
nothing else matters.

V.

I said, "There are no words for it"
and began to write.

I said, "It has no form",
and the shape became clear.

I said, "It has no end",
and found myself at the brink.

I said, "No one can hear"
and began to speak clearly.

VI.

I'm sorry. I said what I did not mean.
I said I was sorry; and that was not what I meant.
Sorrow was meant; but not to be sorry.
I didn't mean what I said; and there's sorrow in that.

Is there anything left

Is there anything left
when you've spent it all,
finished the last pint,
emptied the pack?
Is there anything you've got
out of all you've had,
or anything you want
that you've got?

Do you know what you want,
or how much it's worth?
Is it worth that much,
as much as you've got,
as much as you're worth,
as anything is worth?
Is any of it worth
what it costs?

How much has it cost,
has it cost you much,
to get you this far,
as far as you've got?
Is it worth what you pay,
the way it's going?
Do you think you'd buy
the same again?

Who sold it to you,
and on what terms?
What did they sell you?
Who sold you up?
Did you take on more
than a man could take?
Did you read it through
before you signed?

It's a proper business
and no mistake,
with a wife and a home
and a decent job.
You did the best you knew
but you didn't know.
You're not even sure
what the hell went wrong.

Do you know what hit you,
what got into your drink?
How long have they had you
by the balls like this?
It's not your fault.
Nobody warned you.
Is it all that easy
to do you in?

Have you far to go?
Are you going somewhere?
Have you any notion
just where you stand?
Can you stand by yourself?
How long can you stand it?
How much longer
can you stick it out?

All right

All right, I'll say it:
  he bores me stiff.
All right, he is,
  he is very kind.
All right, it's true,
  he's a good friend.
All right, I wish
  that we'd never met.
And so it is,
  and it isn't right.
He does his best.
  I do my best.
I really like him;
  but I can't stick him.
All right, I'm wrong.
  All wrong, I'm right.

Don't Know Blues

No, I don't know,
not any more,
not like I did –

   though I do know more,
   more than I did –

if you know what I mean
and you ought to know
if anyone knows –

   how it is,
   how it goes –

that it isn't the same
as it was,
because
I don't know any more –

   if it comes to that,
   and it comes to that,
   that I don't –

no, not like I did,
and I did, you know.

I'm sorry

I'm sorry that it has happened like this,
   that I should now be sorry for what has happened.

The mistake was mine from the beginning,
   not to have declared that it was all a mistake.

Once I could look you in the eyes,
   because I merely looked at your eyes and not at you.

It's too late now, much too late,
   to postpone anything any longer.

I scowl in shame,
   that I should have smiled so pleasantly so often.

How can I begin to love you
   until I have opened the full measure of my hatred?

She'll come

She'll come.
I'm a bloody idiot.
Something is tearing inside.
I can't stand it.
She'll come back.
I can't believe it.
There's a noise of ropes creaking.
She'll come back to me again.
A harshness of great cables winding.
Back. Back again.
The labour of her presence in her absence.
And to me again.
Will she?

How far?

How far was your head?
Three? Two feet?
Not even that?
It's hard to tell in the dark.
Turned from me.
Next to me.
Where did you go?
As if past barbed wire
across a range of sand dunes.
A demarcation. A frontier.
Half a pillow length, or three quarters.
Scarcely more.
Perhaps less.

To think here

To think here of you and of your question,

or not thinking at all, perhaps, but just trying to be aware, to
question myself and to know the grip of it,

as you asked me and thus in a sense for me, whom I also ask now in
my own and reciprocal cry,

"What's it all about?"

and so it is, all of it, about or in this, however under or around, this
ask that demands, that seeks only the asker,

and with no end, as it speaks, either to us or for us –

but to end. To stop short. To go on as before . . .

into it all, that question, and thinking of you.

A Well Known Road

Travelling a well known road:
   but it isn't the same –
past the familiar landmarks:
   what do they mean? –
going back to that place:
   where is it now?
and there it is:
   and it was –
and it's all utterly false:
   and all so true.

I would speak of him

I would speak of him who could not speak –

in that soft distance full of milky light where residues of long since flamed and sunken coal now float as minute fluffs of carbon in a depth of air –

who could not speak of what concerned him most –

curdled by fumes from the barred chimney stacks of chemical works that rise like masts above the seal-skin slates of droplet burdened roofs –

who was concerned instead with his allotment –

out of the fog that crawls upon the ochre bricks of caterpillar housing rows and spreads like grease upon the iron furrows of a railway yard –

his piece of ground he worked, a garden there –

and in the alleys where the children's footsteps sound like kettle-drums whose beat is lost into the cracks between the paving stones –

who was proud of his garden and spoke of it.

So the Heart

As the verdure of Aprils
long past, decomposed,
annealed to ebony
under the weight of time,
now heats a room;
as embers flare
in a half empty grate,
spangling the walls
with radiant dancers;
so the heart must serve
as its own coal
on a dull day.

Yes, sunshine

Yes, sunshine. A warmth.
The waves, brilliant.
We walk on the sand.
We speak and hear
and understand each other.
The sea breaking,
back and forth, unwearied.
The light changing, decreasing.
A faint breeze. The tide
coming in. The ocean
destroying our footprints,
grinding the sand even finer.
A glow slanting now
on the surf. We touch,
a moment. Goodbye.
A fine afternoon. An hour.
A warmth, and a brightness.

A Breath of Autumn

A quaver of light.
Trees sift the dusk.
Far sounds curl
in the ear, falling.
Days ago were
and are not now.
The earth moves on
around the sun

This moment slides
away but a roughness
abrades the air –
a singed aroma:
gone as a stone
into a pond,
the ripples only
expanding, coiling.

For an Anniversary

It's been a long time, even since yesterday. Many years, since this morning. And tonight may never come at all.
                                        Yes. Perhaps. I don't know.
Never mind.
                It does make something to say. I did have something to say, didn't I? If not that pressing.
                        Or even so different to what I say, much of the time. But there, that's it – I do.
                                That is talk. And to you. If not all, most of the time.
                        Just to say something. And that, pretty much what I say at any time.
                        Something to pass the time. To assure me that you're there. To remind you, I'm here.

He and She

Tell me why it happened?
  – What happened?
Exactly what happened doesn't matter.
  – Does it matter?
It matters what you tell me.
  – Can't you tell?
I tell you I must know, I must.
  – Must I?

I look into

I look into your eyes and see –

    but no, not your eyes –

rather, the corners of the lids where the wrinkles
      flare out –

    and yet, not there –

instead, the forehead, the creases tightening upon
      the root of the nose; or the remnant of a
      child's freckles on your cheeks –

    is that where? but no –

I look into your face and see –

    but no, I don't see –
    is it possible? is it so impossible?

your hair going grey at the temples; your dry lips;
      your dimpled chin that might have been that
      of a bacchante

    (that might have been, that perhaps was, that
      is not, cannot be, that by the very suggestion
      mocks itself and you)

where have you gone?
that I look at you and see a face –

(where have I gone?)

why has it come to this?
that I recognize the distance, that it is the
      distance that has become familiar,
        a landscape of separation upon which I depend –

is that all?
a question mark sunk into a face, overgrown by
      granulation, festered and scarred about,
      become part with the resentful flesh –

    (like a grenade fragment long years after the
      explosion, the battle itself almost forgotten,
      but still there where the surgeon in the
      casualty station gave up the struggle to
      find it even then)

what was it?
that you did not understand, that bewildered you
      and left this quizzical brandmark
    (that I do not understand, that bewilders me)

is the light too bright?
that we peer at each other, frowning not in enmity
      but to protect our eyes –

is an ordinary day
too much for us?

You and I

You and I,

and the nearest star visible in these latitudes,
    which is Sixty-One Cygni. God knows how they're
    so sure, but it's possible.

While you and I,

what will become of us? God knows! What could
    become of us? What have we become? Not much,
    I don't doubt it.

While you and I write,

a coolie watches his children starve. God knows
    where. Anywhere! A snowdrop buds. A man
    stumbles on a cure for schizophrenia,
    unwittingly. It's possible.

While you and I write to each other

to keep in touch, as they say. To exchange views.
    To come to some sort of conclusion, though
    God knows when that could be, yet I don't
    doubt it.

While you and I write to each other about what
    matters

which is . . . ? Who knows? Or if we're meant to.
    But it's possible

even for you, even for me.

To be shaken

To be shaken at heart is to be taken by the heart
and mine scarcely known until surprised as if struck,
almost toppled by a few words which I took to heart –
In themselves perhaps groundless and scarcely heard
yet in which my heart was discovered
and I in its grip, taken
in the same shift, as it shook, shaken.

A Hill

At dawn: first sight: black against orange,
a profile of giant rubble,
it barricades the sun.
Orange out of black,
a foliage of wrinkled copper,
light germinates in a furrow of the hill.

The phrases are apt.
The scene is not unusual.
The joy is in the attention.

The description is not a circumscribed likeness,
that is, of a delimited hill.
If never finally exact,
it is not exactly at random.

The description portrays a hill
which is discovered in the action:
an unknown hill which becomes known,
which is a likeness
and which becomes likely.

It is Bredon Hill. A name. But not merely.

Then is it a whale, dark indigo, partly submerged, the dorsum crusted
    with shellfish?
Mount Badon, with Arthur and the Table, and the last outpost of
    Empire?
Asleep, with drooping mouth, sunken eyes, an old man taking a nap?
Awake, a heraldic beast, its nostrils alert for the Malverns, staring
    beyond into the hills of Wales?
The Savages, their seventeenth-century bones at Elmley Castle, under
    the garish monuments, newly repainted?

Archaeologists from Birmingham, digging in the earth-works near
  Overbury, defining storage pits in the chalk?
A young couple who have modernized an old cottage at Great
  Comberton, with a Van Gogh print in the living-room?
The damp, dripping through the bracken, settling on the backs of the
  sheep between the filaments of wool?
Or an afternoon yet to come, a picnic with sandwiches and cider, the
  children running happily on the turf, with bees in the gorse?

And it is not. And it is.

The description attests.
The attention becomes explicit.
The implicit becomes familiar.

It becomes an accumulation, not a hill.
But it declares a hill, a very particular hill,
a remarkable hill:
a hill which it is possible to know.

La Sainte Face (a painting by Rouault)

Dot, diddle, dot, diddle,
so many pretty colours –
forget-me-nots, marigolds –
set around a box to frame:

a face

crowned
with rays, bright rays
of spangled yellow thorns –

decapitated
hung

in order to look at you
without any curiosity at all.

At Mareta

The poor are starving at Mareta,
not exclusively at Mareta
but particularly.

The poor starve slowly
if not unusually.

The sun doesn't starve.
It shines
especially at Mareta.

The rich think this remarkable.
They often think about the sun.
The rich like to think
even about the poor.
The rich know how to think
as the sun knows how to shine.
The rich are remarkable.

The poor are also
but differently.
The poor are hungry.
Presumably the poor know how to starve
or should.

Certainly they learn.
But are they satisfied?
Could they be?
Do they have to be?
Are the rich?
Is the sun?

Even at Mareta
where it shines so much

and the rich are so very rich
and there is so much time
to be satisfied.

The sun comes and goes
according to the seasons,
as do the rich.
The poor remain
and will remain poor
and will continue to starve
while the sun goes on shining
as usual.

The sun is remarkable,
as remarkable in its way as the rich.
The sun can't think
any more than the rich can shine.
As for the poor
they can't do much of either,
usually.

The poor can starve.
The poor are very poor.
They are very hungry
at Mareta.

The Mind Turns

"for the sun rises . . .
upon the just and the unjust"

upon all,
           and the mind turns
upon such words that call
to all who hear – we
whom the light falls
upon and warms –

as it shines, justly
or not, upon this phrase
itself that sounds
in the ear
           and sheds
also a warmth
             and recurs
to the mind
             and affirms
its light
         and does
not fall.

A Western

Who starts last
but shoots first
does not miss

on the draw
standing up
face to face

to kill him
who moves first
and thus betrays

himself and is
too late
in his haste.

At the Mineshaft of a Ghost Town in Southern California

They came with great labour
across a great distance.

They dug with great labour
a great distance down.

They took all they could
and went away

leaving as their monument
a great hole.

Death Valley

We shadow our eyes,
scarcely believing
but forced to concede
this virtuosity
of crumbled brilliance:
arête and wash,
flare and stipple,
silt and erosion
curdled by the sun
into a splendour
of peacock dross.

Not a landscape
to be dwelt by men
but rather a scope of land
which here escapes
the grasp of man's regard
into an exaltation
of chromatic debris
in which we linger
as willing intruders
scarcely able to relinquish
what has cautioned us.

George Fox, from his Journals

Who had openings within
as he walked in the fields

(and saw a great crack through the earth)

> who went by eye across hedge and ditch toward the
> spires of the steeple-houses, until he came to
> Lichfield, and then barefoot in the market place,
> unable to contain, crying out,

and among friends
of much tenderness of conscience,
of a spirit by which all things might be judged
by waiting
for openings within, which would answer each other

(and after that crack, a great smoke)

> and in a lousy stinking place, low in the ground,
> without even a bed, among thirty convicts, where
> he was kept almost half a year, the excrement over
> the top of his shoes,

as he gathered his mind inward,
a living hope arose

(and after that smoke, a great shaking)

> but when he heard the bell toll to call people to
> the steeple-house, it struck at his life; for it
> was like a market-bell, to call them that the
> priest might sell his wares,
>   such as fed upon

words, and fed one another with words until they
had spoken themselves dry, and who raged when they
were told, "The man in leather breeches is here . . . "

a tender man
with some experience
of what had been opened to him.

Twenty Words, Twenty Days

I

at a certain hour of the morning of a certain day of the week –

time,

like a bonus, to be expended, not used –

a depth, a largesse –

and within such magnificence nothing for it but
to dilly-dally, fritter –

as a BOOMERANG –

thrown overhand to spin vertically will curve up and to the left, circle,
then glide back –

an effect discovered by observation and refined by
error, not deduced from principles –

the arms at right angles or less,
each surface pared smooth (but with a thickness on one side at the
leading edge of rotation) –

in the air, a phenomenon and a byword –
to be understood in both senses: as 'rebound to hurt' and as 'restore to
safety' –

so this moment, in a gust of days, hovers –

in which I mess
with the car, clean the guinea-pig's cage, fix the girls' bike, walk with
Jonnie on the pier –

from where we can watch the surf riders on their
boards, the sea very still, with long slow, very slow breakers –

coiling,
uncoiling, recoiling –

returning, turning upon the shore –

II

going to the Arts Centre in the next town in a rush, and we get there
too early, a mistake in the time, and the children are patient, even
eager, despite –
                        the hospital calling, can't find anyone to help with a
case and wouldn't I? –
                        but I can't (and they manage just as well, after
all) –
            an afternoon frayed at the edges, but without irritation –
                                                                    let go
as it may –
            not quite paying attention –

and the girls dance, a Round, arms linked, legs swinging, something
peasant –
            the music draping them in long skirts of thick weave, with
smocked blouses, the music giving them bare feet, the music turning
the hardwood floor into dark earth, well stamped –
                                                        nimble to the
throb of it, gay, approximate –
                        and I move also and am moved, in
vague unison, and throw back my head to let all go to that pulse an
implication of soot, of grease, of uncombed hair –
                                                        a stale odour,
almost rancid –
                        but a comfort in the dusk, in the thickness, the sun
dropped behind the hills, the air abruptly cold –
                                                    as if abandoned, as
if gone into next year already –
                        a SLATTERN –
                                        inconsequential,
not straight in the eye –
                        lacking something –
                                                if not lacking charm –

III

a world awry as I read –
                    a letter from a friend –

" . . . from a Presbyterian standpoint what I'm doing is unthinkable
– from a French standpoint it's simply poorly handled – but from
the standpoint of authentic something or other it's right and I don't
regret . . ."

and myself snagged, almost throttled, as if I had been the one –
                                                        but
which one? –
                    " . . . we hiked all through the Sierras, living for three
weeks off the fish . . . attempted to break it off, but she had restored
to me a sense of joy and I was at a loss without her . . . to see my wife
suffering was also unbearable . . ." –
                    as a cord pulled together –
a DRAWSTRING –
                    and I, in reply, tumbling words, with nothing to
say, nothing –
                    except,
                    "Yes, of course . . . of course, yes . . . and I
know . . . and I couldn't . . . and can . . ."
                                        eager, eager for the bait,
that source and lure, there at the bottom of the bag –
                                        the loop pulled
tight, lifted into dark by the hand of the hunter –
                                        the fabric taut as I
strain –
                    myself taken, snared –
                                        by a thin line straggled on paper –

IV

grape-like, a cluster –
                    the technical word: a MORULA

a condition of growth occurring after the first divisions of the
embryo but before the blastula, before any structure is apparent –
                                                            an
interim, at a certain density –
                    clumped, almost ready to start the first
breakdown, the first cavitation –
                    but as yet all intact, each cell equally
present –
            unlike this day, already gone beyond any balance, already
beginning to liquefy in places –
                    a deliquescence, and of event, as I
remember –
            how I held the baby, feeling her tremble as she drew,
making circles in pairs, over and over, elated at herself –
                                                    and
remonstrated with Carol after Joan's anger had detonated, the echoes
lurking –
            and read Mead's pamphlet, the first proofs, and wrote to
Newcastle to say, "Remember, a date!" and "Yes, how handsome!" –

and watched a child nearly choking during a tonsillectomy, lips and
ears cyanotic, with blood clots in its pharynx, and had pleasure in my
skill as I cleared the airway deftly and re-inserted a tube –
                                                    and
collapsed on the bed at 5.30, my knees aching, almost nauseous –
                                                    with
the islands visible under low clouds, smudged with graphite –
                                                    the sea
like a puddle, a huge rain-freshened, rain-muddled puddle –

V

my daughter, gone into her own world, already cut off, sitting out on
the front steps in the dark –
                    a cold evening, in a thin dress, staring
intently, but not seeing us –
                    locked in battle with . . . with what I can
only guess . . . where I can't come –
                    and I resent this, resent her,
almost hate –
                    who sits there, barricaded against us in desperation –

voyaging where she must, assuaging what she must, hurting whom
she must –
                    there being no sequence of words, no means of saying,
"Yes, of course . . . and having secured *that*, then *this* moves into place
. . . and the rest foreseen . . . and so forth . . ."
                                        no domino count end
to end, no source or destination explicit –
                                        however hard one tries to
demarcate its parts, however closely one searches for some cleavage –
INDIVISIBLE –
                    as reduced to an element, each element such by
definition, beyond which there can be no further process of
fraction –
                    or, touch at one place, at any, and the whole edifice
trembles –
                    an experience, obdurate and yet perhaps equally yielding,
affording no access upon itself –
                                        and the soldiers cast lots for Christ's
cloak, there being no seams to unravel –

VI

after the radio voices, television faces, all clatter, flicker and stippled
print, berating us with headlines, bulletins –
                                            impaling the day with
words –
            blood: bullets: assassination –
                                    as one struck, so all struck –

the children too, on edge, shaken, aware of an adult world disrupted
by an inexplicable . . . by a . . . by what can be named but not
identified –
            a grief, undirected –
                                    yet become direct, threatening and
revealing –
            that persists, is everywhere –
                                        a nausea in the air as of
some sort of gas leaking –
                    and implying . . . no, more than that . . .
insisting upon a realization of our
                            UNDERVALUATION
                                            of all that
'other', that unbelievable and extraneous, that fairy-tale of king's
daughters and wicked magicians that is history –
                                        now grubby with
detail –
            smeared on the seat of a car, soaked into the pleats of a
skirt –
            in bright sunlight –
                            what was so surely meaningless, no
longer supposed that –
                    become, of a sudden, a membrane lining the
throat, an adhesion in the cavity of the mouth –
                                            a cramp in the
tongue –

VII

urgent, requires answer, a query:
                                "... can you think of some gay title
for the reading ..."
                        at once, it's no problem –
                                but instead, I think of
my forefathers, namesakes, Borderers, near Jedburgh and Melrose,
and one day every tenth man hanged for cattle stealing, on 'general
principles' and 'as a caution' –
                        that father of mine, was he one of the
nine-in-between, his luck good? –

ah, great luck, to survive to write this and foresee –

myself, in a far place, a future time –
                        an APPARITION –

a thousand miles, a few weeks hence, all planned, where and when,
and I anticipate –
                        that self, there, genial, speaking as if with
knowledge, to whom others attend, a public occasion, with crowded
faces –
                asking to be shown ... to be held ... to be astonished –

as birds in migration –
                        as cattle thieves –
                                gay, titled –

that is: apt, which means both relevant to the material and having an
impulse within itself, an identity as to phrase –
                                a pressure and a
presence –
                and happy, that is: containing joy and contained by –
                                        as this
evening: the sunset, a fine twilight, clear air, with a cobblestone drift
of rose-petal clouds –

as my thought moves, is able –

appears obvious, hits square –
fills out the sky of this paper –
and
replies –

VIII

described by Miss Ann Dart, as he was visiting Bristol, while still a
youth: Turner –
"not like other young people but singular and very
silent . . . no facility for friendship but never other than pleasant . . .
seemed uneducated, difficult to understand . . . sometimes going out
sketching before breakfast and again after supper . . . desirous of
nothing but improvement in his art . . ."

a VALENCY –
defined as: an expression in terms of small digits of an
ability to unite with other like integers –

a ratio, denoting specificity, an exaction –
and at approximately 4.45
p.m. a child brought into the hospital that had tripped, struck her
head –
not much more than dazed at first, then slowly lapsing, until
rapidly depressed, the breathing almost arrested –
"linear fracture
of the skull in the left temporo-parietal area" a decision, and with
decision –
to surgery, each of us in place, to accomplish what must
be –
an incision –
at 5.17 p.m. the fault exposed, a torn artery ligated,
a clot removed, the brain free to expand –

without words or only of
trivia –
bonded by our intent and intent upon it –
made explicit though
unspoken –
an obligation assuaged, as discovered –
and a unison –

IX

at ease, on my back, dozing, I look up –
into a sky which becomes a
ground from which all pigment has been absorbed, leaving only a fine
dust, an indeterminate bleach –
a purity, of a sort –
then the air
fragmented by diesel engines, bulldozers and earthmovers, on an
adjacent hill, cutting roads, levelling terraces –
masticating the dirt,
excreting –
acromegalic locusts with rumplestiltskin secrets –
GARGOYLES –
as corbel stones, carved at variance, obscene or
ludicrous, upon a sanctuary –
then later at dusk as I walk on a strand
of rocks, the waves pulsing, the sun as if corroded by salt and annealed
into the horizon, but the air still flushed, still holding trickles of
radiance –
among the pebbles, one pebble, small, seen from afar, as if
arc-lit, a brilliant rose colour, halting my glance –
as if ignited, as if
conduit for all the brilliance drained from the twilight –
but closer:
pitted, chalky, with filaments of slate-grey –
taken home to lie on the

table among the supper dishes –
                       and become dun, grotesque, eroded
into sworls, almost a parody of the foam that shaped it –
                                and cold,
inappropriate –
            unyielding –

X

did I dial the right number? did I dial it correctly? or if dialled, did the
number go through? and etcetera . . .
                   at war with distance, and a
gadget –
        in quest? or on a ramble? –
                to find a place knowable,
circumscribed, having identity –
               perhaps a VILLAGE –
                       within range
of a good shout, "Hello, Hello" and a direct reply, "Yes, I hear . . . I
hear you . . ."
            where all that's needful may be found by a stroll and
one face missing is a clarion –
              a comfort too, that might smother,
against which it might be necessary to rail, to mutter, "Damn them
. . . *must* they . . ."

who are but us, behind partly drawn curtains or in half opened
doorways, peering out, anxious to miss nothing, as if anything *could*
happen –
         seeing all that is within range –
                   a constriction and a
perspicacity –
           to which and from which there is a lane, an access and
an exit, always open, between hedgerows –
                   as the Past might be

invoked, summoned, in exorcism, to contain the Present –

against

disparities –

and the long distance telephone call –

XI

". . . a white object floating on the river, though its whole surface is light against the water, yet the reflection has not any light but on the contrary is dark . . .

and not only darker, but the reflection appears longer than the object which occasions it . . ."

perhaps often seen but not hitherto remarked –

a peculiarity –

as a catalyst, the reaction proceeding –

IRREVERSIBLE –

and heat, as a bonus supplied, an excess of energy liberated –

or absorbed –

and I, with a friend, suddenly aware that I'm talking more rapidly than I was, as if to convince someone (perhaps myself) of an opinion that I've swallowed, a refrain –

of injustice in the courts, a man hung in error, documented, palpable, gross, and not yet even partially acknowledged –

with conviction as fuel, as acceleration, my face flushed, and my words –

a reflection of light –

now dark –

disproportionate –

past recall –

XII

of or having to do with a method of helping to bring out ideas latent
in the mind –
       from the Greek, literally, 'obstetric' –
                    forceps needed
on occasion, the child willing to come, and willed, but yet unable –
                             or,
"Push, you've got to push! A deep breath and hold it! Then relax, you
must relax in between, until the next one!"
                  and also the value of a
long black cigar, smoked to maximal savour (that is, to a measured
pace) –
       doing nothing, with precision –
               and this evening, by chance,
as we visit some friends, their voices, the sound of guid Scots –
                       and
the taste of it –
       MAIEUTIC –
             our tongues loosened –
                     animated,
almost garrulous and then surprised, "Did I say that? Or said, did I
mean? And if meant, then . . . ?" and "No, it couldn't . . .
but . . ."
      and laughter bursting, at such recognition –
                   ". . . a shame to
spoil by diluting . . . and if you don't care for the flavour, why take it at
all?"
     taking a glass together –
             or perhaps looking at, reading the glass
to foretell the weather –
        or through a glass, to approach detail –
                      or
just in the glass, a long look at oneself –
           then faltering, with gaps,
reticences –
     unable to speak, and listening –

to the pauses, their
conception, their gestation, their deliverance –
that nothing hinder –

that all come forth –

XIII

bloated from over-eating, picked bones on a plate –
and the fallen
leaves too damp to burn properly, smouldering, the smoke like
resentment contaminating the air –
yet a deep smell, as of a
completion, to be inhaled, a savour –
the year too, shrinking, seeking
another level –
a CARCASS –
and on the wireless, a jetliner down,
just north from Montreal, 118 people on board –
"... seemed to
explode . . . just came apart in mid-air . . ."
in driving rain, near
freezing, masses of mud, with no survivors to be expected –
and I go
out, restless, to try to walk it off, a thick taste in my throat –
on the
front steps, the remains of a mouse that the cat hadn't finished, just
one leg and an ear, some whiskers, that I carry to the dustbin –
to go
off scuffing the weeds, down back lanes, along a railway line, past
shops gone out of business –
by a scrap yard, with rust like scabbed
ulcers, speckled ochre, eating away the metal –
desultory –

XIV

obviously how it must be –

you really knew all the time but just tried
to pretend –

go at it how you may, it will end up the same – strident, a
voice from a box:

". . . a man protection, the effective protection he
needs, with three times the power of any other deodorant . . ."

did you *have* to be told? –

a NINCOMPOOP! –

and Jean-Louis
Barrault, in *Les Enfants du Paradis,* lugubrious, in front of a raucous
crowd, with unguent limbs, drooping sleeves, pantaloons –

moving
as if to move were to betray all (and yet his only hope . . . his hope of
what?) –

and his eyes as if the lids were shut tightly but behind rather
than in front of his eyeballs so that at first glance he appeared to be
looking out but in fact was looking in and had shut his eyes at that
sight –

yes, there he was, a posture! –

fixed in it! –

and you, where
have *you* been . . . ? nodding . . . ? –

a silly ass, to suppose that the
answers aren't given at the back of the book –

an utter goof, to expect
anything –

more than the obvious –

XV

> "I'm sure I can find
> a thing of some kind,
> a good kind of thing
> to do with my string"

the forward path of the poet into the labyrinth –
                                        not a poet, be it
noted, but *the* poet, that flourish –
                        but Theseus used his to find his
way back –
            an INTELLECTUALISM –
                        as a prism to spread the light
for its parts (but looked through one sees only a jumble) –
                                                a great
fankle, sometimes, to be unravelled –
                        or a spider, hanging its web for
what might be snared, arrogant in patience, and sticky –
                                        or a child,
collecting bits of twine, knotting them end to end –
                                        (how big will it
get)?

> "with a big ball of string
> I could do anything!"

XVI

awakening this morning, as the alarm rang, a guilt –

unexpectedly remembering a girl I met once years ago, while on
holiday, out walking in the Appalachians –
                        how I came upon her on
the trail, high on the ridge, having seen no one for two days: she in

shorts, with rucksack, plodding the same direction but more slowly,
a student from some university and taking . . . what was it? . . .
geology? –

and she wanted to talk, so it seemed, a bit lonely too I
suppose, a gawky kid and more than slightly eccentric to be way off
there by herself –

and I turned, turned from her because my mind
said that she was ugly, not attractive, a physical aversion, a disdain,
not the woman I imagined for myself at such time and such place –

and I walked on ahead as quickly as I could, as if in flight, as if
actually pursued –

as I flee the vague guilt, the regret that follows me
closely even to this moment –

that I should have feared such an
ordinary smile, of some-one out there on that mountain, trudging
the same route, sweating the same pack, seeing the same endless
trees –

assuaging the same oppressions heavy on me –

yes, surely the
same, surely, however different –

or at variance –

and yes,

PRECONCERTED –

the whole thing 'fixed', 'rigged', a 'set up' –

granted the facts of my birth, natural disposition, upbringing, and so
forth –

no escape; and all now escaped, gone –

before I knew fully,
without possibility of appeal –

as I do appeal, nonetheless, not
knowing to whom –

as gesture –

and indictment –

XVII

to prevent abrasion –
                    DEMULCENT –

an agent and an action –
                    and I, up half the night working, so today
my eyesockets burn, my lips tingle –

my attention drifting in lapses, despite effort, despite all resolve –
                                                            with
flushes, then chills –
                    clarity through a haze –

nausea upon euphoria –
                    and I cling to one strand . . . the next instant
. . . and the one after . . . and . . .

and pause, to breathe deeply, and hear within my ears, a sound –
                                                            as if
all carried by wheels on rails –
                    chuck, chuck . . . chock, chock . . . a
pulse –
          the universe unfurled, sliding yonder where I was, where I
may be –
          to an end-point, to a fixity –
                              with sleep as a pit –
                                                  and
fatigue: a mercy, an opiate –
                    and as reported in the paper: the Wankel
Engine, for the first time in a commercial car, at the Motor Show –

essentially a single rotary piston without reciprocating parts, attractive
for its simplicity and excellent torque –
                              with an almost complete lack
of frictional surfaces at which wear could occur –

XVIII

as against: ". . . the first genius of our age . . ."

Turner, according to a contemporary –
                         this afternoon, reading a
magazine, a collection of poems by living authors, all their writing, the
mass of it –
           so prolix an effort –
                       and gloom, not that it can't be read,
but can, so much of it, so apt, with such singleness, such a pain to be
urgent –
           and I, busy as with a Meccano set, a language of nuts, bolts
and tin struts, contriving phrases as one might improvise toys –
                                      for
ingenuity, and as a pastime –
                     "Turn the handle. A string runs on a
pulley. A hook lifts a matchstick.
It works!" –
           a LATTICE –
                     of bits, lacking better, a patchwork –
                                         as
against: Watercolour, the 'English Medium' –
                         where the texture of the
pigment is determined not merely by the brush but by what is given up
as the strokes dry, by what is lost from the paper –
                       a purity; but in that,
without body, without protection against air, against light –
                         so that what
we have now in the galleries, mostly but hints –
                     even Ruskin, in *his* old
age, saying, ". . . have lost something of their radiance, my Turners . .
. though the best, in that sort, are but shadows . . ."
                       of the day rising
up, of the sun shining through vapour . . . through interstices of cloud
. . . in crannies, the light precipitate as dew the colours flared. . ."

". . . with blue and yellow close together in some places, instead of
green" one critic grumbled, "as if *that* could fool anyone . . ."

XIX

Weyland Smith, worker in iron, shoer of horses, linker of chain-mail,
himself perhaps chained –
                                      a captive, a refugee, and said to be lame,
perhaps hamstrung when taken, who toils for a master –
                                                                            by the
Ridgeway on the Berkshire Downs, a ruined Long Barrow, ringed
with elm, once used as a forge and given his name, where the turf is
alive under foot and the granular stones, dark as rain clouds on the
horizon, lie half submerged where they have tumbled –
                                                                            and I
remember it today, Pay Day, collecting my cheque, my ration, to be
used and hoarded –
                          I sign for it, a slave's mark –
                                                          yet bread in my
mouth, and a roof –
                          a FAMILIARITY –
                                                of disgust and of necessity –
and in that, a sort of reassurance, a persistence –
                                                          even a pride, if not
always of craft, then at least of a certain minimal agility –
                                                                            as if
also at the anvil, squeezing the bellows to heat the charcoal to
incandescence, the iron thrust deep until softened, to be hammered
and rehammered –
                          day upon day –
                                                sweat dripping onto the
metal, sizzling in beads, engraving the surface with whorls, with a
lace-tracery pattern –
                          myself imaged and marked –
                                                                  as bondsman –
and contriver –

XX

last night, crying out in my sleep (so that Jonnie had to prod me until I
stopped), ". . . but it's murder . . ."

　　　　　　　　　　　not in fear, but amazement where I
was –

　　　a valley between mountains, with boulders, bracken, straggled
clouds down to tree top, tents, canopies, dripping guy-ropes, banners –

and men: hulking, spare of words, their eyes bloodshot from urgent
travel and the smoke of charcoal braziers, with rich brocade under
their jerkins –

　　　　　　inhaling each other's thought as one might scent –

　　　　　　　　　　　　　　　　　　　　their
inmost being finding sustenance far down, as plants with long
tap-toots growing out of a shale slope –

　　　　　　　　　　a world imagined, become
imminent –

　　　　　but not mine and blundered into as I slept –

　　　　　　　　　　　　　　　Powys (John
Cowper) and his novel *Porius* –

　　　　　　　　　　read so long ago and so ill-
remembered, yet unmistakable –

　　　　　　　　never POOR –

　　　　　　　　　　　　　but a plethora, a
gallimaufry –

　　　　　　　　and this evening, the baby, as she fell asleep after happy
struggle in a corner of her crib, almost upside down, so abruptly, she
was so tired, with one last wail as if tumbled into a chasm –

　　　　　　　　　　　　　　　puir wee
thing –

　　　　　　and I remember an Edinburgh room and one saying, when I
asked what he'd done that day, how much –

　　　　　　　　　　　　　"I tore it up . . . I
wisnae pure enough when I wrote . . . I wisnae pure enough . . ."

Briefly

Briefly
such an ease
of splendour
as she strays
out of childhood
held amazed
by a glimpse
of her domain,
scarcely as yet
a woman but
suddenly all.

Done speaking

Done speaking
in the silence – yet
for the spoken words
composed – silent,
she kissed him

and stunned,
at a loss,
he almost lost her,
reaching for some word.

However

However long
or far
we may
or must
part, don't
ever doubt
you have
my heart.

Simply

Simply
to hear
as before
your voice
your breath
in my ear
saying no more
than, Yes
I'm here.

Be so

Be so
as you are
in my need
when I need
as I need you
now.

The ever-presence

The ever-presence

of your absence.

Make some

Make some allowance
for him who casts
his heart on a whim
but more
for him who cannot.

A song

A song
gone
along lanes
alone.

Where

Where it rains:
    here.
Where the rainbow ends:
    there.

Not piecework

"Not piecework. By the hour!
With overtime. And tea breaks.
Fringe benefits. The lot!"

Better pay, elsewhere? "Maybe . . .
but short-time . . . lay-offs . . .
not with this! It's steady"

And the rock? Sisyphus shrugs,
"Dunno. Not my idea.
Someone's got to, I suppose."

Thighs gripping

Thighs gripping, hips
moving in pace – her face
suffused – each breath
short and quick
through spread lips,
she is possessed
and lost in the act

trotting
her horse down the lane.

Two Jibes

(1)   Nice
to be in your place
where you squat.
But to get there,
all that shit
you clambered through,
how could . . .
So easy?
Natural?

(2)   It's true
you do get paid for it –
but to smile as well?

A blindfold

A blindfold
on a condemned man:
the mercy
not to see
his eyes.

Rightly

Rightly correcting
after every shot
when not to remark
if it miss or not
would hit
more likely.

Didn't ask

Didn't ask from where
or how etc., and no stint,
and must have known
it was all on tick,
a freak of an overdraft.
Can't grumble. Had my bit
and to spare. And now
the bailiff. Out,
or pay! That's it!

One word

One word and clearly
and from the heart

when I had swum my utmost
and felt my breath give out

was enough
as the water lapped my mouth.

Homage to Jean Follain

I think you must have written them on postcards, your poems, like
   something one sends home while visiting abroad;

or like woodcuts that one finds in an old book in the attic and stares
   at on a rainy day, forgetting supper, forgetting to switch on the
   light;

but not antique, though out of time, each fixed in its moment, like
   sycamore seeds spiralling down that never seem to reach the grass.

What became of the freak, the girl with animal fur, when the fair
   moved on to the next village?

and the old souse, when he got home from the wineshop, did he beat
   his wife or did she beat him? did his daughter run away?

and that horseman coming home from a thirty years war, did the
   dogs know him? why should that one bird cry to announce him
   from so far?

and the police, toiling day and night to manacle the world, did they
   finish the last link, or did their ink dry up? did their slide-rules
   crumble?

But you don't tell us, and perhaps you don't really know, as you drink
   autumn wine in the evening, leaning over the battlements of an
   imaginary tower, watching the unwearied insects hovering in the
   immaculate air.

Sunday Afternoon

The houses crouch. Their eyes are shut. But they
    are not asleep.

They purr silently. They are digesting. They
    speculate vaguely on the next morsel.

I have never seen them pounce. Perhaps they don't
    have to. Like carnivorous plants, they hunt
    without moving.

Nothing moves, except a few sparrows. I hesitate,
    and look over my shoulder.

One street is like another. My heels echo on the
    pavement. I try to walk on tip-toe. I pretend
    that I'm going somewhere.

The houses smile inwardly. They bask in the sunshine.
    They exhale a few trickles of smoke. They wait.

The Priests of Paris

The priests in Paris are the Priests of Paris.

The black ones, striding along the pavements, always striding
somewhere, always purposefully going,

some with hats like platters, some in skull caps, some with shaven
pates,

some carrying valises full of important documents concerning the
distribution of souls,

some with their hands folded under their black capes, making
invocations with their fingers to conjure new souls into being;

black flapping drapes of the priests of Paris as they go past on their
urgent errands.

Beneath their charcoal robes they guard the secret purposes of the
city, they guard the delicate pollen of happiness,

that Paris may flourish and its leaves wave gently in the slow air, that
its white roots of flesh may be moist,

under the dark earth of the priestly garments they conserve the deep
juices, withholding them, intently feeding them,

on their errands as they go past, and no one talks to them, no one
looks at them,

as if to pretend that they were not necessary, as if to pretend that
Paris could flourish without them, as if to pretend that their
purpose was towards some far-off non-Parisian heaven.

'Les Toits'
(a painting by Nicholas de Staël)

You have hidden it, that, there under the paint,
a colour, the subject of your picture,
which is there, somewhere,
under the tiles, slates, casements, chimney-pots:
that, whatever it is,
which you don't dare (you don't want)
to see anymore,
a colour you once saw
which may still be there, which must be
there under the greys, greengreys, bluegreys, rainbowgreys:
that
colour of a knife, implacable colour, one colour
which you have covered up, pretending to paint a picture
of roof-tops –
to declare with such astonishing candour
what you could not conceal otherwise.

Victoria Regina Imperatrix

The guardsmen stamp their feet and the tourists gape and the Royal
Standard flies up aloft and the boys with their girls throw crumbs to
the ducks in St James's Park and the cars whizz round and round,

> and yes, it's true, all, every bit; and it's no joke to *Victoria
> Regina.*

A plump old thing on a pedestal. Her bottom must be pretty well
chilled by now. No wonder she looks a trifle grim.

> It's true. It's no joke to be sitting up there that long in the
> damp. Indeed, it's no joke just to be *Victoria Regina.*

Her Albert's dead, and a long time too, and now it's spring and the
trees in the park are green. Albert, who gave her so many kids. She
loved him, yes, she did.

> It's true. And he died. And that was nothing to joke about for
> *Victoria Regina.*

While the cars whizz round and round and the tourists gape and the
jets are smearing their vapour trails all over the sky and the pigeons
perch on her crown and the droppings fall all over her dress, she
must say to herself,

> "Surely it can't be . . . Surely it can't . . . ?" Though she's still,
> indeed, no doubt of it, *Victoria Regina.*

Then I call to her, "Don't you believe it! Tricks, that's what it is! A
packet of nonsense!"

> And it's true, it's all of that, just a sort of a practical joke,
> sort of . . . on *Victoria Regina.*

Thoughts on the One Hundred and Eighty-Third Birthday of J.M.W. Turner

A charge was inserted under the foundations and detonated . . .

The sun has disappeared leaving part of itself adherent to several fragments of vapour. A gold sovereign comes in handy as replacement.

The sky has been pried loose from the horizon. The blue has taken the strain by splitting into radial fissures of indigo. Tack it together somehow with rivets of carmine.

Then go home, have a glass of sherry, and look at it again.

Tomorrow we will begin the reconstruction of heaven. Meanwhile, this evening, demolition has its attractions.

Accidents, too, can be very useful.

Not to forget the weather. A very proper subject for conversation. The damp has penetrated more deeply than we might have supposed. The light itself is warped. Even the clouds are affected by mildew.

Our text for the occasion being: " . . . to preach deliverance to the captives and the recovery of sight to the blind, to set at liberty them that are bruised . . ."

The colours imprisoned in daylight.

Six Fancies

Il y a un poème à faire sur l'oiseau qui n'a qu'une aile
APOLLINAIRE

A Fragment of Truth

While working in the garden recently, I dug up a small fragment of truth.

It was stuck all over with clay and must have been buried for many years but I recognized what it was almost at once.

At first we kept it on the mantelpiece in the living room, but it was often embarrassing because of visitors and I eventually put it on my desk in the study, for a paper-weight.

I asked several close friends what they thought I ought to do with it, but no one was sure. "Keep it for your children," some said. "It's a great curiosity." Others suggested the local museum.

While we were away on holiday, someone broke into the house and stole it. The police said that they would make inquiries and asked me, "Could you identify it again as yours, if you saw it?"

Perhaps. But now I'm not sure if I do want it back. After all, if whoever it was should have found some use for it . . .

Learning to Breathe

I've been learning to breathe under water. Don't laugh. The flood
level has already risen overhead and is still rising. It doesn't leave
much time.

Of course, I'm not the only one to be submerged. Several of my best
friends have already drowned. They sway here and there as the
eddies carry them. I try not to look.

Gradually the lungs fill up and it begins to seep into the circulation.
The crucial moment! Don't think it won't flow in your arteries.
Only too easily!

Concentrate rather on one cell in your brain. Keep that dry. To try to
save the whole brain at once . . . you'll only end up by drowning.
With one synapse, even one cell, it's quite possible to survive.

I'm learning to breathe but it's slow work. As of today, I can breathe
perhaps twice, or if I'm lucky, three times a month.

This may seem a negligible accomplishment. But then, perhaps the
flood level hasn't risen so high in your part of the world, as yet.

A Wild Joy

A number of ancient customs are still observed in this part of the world but none is more curious than the yearly capture of a joy.

That is, a wild one. Some are still natural in the country districts. By tradition the whole town participates in the pursuit. Crowds come from great distances to watch, as, except for circus specimens, they know them only by description.

"Poor thing!" I said to one of the spectators, "to be tracked down like that! See how it trembles!"

He corrected me. "On the contrary, they are remarkably hardy and can survive for long periods under conditions of the greatest privation.

"What's more, they are treacherous. It's no secret that more than one great man has come to grief here, thinking he might get one for his own."

No Instructions

There were no instructions on the label.
There were no instructions inside the box.
I have gone through the packing carefully without finding a clue,
and the postman refuses to take it back, saying,
"Delivered to you correctly. No return address. Sorry chum, but
    you've got it now."

Yes, I've got it and I bought it and in fact it begins to look as if I'd
    been properly had.
I saw the announcement in the classified section and I sent away a
    money order for happiness (it sounded just what I wanted)
and they sent me the complete kit as they promised, every bit,
but without any instructions, not a word.

An Accident

As I ran to catch a bus, my heart fell out. This was quite painless, but
    I was startled as you might imagine.

It didn't appear to have been damaged. Feeling rather sheepish, I
    picked it up and put it in my pocket.

No one seemed to have noticed but when I got onto the next bus
    some school children at the back began to giggle.

How could they tell? Is this a common occurrence? Should I call my
    doctor?

Meanwhile, I keep it in the refrigerator. This is a warm summer. If it
    should spoil, I might have trouble finding another.

The scratching sound

The scratching sound, in case you ask, comes from my fingernails,
working at a small crevice which I've discovered in the plaster,

beyond which, you don't have to tell me, there are probably bricks
and even concrete,

and certainly most of my time is taken up with routine or even
compulsory activities, which is just as well since my nails would
never stand up to it for long at a time,

and admittedly there is an element of deliberate eccentricity since
the scratching has a bizarre effect upon many of my companions,
which does help to pass the time –

none-the-less, this particular crevice is far from exhausted and, finally,
I can see no other way out.

A Case

They call me that we have a case at the hospital. It is a fine night, not late, only a little after eleven. When I arrive, they tell me, "Mr H– is going to operate. The patient is in the first bed on the left in the men's ward." I go in.

It is dark but some light comes from a wall fixture above the bed. He is a man in early life. I begin to ask the usual questions. I explain that I will give the anaesthetic for the operation. He says, "My name is Pisgah." I nod and go on with my questions and examination. He appears tired and in some distress. The exact nature of his condition is still in doubt.

It is true, when he tells me his name, I have a momentary surprise, which I suppress. The name is that of the mountain mentioned in the Bible from which Moses is said to have viewed the Promised Land. As a child, the name had intrigued me. It also occurs in a hymn, as if it were a man's name: Pisgah's Mount. I had often thought, singing the verse: who was Pisgah? I had used the name later, rather at random, for a person who existed in a story I was writing.

It was a story upon which I had exerted myself and then, in one sense, abandoned. Pisgah, in fact, was the person in that story with whom I was most concerned. I had written two extended versions, and others more fragmentary, without being able to bring them to any satisfaction.

That I had not finished those pieces did not mean that I had abandoned the work. To abandon a piece of writing is one thing. To abandon a work, is another. A particular piece of writing is a means, for a writer, which may not always finally serve the work. Thus, I write this, which also serves, for the moment.

I give the anaesthetic while my friend Mr H– does the surgery. The details of the case are of no consequence. It goes well. Towards the end, when my attention is not too pressed with technical details, I have the chance to look more closely at Pisgah's face.

It is the face of a man asleep. As he sleeps, he is remote, both from himself and from us. Yet he sleeps by my will. I check his pulse, his blood pressure, his colour, his muscle tone, and gently assist each breath.

In the story I had often had the experience that Pisgah was difficult to lay hold upon. His character seemed to change. Even the details of what he did or said. I had wanted to discover who exactly he was. So that I could, in some way, come to terms with him, to finish the story. Now, suddenly, I felt him alive against my hand. And that life dependent upon my attention. If my attention should fail, I might lose him for ever.

I speak occasionally with Mr H–. Sometimes about the details of what he is doing. Sometimes about other things entirely. Neither of us speaks of the man with whom, in our several ways, we are involved.

Later, before leaving the hospital, I make a last routine visit to Pisgah's bed. He is now partly awake and responds to a touch on the face or a simple question. I look again into that face, somewhat firmer now, and occasionally tightened by the first twinges of pain from the incision.

"Who are you?" I ask. He smiles faintly, out of his half sleep, as if amused that after all this time I should not know.

The Sierra Nevada

Breath taking, in both senses,
   as I climbed out of the valley floor,

through scrub timber,
   over glacier polished rocks,

step by step, with vistas of sheer cliffs
   and narrow torrents of foam,

my map recording elevations,
   so many feet, so many thousands of feet,

and what had seemed ground level where I had slept,
   was indeed ground and level

but already a day's climb above my former ground,
   itself far from the sea;

and so above the tree line at last,
   as if approaching the sun, without shade,

to peer at serrations of peaks still beyond,
   still layered with snow at midsummer,

on a scale that is not to scale,
   not to be subsumed to the length of a man's footprint,

and yet trodden, marked by steps, laced with tracks,
   approached and touched, breathed upon,

even remembered as intimate.

For a Friend

I fell asleep
reading your new book
at ease in the sun
by a mountain stream
listening to the current
as to your words:
the currency of the phrases,
the concurrence of the thought.
It's one of life's pleasures
to be able to doze off,
to read your poems,
to hear your voice,
to sleep when tired,
to wake refreshed.

An Actress

She knows how. And how to do nothing.
Which is, in itself, nothing. But in place:
at the precise turbulence of a breath
at the precise angle of her throat,
stopped! For a duration. An area.
A prairie horizon of an instant.

Her head lifted. Not lifted further.
But held, resting. And holding us.
Who attend, moved, in her grip.

As she knows. Who is what she does.
Knowing us. And not moving.
But waiting. For that moment, not yet.
That next. That exact one.
In which she can move. And must.

A kite

acquires life
by grace of a string;

hovers, a hawk
in arrogance, then tumbles
undone by a gust;

darts at the least slack,
a hooked fish –
in its bondage making explicit
the intimate texture of the air;

skimming a thrust
from the bounty of the wind,
a tethered missile –
it swoops to display an energy
not its own yet flourished
in a paper tail;

and tugs at my hand
pleading to rise
that would fall
were I to release it.

By Auction in a Marquee in the Grounds

In the Staircase Hall:
Lot 498. Two iron bootscrapers, a handbell and two coconut fibre mats.
Lot 499. An oval two-flap gate-leg table with spiral legs.
Lot 500. A country-made single chair with solid seat.

"Tread softly damsel, with your stiletto heels and beehive hair.
A sediment of love is on that stair."

Our cars are ranked
in an adjacent field.

The last owner, an antiquarian,
died hoping that all would be maintained,
but lack of funds . . .

The lots to be taken away, whether genuine and authentic or not, with
all faults and errors of every description, and to be at the risk of the
Purchaser.

The bids inaudible outside
where the late summer air
stirs the matted trees.

Lot 501. An Eighteenth Century bracket clock with a white enamel dial
and eight-day striking movement, by James McCabe of London, in a
case.

"Dip your head, sir, as you go through;
that lintel can deceive.
Its height is less than what you might believe."

Stagnant moat water
and a swan
immaculate.

The auctioneers do not hold themselves responsible for the correct
description of, or any fault or defect in . . . and make no warranty.

LOT 502. An Eastern prayer rug.

In Gothic Script upon a wall:
O Lord support us all the day long of this troublous life,
    until the shades lengthen and the evening comes . . .
    then, in Thy mercy, grant us safe lodging . . .

LOT 503. Seven framed engravings, various.
LOT 504. Other items, various.

Sharing a common lot,
as if by lottery.

"You bid against Time's sand. Be generous.
Not even the catalogue is free.
There are no bargains here, or in history."

Birtsmoreton Court, Worcestershire
25-27 August 1964

I, Maksoud

I, Maksoud
of Kashan, a slave
to splendour,
wove this pattern
and these words
(each thread,
tied with a knot –
four hundred,
less a score,
width of a thumb –
for the sum
of the lifespan of a man)
till it was done
as garment
to no ordinary floor
beneath the eye
and tread of God,
here, where you kneel.

A sea-stone

A sea-stone – by the tide
(grip-sized, with carapace
of shards: a tooth,
polished, eroded, carious
from the jaw of time)
spat up, once only – held
and then dropped back.

For a Jazz Pianist

Seen (through
fogged goggles?)
submerged against
a cellar wall
(of museum dust?
of lumpy porridge?)
where we congest
and thicken (compost
air? scrapyard
breath?) to hear
few bubbled
gritty noises
(patterned?)
from a black
and polished upright
slotted box
(a camel's coffin?)
you (a swaddled
clockwork torso?)
sit before
and prod.

Riel

Perhaps I railed.

Is the truth
insanity?
Can we live on muskeg?
blackflies? air?
Even our mothers' words
cast out?

To break us, break
all trust, by promises.
Till murder was.

You must swing, Riel!

Like a silver bell?
Or a beast, to bellow
till the rope jerks?
Better, a vial
in God's grip,
poured or kept.

Where I have not been,
north of the trees,
the Indians tell
of how the caribou still come
from nowhere, suddenly
a host, uncountable –
and go.

And no man stays
to winter
on the Barrens.

John Bunyan: of Grace

mere foolishness
to those not knowing
the cogitations, torments
sometimes headlong
scattered, groping
amid tombs
bewildered, numb
with often glimmers
longings and breakings
sometimes pleasing
but stumbling ever
the very sinews
knotted in me
cankered, scurvy
bound in chains
upon a ladder
rope at neck
head in a bag
stopped at the throat
what guilt is
felt the smart
when broke upon me
seemed to spangle
'is sufficient'
not my will
'not cast out'
cling to that
relief and shelter
burden from me
sweetness in it
drops of honey
ease to speak
O now I know
such overflowing

all the goodness
such abundance
scarcely bear it
so out of measure
even to utter

Hommage à Cythera

How
lovely   a boat
slowly   rocking
a wave   gently
stirring   a leaf
softly   turning
a breeze   easily
safely   a shadow
lightly   a wing
beckoning
clear

After Catullus

You ask me? – her? – flat chest, varicose veins and teeth in
need of care –
               true, agile hips, smooth belly and snug crotch
(despite four healthy children) –
                       but slow to come and
hysterical – gabbling in panic – incoherent phone calls
– always writing that she'll write a proper letter next time
(always next time) –
               clutching in desperation –
                          then most
circumspect tomorrow –
               primping, but anxiously, before
her glass –
            sometimes nothing else to do but laugh at the
idiotic things she's got me into – while (I ask you!) swearing
all she wants is quiet, home, domestic unevent –
                   and I ask
myself: why her? – with her damn crook nose and a way of
looking in my eyes (I swear that hers change colour) as if she
glimpsed – but what? – or sought? –
                 ach, I'll break her bloody
neck, I will, one day, she holds her head so straight and walks
with such a swagger, such imperious sway, on quick light
steps, on air – but mincing! –
               and her heart, if I can, if she
has one – yes, she has – I felt it tremble once – and more than
once – God rot her – ludicrous –
               and I, at the age of forty-
three (know better?) – with wife and kids I'm fond of, more
than fond – to fall in love –
              and she, hung up on her husband,
anyway –

A Song

The river runs into the sea.
The sun returns to the west.
But tonight
    I can't rest.

The wind comes and it goes
Blue sky, and then there's rain
Some day
    in her arms again.

No man can foresee his end.
Nor remember from the start.
But I know
    who has my heart.

The sun returns to the west.
The river runs into the sea.
She will
    come back to me.

Walls

(1) For Matthew Mead

Graffiti on a wall
pockmarked by bullets?

Not without reason
but for all the reasons.

Is a wordless song
a song without a tune?

If I know you
then tell me who I am.

(11) For Pete & Spike

with back
against the wall –
that stance – a stand
taken, made –
indeed, the stand
at which to stand up
and command –
confirm the world
as present to our
presence – and
attending – its
attention granted,
held – voicing
its silence – to
allow us
voice

(111) For Ian Hamilton Finlay

To find that little right point,
even the tiniest one, as a start –

or a star, startled . . .
ah! – glad

it isn't too near
or far –

how else to manage? there is
so much to be managed

and syntax too slow
for what we know

at a glance, then ponder upon
and on.

Even four walls, a roof, a floor
are not much help –

the world leaks in
and so much else drains out.

Only a few words – pebbles
fondled dearly in a pocket –

may be kept
and keep.

(IV) For Charles Tomlinson

to delineate
what is perceived
with glance intransigent
as mason's chisel
struck with mallet force

yet deft enough
to match each shift
in a familiar landscape ever
redefined by sudden
inflections of the light

to cleave, from a wall
of sedimentary words,
a quarried speech

(V) For Robert Creeley

But to make sense
despite all,
that sense, above all
important,
of where you
or I or any
are
or go
and the pace necessary
just to keep pace,
knowing how far
and how long
it is
and takes

through that wall,
that door
to be passed
by some means
by all means
by any means
to be had
or used
as best we can
sometimes
even another man, perhaps
for the pulse
and impulse
of his voice.

(VI) **For Robert Duncan**

Made up (contrived,
as if a poem,
of words) to whom
often I turn
and may return and be
always at home –

wrapped in by walls
where the echoes speak,
are clear (resounding,
many men, as tides
caught in the ear,
as if a shell
held near) and dear
with remembered names
that chime
of rhyme and Rime;

and of that rime
(condensed by chill
from the void, a precipitate)
where Ymir woke,
hoar and gigantic once (a tale
told and retold)
the source
of all that's shaped.

(VII) **For Pierre**

an absence in myself, that I seek in
you that missing bit? –

                or the lack
in you perhaps of something which I
have? –

       but no, nothing to do with
have or have not –

              then just that I
need your good regard? – I do – but
indeed why you I could not say – though
I have that need –

           to attest that all
was real? to exult for me? –

                but no,
nothing in that –

          I have lost touch –
not knowing where you are, I am cast
astray –

        not even a wall to knock
against or an address – gone into
uncertainty and taking part of me –

but no, not taken – I have given it
away, not knowing where –

---

                but no, not
exactly, for I do know where – knowing
that it must always stay with you –

(VIII) **For Michael Shayer**

Once, climbing –
        loose shale
damp moss
        with an overhang
not a belay
        the route lost
night falling –
        we blundered
out on a ledge
        stood up, discovered
in the wall
        just above us
enough there
        to keep going:
a foothold
        and a handgrip.

(IX) **For Cid Corman**

We touch our feet
        to the same ground
joined by the depth
        of the globe itself.
There are no walls
        around
this earth we claim.
        I hush

and hear
    almost inaudible
yet clear:
    my lungs –
each breath
    drawn in
and then cast free –
    repeating
how we also share
    a common air.

(x) For Basil Bunting

not words
but a man

no wall

and a voice
to shape

delight

It's dark

It's dark
and late
and still.
Let me hear
your voice –
once again
once more –
the sound
of your voice
as you speak
my name.
Let me feel
your touch –
and again
as before –
against
all the cold
in the night
out there
kept away
by the fold
of your arms.
Let me be
as I am
with you
as we are
like this
while we can
still know
while we are
still here
while you are
as you are –
no one else

nothing more –
that is how.
There's time
even yet
even now.

Seven Snapshots, Northern Ontario

I
Living alone. A homestead in the bush.
Not well for a week. Now worse.
Gasping each breath. I tell him,
"It's the hospital for you!"
He shakes his head. Looks sullen.
Embarrassed? Scared? Then what?
At last, "My horse.
In the barn. Who'll care for her?"

2
The road, a tunnel. High banked snow.
We, jammed in a bus. To glimpse, ahead:
bronze body, neat black feet, sharp nose,
with tail fluffed, floating out behind. It runs,
swerving and jerking, crystal puffs of panic.
To shouts of, "Go on! Get him! Faster! Faster!"
Then gone. As we get off, "No market –
fox, hardly worth the trapping."

3
"Allo? Le docteur, là? Oui? Viens vite!
C'est moi. Chez nous! Ma femme . . ."
I rush. Neighbours and relatives
crowding the door. A babble. The priest
just coming out. We greet, shyly.
Then he whispers,
"All right, I think. Bit frightened.
Not the first time she is dying."

4
An Indian, "Sick." Stares at the ceiling.
Repeats, "I'm sick." Won't answer questions
or be examined. Just, "I'm sick. I'm sick."
Then snaps, "I told you." Rolls over,
face to the wall. A doctor?
What's he good for? Not to know?

5
No joke, it can really stop you dead,
charging the headlights on the road at night –
a thousand pounds or more, full gallop,
plus the speed and weight of car –
that's impact for you! With result?
A write-off. And the moose? No less.

6
Dabbing his handkerchief,
"You know it's got to come –
but when it does, it's sudden.
Forty-seven years together, and
we got along. Couldn't have asked for more.
I've expected it. But you can't, you can't."
His bobbing throat:
an overturned canoe in rapids.

7
"My shin? Oh, that! Did it myself.
Out on a trapping line alone, once.
Deep snow. My axe slipped. Clunk.
Right in. Quite a tug, to get it loose.
Lay up in my shack. It ran, pretty bad,
and stank. Whew! Had my flour and coffee.
Got out when the thaw came, somehow. Yeah,
guess I was lucky. With enough firewood
already stacked. Or I'd've frozen."

Six Country Pieces

longings
gone
along lanes
alone

★

shedding
to cover a field
beneath,
the leaves,
shed,
uncover fields
beyond

★

burning
the leaves

turning
over the earth

turning over
the earth

the leaves
returning

★

it's raining
again
out there
fresh rain
from the air
fresh air
air freshened
by the rain
it rains
refreshment

★

a cloud shadows
the sun's light

sun lit
clouds

light cloud
shadows

shadowed
sun light

the sun lights
a cloud's shadow

★

snow
flake
drops

In the silence

In the silence – yet
for my spoken words
composed – silent
she kissed me

and stunned,
at a loss,
I almost lost her,
reaching for more words.

Maria

Nights
with Maria –
and days
as bright.

A Girl

"April – and all
full leaf – and love –
and mine, he's gone –
like that – don't know
even where – who'll
kiss me now?"

Inventory

My glasses:
for astigmatism.
My corset: weakness
after polio.
For bread and roof:
a medical degree.
Daily, what
I depend upon.

Cigolando

Flame torments the sap
where the axe has cut
whimpering in the heat
as it splutters, as it frets
      it goes, it cries
            cigolando, cigolando –
green wood, green wood
talking to itself,
grumbling in the fire.

In the words of Tuscany
fresh wood as it burns,
as it crackles, as it spits,
as it smoulders, it complains
            cigolando, cigolando –
green wood, green wood
talking to itself,
grumbling in the fire.

For Us: An Invocation and a Processional

for us

a brightness
impelled to be uttered

for us

a season
sea-mark sheer

for us

a memory
so they can't take away

for us

a love
though gripped, set free

for us

a voice
while breath persist

for us

an hour
retrieved from shambles

for us

a joy
to be lifted up

for us

a dream
where no word was

for us

a sleep
and not by thought

for us

a day
brimmed and to spare

for us

a gift
against mere limitation

for us

      a dance
before the bolt is sprung

for us

      a moment
against the onslaught

for us

      a voice
with no need to reply

for us

      a hope
and there is no mistake

for us

      a silence
where light may seep

for us

      a touch
each day, as bread

for us

      a year
to keep what is

for us

      a savour
not choked back

for us

      a birth
at the rim of the pit

for us

      a work
and not perhaps

for us

      a place
lichen bright

for us

      a look
in the press of the chamber

for us

      a life
erased, new cut

for us

      a song
as a weight shaken off

for us

      a breath
to endure on the tongue

for us

      a word
before the door is shut

A Sea Story

really just an incident – and mostly for the sake of what a man said once
– in a little boat somewhere in the North Atlantic – nine hundred or so
years ago – and written down fifty or a hundred years after it happened
– so that though we can't be sure of exactly what he said, it must be
pretty close to the feel of it – or it wouldn't have been remembered

and his name was Bjarni – Bjarni Grimolfson – and he'd gone with
Thorfin Karlsefni with three ships from Greenland to Labrador and
Newfoundland – which were warmer and more hospitable then, than
they are now – but they'd had a rough time of it – because of the
Eskimos and Indians – and quarrels among themselves – and had
turned back

and this Bjarni was in one ship and the rest of the expedition in the
other two with Karlsefni – and had got separated and lost their way and
the ship began to leak – badly – the story says some sort of sea-worm
had chewed up the bottom – until they could see they'd really had it
– and still far from land

but there was another much smaller boat – towed behind the main
ship – a long boat or cutter – which had its hull protected with a sort of
tar made from seal blubber-so it hadn't been damaged – but much too
small for all of them – so they drew lots – who was to get away in the
little boat – and this Bjarni (it was a fair lottery – even though he was
the leader, he took his chance like the rest) drew to go in the little boat
– with about half the men – but when he was in it, one of the men left
behind (a nephew or some sort of relation) called to him – that when
Bjarni had invited him to come along – back home in Iceland – he'd
never thought then, that he'd get ditched like this

and Bjarni said – "if you're that bloody greedy to live – you can have
my place" – or words to that effect – and the nephew (or whoever he
was) got to the coast of Ireland in the little boat all right – while the
others in the other ship drowned – at least, no one ever heard anything

of Bjarni Grimolfson again – except, of course, for the story – and no
one even remembers the name of the other man – whoever he was – or
what he did with himself, afterwards –

Five/Four Time

bramble hedge roses

weave and unravel
wind and regather

loop and turn backwards
twist and curl inwards

scent of deep thickets
thick with rose brambles

tint of frail petals
pale on dark lattice

roses in tatters
scatter your blossoms

bramble hedge roses

At Witley Court

At Witley Court
all that remain
are stones and stones
under the rain

and nests for birds
ivy and moss
all gone the same

merely a name
fountains of stone
absence and loss

tatters of wall
a roof of sky
and doors of air

so pass so pass
all that proud fame
fallen to earth

the years how long
and time how short
at Witley Court

A Meagre Song

Sparrow, sparrow, stop and start,
dull of feather, quick of heart,
how you live, while you can –
    wit and courage,
    dust and straw –
take this homage

Sparrow, sparrow, hop and fly,
pale of throat, black of eye,
how you live

Sparrow, sparrow, dodge and try,
scratch the gutter, plunge the sky,
how you live

Sparrow, sparrow, you and I
pair and mate, breed and die,
how we live, while we can –
    wit and courage,
    dust and straw –
take this homage

Dandelion Seeds

as dandelion seeds
upon the air
so the phrases go
are gone   and are repeated
lifted up
and drifting out
so each one goes
fall where it may
the dandelion seeds   abroad
upon a day in May
across the fields
above the town
blown by the wind
cast free   and strayed
playing upon the air
dancing   upon themselves
upon the chance
upon the chancing movements of the breeze
so fair
so fair a dance
so fair a day in May
and the dandelion seeds
they go   are gone
and none knows where
upon a whim   a gust
upon a chance of air
as if a haze gone up
blurring   as if a smoke
seeking their end
seeking a rest
restless to find a rest
a place to stay
and they are lost
are lost to us

and each alone
to find their home
their resting place
twirled up   and driven on
rocking   at ease
not caring   drifting down
to disappear
and not come back
so they must go
as we must go
as the phrases go
by chance
one afternoon
one afternoon some day in May
the dandelion seeds
upon the air
some afternoon
towards the end of May

Lake

I remember once
in a far off country
it doesn't matter where
or even when
it had been a hot day
and a lot of work to be done
and I was tired
I stopped by the road
and walked across a field
and came to the shores of a lake
the sun was bright on the water
and I swam out from the shore

    into the deep cold water
    far out of my depth
    and forgot
    for a moment
    I forgot

where I had come from
where I was going
what I had done yesterday
what I had to do tomorrow
even my work
my home
my friends
even my name

    even my name
    alone in the deep water
    with the sky above

and whether that lake was a lake
or the shore of some great sea

or some lost tributary of time itself
for a moment
I looked through
I passed through
I had one glimpse

    as it happened
    one day in that far off country
    for a moment
    it was so

Amber Toad

getting up and lying down
  and wake again and keep in time
with the amber toad who squats beneath the
    purple celandine

starting out and coming back
  and going round and keep in pace
with the khaki beetle climbing through the
    blades of meadow grass

take me where I want to go
  and don't tell me until I'm there
with the crystal dragonfly who trembles on
    the sunlit air

how it is and where it was
  and rain upon the jungle trees
with the golden hummingbird flicking through
    the scarlet leaves

patch it up and knock it down
  and start again and keep it tight
with the midnight spider weaving dew upon
    his web of light

edging sideways, falling over
  knock it back and have your fill
with the daddy-long-legs scrambling on
    the bathroom window-sill

many places, many times
  but always patient by the wall
where the slugs are happy
    and the damp will never fail

there he is
night or day
there he is
rain or fine
    watching what may come his way
the little amber toad who squats beneath the
      purple celandine

For a Chinese Flute

```
    as if a squall      gone past
bare trees       finger the air
    perhaps forget      what went before
and now and       not my voice
    crowding      clouding the attention
tending       turning towards
    new gaps      of sky
one voice       another's
    various      what was
not chosen       choosing
    some early morning       golden sun
to run       outside
    all holiday       games
make believe       believing
    started      tried
not hard enough       perhaps
    disdain      even of summer
why not       why
    going back      restating
all in the error       all
    in the diffidence       and another's
and was born with       bourne with
    burdened      slipped
let slip       and find to find
    even today       year of a life
indulgence       drowsing
    drifting      rest
no rest       but tears
    relief      and silence
silences       in stillness
    steeped      light
silver grey
```

There is no Why

turn, the thought may
burn, the mind's con-
cern, it will not
learn
      (it will not learn

know, that love may
go, the heart is
slow, but it is
so
      (for it is so

sing, what thought may
bring, the mind may
cling, past every-
thing
      (past everything

cry, that love may
die, the heart may
lie, there is no
why
      (there is no why

    it will not learn
    but drift and turn
    for it is so
    as time must show
    past everything
    that time may bring
    or song may try
    there is no why

Where the Wind Blows

Where she comes from,
    no one knows –
now she's gone
    where the wind blows.

She, I loved
    and do love still –
always the same
    as the leaves tell

as the river sings
    and the birds cry
as the stars shine
    in the far sky –

who made me glad once
    with her smile,
who stayed with me
    for a brief while.

But where she comes from
    no one knows
and now she's gone
    where the wind blows.

Mid February, Snow on the Wind

her finger tips
graze chill
beneath his shirt
along the ridge
and furrow of his ribs
to press for home
in the heart's fold
    till skin
and sinew quake
and pulse
    rewake

A random sapling

A random sapling
you sprouted obviously
in the best place
where you weren't meant to be

and twice I cut you carefully
down level with the ground
but you grew back

then I tore you up
and shoved you roughly
into an unwanted corner

where you took root
and flourish now
even more vigorously.

A Regret

Not that we loved
or it came to what it did
or we had so little time
or even all the pain that others knew

but how, one summer day, we never took
that one mad dip in the surf I'd promised you
because I lacked the carelessness to squander
even those few moments from your arms.

Went to Hell

Went to Hell
(not for the first time).
Thought I'd seen the last
of my old girl friend
but *"You rotten bastard*
(she started) *all your fault*
I'm stuck in this
bloody awful place."
"Come off it (I said)
that was your hang up,
not mine. Lots of birds
I fancied better'n you."

How Could I Not

Snapped off,
crushed, faded,
once a living flower –
was that what I sent you?

Yes – and yet
how could I not
grasp at such loveliness

or not want for you?

A textured mist

A textured mist
    clouding the Malverns –
your touch enfolding
    the hillsides of my heart.

Happiest

"Happiest
like this"
she said –
happy
with him
like that.

Residues: Down the Sluice of Time

glitter of what's far off,
flash of the unseen
casting back the light

      pulse of the stars – and the dark
      consumes our sight – in a shuttered room,
      a candle flickers – and her eyes ignite

to rekindle
at source
the first fire –
need, need
against need,
the need fire –
to consume
with a need,
to blaze forth –
to ignite
the last void,
to flare silent

      and a girl walks away down the street – her
      hair hangs in a braid down her back – as
      she walks, she moves, that braid moves,
      my heart moves – desire moving, shaking
      the heart

by the heart, taken
and from the start

      though sometimes glimmers – finding what
      lightens – words that cling, that delight –
      one word: alula – meaning: a tuft of feathers
      to prevent stalling, on a bird's wing

against the falling
of the wind's thrust

    as I remember walking with you, too early
    for a northern spring – the sunlight
    bright on the barren trees – the air still
    coldly abrasive on my face –
                talking of mutual
    friends – gossip of Montreal, Kyoto,
    Albuquerque – around the world as if next door –
    their losses and achievements part with yours
    and mine –
            near and beyond, as then, as now –
    a landmark sure by which I can navigate – by
    which all other bearings can be judged

and yet I have lost touch with you –
as if we had mislaid our hands?

    and once when a child, I saw in the British
    Museum, a man from three thousand years ago,
    preserved largely by accident and the drying
    action of the sand, lying on his side in a
    slightly huddled position, in exactly that
    position in which I sleep myself

against all rest, all trust –
to find the courage to write
that I don't want to write to you
ever, ever again

    riddled with cancer, scarcely able to sit up,
    old Charlie Oliver, as I drove him to the
    hospital: "You do realize that you've ruined
    my day? I was planning to go pheasant shooting"

potency of nostalgia,
in farewell, such fury
overwhelming impotence

> gold green of the hop vines – late September
> sun – viridian saffron – dangled veins – all
> summer stored in their crispness – aisled
> profusion – topaz shadows – xanthochromic
> light

how was it then, Lord Gilgamesh,
those days you walked the earth,
those days after the Flood?
how was it? was it good?
the sun, the air, each breath,
those years you had in Erech, king,
a famous man, you lived, you knew,
you were . . . what? can you tell us?
do you speak? have words?

> of receding splendour – clarity in the
> morning air – after night of party, drunk
> and high, good friends and whisky, clowning,
> kisses – firelight dappled faces, rosehip
> colours – sinking down, releasing – to a
> light-grey, silver-sifting, soft as
> memory, ash

of what can be no more
and all that went before

> and there in the paper, reading
> of Arletty, blind – and Winters,
> with cancer of the tongue

this one, that one,
their names embarked on history

old Mr King, of the Kedges, farmer, cattle
mostly, yesterday at the Gloucester market,
bread and cheese in the pub as usual but
"hadn't tasted as it should" so sent for the
doctor "never happened before" (except when
he'd missed a turn coming home three years
ago and smashed his car – concussion, broken
ribs and a hip, some weeks in hospital –
"damn nurses ordering me about . . . and now,
won't let me drive") standing astride before
his open fire "you'll have some sherry,
won't you?" and this morning "only toast
and tea for breakfast . . . must be something
wrong" – at eighty-three – "and a lot to see
to, later on today"

well, he's gone now

       after grudging struggle – incoherent,
       paralysed – his buttock ulcers bleeding
       through the crusted pus

and every man immortal
till his day is come

       a January afternoon, transplanting raspberry
       canes – knocking the sticky earth from off
       my boots – warm in the pale light, in the
       saturate air – for half an hour, three-quarters:
       bliss

to distend the heart
and break it

       dried blood bracken,
       stained in autumn burn

and from the Tolbooth of Edinburgh, August
5th, 1684: "And we bless the Lord that
we are not a whit discouraged but content
to lay down our lives with cheerfulness and
boldness and if we had a hundred such we
would willingly part with them all. Our time is short
having gotten our sentence at one of the clock and
are to die at five this day and so we will say no more
but farewell all and welcome Heaven . . ."

signed: Thomas Harkness (of Locherben)
   Andrew Clark (of Leadhills)
   Samuel M'Ewen (of Glencairn)

   down the sluice of time

and near the head of Chapman Cleugh, in the
neighbourhood of Nether Clogg, lies one – but
neither his name (nor the names of those by whom
he died) is known

   where the wind is keen
   even in summer

a weapon called the Galloway Flail: the handstaff,
tough and durable ash, five feet in length – the
soople (that part used to strike the barn floor) made
of iron, three feet in length and with three joints –
one stroke could shatter a sword (or a skull) to bits

   stroke upon stroke – day break, day
   break – threshing the world for seed,
   the reaper sun

something burning,
burning itself out

and the faded watercolour I found of a
little boat with one sail and one man (with
massed rocks and ringed mountains beyond)
out of the mouth of the cave tunnel, out of the
darkness, it moves forward, it floats serene

and towards?

not there, not there

why should it be so painful?

nudge of her breast
through a muslin blouse

so painful

time, all time – that time – those
days – her head within my arm – my thigh
close held by hers – one room – a bed –
how shall it? – shall it end?

as a flare
of breath on the air

or a flush of fire flung upwards in the
flue from one struck match at the paper,
caught – dry twigs igniting, kindling –
spending out in a force of giving – roar
of draught in the caverned vent – a rush
of radiance billowed in the hush –
unchecked – not spent

and the worthies of the Kirk,
their first question:
the chief end?
and their answer:

to glorify
to enjoy

> this morning, going to work – golden
> nuggets overflowing on the road – a lorry
> load of manure – midwinter harvest – for
> the eyes – and for the nose – and the
> waiting crows

no use to deny

> last quarrel with his wife, in a fury
> struck her, knocked her down the stairs,
> saw she was dead, took gun from wall, went
> upstairs, smashed in the children's skulls
> before they woke and then the dog, went
> down, took paraffin, set fire to the
> cottage, back upstairs, lay down on his
> bed, muzzle to mouth, blew out his brains –

and in the country churchyard by the
ancient yew, beneath the four names on the
stone is cut: *"And the Spirit shall
return to God who gave it"*

> to my friend, my old, my old good friend

and a squirrel runs on the Tree of the World,
it runs and is nimble,
between a snake at the root
and an eagle in the branches,
to stir mischief, make strife,
unwearied in provoking

> with weariness, sometimes – and a time
> to rest – look out on the hills – with
> gorse and rowanberries – punctate
> colours through a tweed-grey mist

intense clarity,
the exception

    with rain obscuring rain
    rinsing the light

"and all forms merely
envelopes for the spirit . . .
but to design outside need and custom
is to write in a language no one can speak . . .
and nothing that is only one man deep
can last . . ."

    wrote Lethaby – at least one man – who
    built his church, in poured concrete,
    rare then, sixty years ago, and reckless,
    not reinforced – it held

where the mind may travel

    and a fulmar, three days out from St
    Kilda, following the herring fleet, swerves
    and drops down, almost lost between the
    crests, its wings stroking the long swells,
    as it turns – and turns back – and towards –
    towards a ledge on a sea cliff

so the heart turns
and yearns

    towards what's known
    in the unknown

as an aroma
seeking forth

in my nostrils, citrus wine – the scent,
specific, suddenly – that I'd drunk almost
three hours before – come back, uncalled
for – on my breath, diffused – a residue,
persisting – named and claimed

not strained – with a refrain of music, heard – an air,
a pulse – of dancers – figures, chorus – limbs and
lungs – each stress, a footfall – syllable, a note –
men, making it, with pipe and drum

       dancing at Upton – Taff, the Ledbury Men
       hot afternoon, Bank Holiday – with Dicky,
       Dave – the crowd, crowding about us, egging
       on – striking across and back and back
       across and on – all sweat and laughter,
       sticks and arms – till blood on someone's
       thumb

and in Welsh verse: all syllable and rhyme
with interruptions, decoration,
sheer gratuity –
but in Saxon: stress, alliteration

       gifts – of breath – of halts of breath –
       a moment, minutes – less or more – not
       thankless, thankfully – but giving thanks –
       for all that's given, is

a label: *Queen of the Border Flower Honey,* from
Peter R. S. Halley of Kelso: "This is the finest honey
in the world. The reason being that we in the Borders
enjoy the rich cultivated pastures of clover blended
by hedgerows of wild flower and hawthorn,
plantations of apple, lime and plane tree, often
finished with a tang of early heather. I do hope you
enjoy it."

I do hope so

with a turmoil of insects on the window
    pane, seeking the light and warmth –
each alive, each separate, each with
    its desire –
and behind them: the night

old Mrs Baldwin, living alone – comfy
in bed – her daily turd in the commode,
glistening and fragrant – still doing
the pools at eighty-seven "you never
know" – with her drop of Scotch and
gas fire purring – night light by her
bed – taking her tablets, sometimes
muddled – "rheumatism . . . heart ones . . .
sleeping . . . yes . . ." – with nurse to
wash her twice a week – until, one day,
a headline in the paper: WIDOW DIES IN
FIRE – first light, the billowing smoke –
found crisp and charred

with a wind at dawn
blowing out the stars

inflections – tides on the air I
breathe – congruities of affection –
rare of risk – beyond all hazard –
random gain

a face
passed by on the street –

so near,
scarcely a breath away

cloud tatters – wavering gaps
of tearing sails – birds flung
on hurling air – wind grappled foam –
wave skelters – nails of rain –
a clutch of scurried hail

all breath away –
a sound of hammered nails

consuming flickers
crests of hate
virago screams
each arm, a flail
child sobbing
blink and flinch
sheet over head
limbs wracked
with spreading
blackcurrant ache
"can't help it, can't"
a sodden pillow
stink of piss
ripped nails on slate

rub out – try to rub out –
repeat – try not repeat –
try – try why not –
why not repeat

uprising – caked with rainbow
slime – a corpse hooked from the
river – sausage limbs – no feet –
with peeled grapes for its eyes

replay, replay the tape
(the only way to erase)
till the mind wears out

or is played out to an end, put by,
goodbye – a station platform, dawn, no
sleep – "have a marvellous time" – going
away, a daughter – cut with diamond on a
window: *Saturday January 21st '99 Mary
Ann went to London* – mine the same, but
never mine –
                 to laugh "and don't forget to
change at Oxford . . . don't forget to write
to what's-it . . ."
                   repeating that – a "don't
forget" – repeat "forget" – repeat –
forget –
           a snick of wheels on rails, the
gaps – snick, each gap – snick, a gap –
each cut, a gap – a separation

incisions – wounds – proliferation from cut edges
to bridge a gap – weaving across, clumping tighter –
often stronger than it was – scarred and fixed –
a mark – a cicatrix

    where the heart lies fallow

and I dreamt I stood before a tree
that tree was rooted in the earth
that earth was firm beneath my feet
my feet still hidden by the dark
a darkness lit by many stars
stars that were mingled with the leaves
leaves that were restless as they sang
that sang the changes of the wind
a wind that came for ever from the sky

    and one evening on the rim of a little
    hill with a view out west over the far
    mountains where the evening sun was bright

and the light was warm upon us as we lay
on the tufted grass between the bracken
and the heather
            and heard the sheep
and the lambs calling to each other and the
meadow larks rising and falling in the
blue
            and looked up into the open sky

as we looked
we saw

    we knew

happily, from the Borders, northern
men, Gododdin, don't say
he was not – he was an oak beam
holding, earning fame, his worth
amid spear forest, rank, that day
with lime-white shield, red tartan, gleam
of gold torque, lake-blue sword, at Catraeth –
spreading glut for ravens, ample prey
for eagles' beaks, feeding their esteem
with carrion. He went forth
when all turned back, was gay
in wounds, made death seem
casual and none on earth
so lavish to his friends may
be or was so steadfast, not again

    not there, not there – voice of
    the heart – what's dear and near, gone
    out – returning – turning in the
    heart – and on the air

such as he who comes for the first time
    upon the head waters of a great river

or he who dozes on a park bench and realizes
    the solution to a mathematical conundrum
or he who goes at dawn to clear the cigarette butts
    and orange peel from a public fountain
or he who takes all the children in the street
    to the circus
or he who scrapes the clay from his boots to
    model a face he saw in a dream

      red, crusted, watery eyes – beneath a
      mane of ashen hair – sagged cheeks about
      a toothless mouth – humped shoulders –
      tottering – whisky on his breath –
      twitching his arms and grumbling "not . . .
      not interested . . . in anything . . . can be
      said in less than twenty pages" – angry
      how, as a lad, they had made him view
      his father's corpse "a rickle of bones . . .
      that's all it was . . . not right that a
      boy should have had to . . . forced to . . .
      and the talk . . . the talk, the worst"
      and in thirty hours consumed two spoonsful
      of casserole, a soft boiled egg, one bite
      of toast – the rest, chiefly whisky
      (malt) – but perhaps a little beer and
      a cup of tea and at least two packs of
      cigarettes – complaining all the time of
      dizziness and his stomach feeling not
      quite right –
            with eight pounds every
      week direct from the Queen (and free of
      tax) –
            telling of Pasternak at a public
      gathering when asked unexpectedly to
      recite his poems but forgetting lines –
      how the audience filled them in for him

where I'd never been: a lane under the hills, at
Rochford where the Teme flows deep. The
guidebook reads: Fine Norman doorway to the
church, with zigzag ornament, carved capitals. For
tympanum, cut in the stone: a tree beneath an arch
of stars

      where I have now been

and the old stories tell
how even the Gods of the North, Odin and Thor,
came to a last confusion, struggled and died,
fighting with giants out of the earth and sea –
they called it Ragnarock, their destiny –
and the god of the sun came back,
Baldur the Beautiful to them returned
who had sailed into the horizon burning
that out of ashes grass might grow –
and in the flight of clouds at dawn
going down in tatters, falling,
men might see
upon far dragon wings the corpses borne away –
walking together in some meadow green
to make concordance and rebuild anew
in stillness and sweet air
one day, one certain day

      morning of early June, full light at
five, cool air before the heat – walking
to early work, after night of dancing,
love –
      her head at rest on the pillow,
there, content –
      with a spray of
elderflower over the hedge to brush
my face – multiferous and stellate –
flooding the air with shimmers –
      drenching the heart

the waking, dreaming,
clamorous heart

> There were no roll calls in that Camp.
> They only counted how many went in and
> how many corpses came out. It was a common
> thing to get a corpse to sleep on in order
> to keep dry. The Sondercommando were the
> prisoners condemned to work in the
> crematorium. They could only be relied
> upon to work for a few weeks. The first
> job of each new member of the Sondercommando
> was the incineration of his predecessor

the first job? the chief end?
and the brilliance of colour
on the belly of a bluebottle –
what possible purpose?

> better Sir Thomas Urquhart of Cromarty,
> who translated Rabelais, and died in a
> fit of laughter on hearing of the
> restoration of Charles the Second

and in 1333 at Hallidon Hill, outside Berwick,
a gigantic Scotsman by name of Turnbull (who had
saved Robert the Bruce from a bull) swaggered out
between the opposing armies and challenged an English
knight to single combat

> well, he got killed for his trouble

or the world
a great ball of cheese?
and we, the mites on it?
or somebody
(Prime Mover as Bottle Opener?)

uncorked the champagne –
bubbles, spherules, cascades –
a milky way of foaming suns,
asteroids, condensed gases,
amino acids, evolution –
and here we are?

> with Comrade Mayakovsky
> at the microphone:
> "Fellow workers! Comrades!
> Poetry! The Party!"
> and a great old party too, it is
> (a friend said, leaving England –
> it was, he meant)
> winding on down the stairs
> past the stares
> of the couples (pairs)
> and the hairs, long shed
> from the pate of Comrade Khrushchev
> who had a great old party, too,
> in his time
> (though not so funny)
> vodka, vodka,
> that's no crime –
> drinking, drinking,
> rhyme on rhyme

and time, please, gentlemen,
time

> with dead men's voices
> thronging in the air

and not a word
but sound
till heard

caught in the ear,
itself a shell –
gap in the skull

hone of the sea
far off,
whetting its roar

and Bunyan saw in his dream that as
the pilgrims came to the gates of the
Celestial City, there was a way to
hell even from the gates of heaven

even from the gates

unclench, unclench

bloom of the gorse,
far spiculed

plume of the breakers,
shoreward

gaps in the haze, in the dawn
light glimpsed, one sight

hearing the wind
through stones – alone –
under the eaves – seeking
from nowhere – going, no
not home – needing reprieve –
where is? – who knows? – with snow
greaved – grieving to the bone

her face
by candlelight –
her eyes
and thighs

so, rhymes and chimes
and other times

and sometimes
not such wintry climes
as ours

  with hours of sunshine
  on some coral isle

and flying fish, near Panama, in the tropic heat, as
our ship moved south past the coast (thick jungle
green unbroken, the same now as Drake must have
seen going north in his galleon once, three hundred
years as not): out of the sea, dart-silver sprays, all
glitter, arching wave to wave, piercing the air,
the water, winged and finned

  shimmer of droplets,
  flare of transparency

falling of winter – fanning of leaves, down spinning,
rocking, drifting – twisting in the rain – a spattering
of crimson gouts – clotting the gutters, matting ruts,
congealing puddles, thickening mud – suffusing earth
to mould, to blood

  and at midnight, cold and old, in
  the absolute of their vastness, far,
  the stars are strewn in the dark:
  a precipitate of shimmers, mica seeds,
  of milky crystals, hoarfrost grains,
  a dust of spicules, flaring glints,
  a spume of shivered silver, diamantine
  flecks, an archipelago of quivered light

from an edge of iron
against a grindstone, thrust –
for a moment held
against the wheel of time

    snow flakes on the wind –
    and her finger tips graze chill
    beneath my shirt – along the ridge
    and furrow of my ribs –
    questing for home, for warmth
    in the heart's fold –
    till skin and sinew quake
    and pulse rewake

Residues: Thronging The Heart

thronging the heart

with utter astonishment
for expression

and on the face of a motorcyclist,
brought into Casualty, who'd missed a
turn, hit a lamp-post, his forehead
split down the centre, the eyes
hanging out

indeed, a sight

a form of utterance, an expression

an abrupt clarity

coming home from work, the hills
against the sun: a blot of indelible
ink, indigo on carmine

down the centre, headlong

today, tomorrow or the day after,
falling abruptly into place

staining the memory,
assailing

out of the commonplace, on impact,
unforeseen

indelibly and sometimes
even of trivia

with a gift of dandelions a child
picked and gave for my birthday,
staining my fingers, the marks
persisting

in the crannies lingering,
little streaks of happiness

and of surprise, and in names, and in
each particular: a jog Scray, a
Wallower, a Smutter – all parts
of a water mill

in a drench of words
and those uncommon

filling the corners, crevices,
crannies of what might

with the first reply
to the first question

by the old worthies of the Kirk:
to glorify – that is, sublime,
transform

and in each particular

like Beastie Dovey of Bringsty
who made a cardboard bassoon
and replied to a query: not for
the sound but to learn the
fingering

no less, no more

until left out in the rain to
come apart at a breath yet
unforgettable

that is, by force of intent,
an alchemy

with every moment less,
one less from eternity

so may we love, be loved
unreasonably, to distraction

in bewilderment at each touch,
each parting, wrapt round by
absence, clutching

seized by each pulse
each breath awakening

hearing the alarm, almost not
hearing, to wake to go out to the
cold, to daily toil, leaving her
bed, still dark of winter

who didn't ask to be born

spewed to the light, a fish
thrust on a shore

expiring in the air,
wrapt in a void

where we were borne by chance of tide,
to make our home, who have
none other

stumbling to rest,
not needing further

      while doing something else perhaps,
      breaking kindling, buying bread,
      tying a shoelace even, realizing

thrust of what must

      with a great pain flooding over
      us at the sight of so much beauty,
      that country called Arcadia, where
      we'd stumbled

helplessly thronged
to need each other

      with gaps in the haze, in the
      dawnlight glimpsed, one sight

plume of the breakers,
shoreward

      thronging the heart

Knarsdale

Snowdrops and stars:
a river sounds in the dark.
The fells, darker, surround
her footsteps cold on the path.
She goes by torchlight
to read names on a stone:
theirs, she never met,
and her own. She finds
no shelter from the wind
in the kirkyard, the kirk,
the ground frozen, the door barred.

There's more
(for the Faithful City Morris Men)

There's more than just these dances
or these songs
to every music played
and each belongs
to whoever makes it
now this evening
or in some yesterday
before our grandfathers had breath
or in some 'yet to be'
when the last memory
of this particular occasion here
is swept away
by the long caressing of the tidal years
and other men will recognise
always afresh these same
familiar moments that don't come again
and feel the beat
of our long practised stepping
in their feet and hear
recycled in their ears
even these words
so long dispersed
on the generations of the air.

The Borders Revisited

Those grasping men
best known for taking
their neighbour's cows by moonlight
and for their endings
in defiant ignominy
kicking the air
at the snug end of a rope
knew what they wanted
if not how best to get it
and taught their sons
more care in calculation,
less trust in luck.

Today, they sell clothes, groceries,
tend farms, keep schools –
still indifferent to opinion
but not over much.
As a signpost states
(from the A698 to Nisbet)
'seven-eighths of a mile' –
no less (or more)
as they watch the distance,
keeping a distance,
guarding their distance,
not so much wary
of what's there beyond
but more aware.

And of how to get there,
who nearly all do well.
Which is just as well.
Or not? Well, well enough.
Enough to live to keep what they have got.

Could it be

Could it be – was it true – that I
drove seven hours for a half-hour –
then mistook the day – wrote abject
letters – sulked – got angry – roasted
in jealousy when your girl friend
came – clambered up drain pipes –
walked on air – fell back in nettles –
made love in the rain, the mud,
under a mackintosh – then left my
shoes behind – once, lonely in a
field, was woken by a curious horse
at four a.m. – just to meet a bus –
once even thought you loved me –
more absurd, that I loved you –
how could I – did I – and still do?

You're right

You're right
but don't get me wrong.
Though I've no gift
for the spontaneous song
and you no use
for the contrivances of art –
be sure of this:
we both strike for the heart.

It's been

It's been a long time
all the time we've spent
and we've had such times
though sometimes not
and at other times
just no time at all
and all the time
hard to find time
for what does take time,
to tell you
they've been good times
and often, countless times,
beyond that and now
it's that time
when there's less than there was
but still time
and to spare,
time enough,
this time,
which is always
a long time.

The Last Fool: Berkeley Churchyard

"His folly served to make men laugh
    when wit and mirth were scarce."
So reads the epitaph of the last
    Fool in England, Dicky Pearce –
died seventeen twenty eight, Court
    Jester. Now the jest's on us
for we've had no lack of fools
    in public places since.

Watching a Burning House at Night

Insects trembling on the window pane,
we skirt the brightness (and our need, the same:
to court the aristocracy of flame –
a ruthlessness we secretly admire –
a fear we do not know that we desire)
unwittingly to honour this disdainful fire
that has disturbed our customary night
who gain but shadows and must shield our sight
and are revealed by the destroying light.

Aurora

Over the north:
aurora
cold splendour
rainbow shadow
flicker of darkness
banner of ice flow
streamer of fading
billow of frost rime
hanging of snow glint
mist haze of glacier
gauze flare of crystal
wind spume of ember
wave fall of radiance
shimmer of flame dust
verging, receding
unfolding, remaking
to glow without heat
to tint without shaping
over the north
cold splendour
rainbow shadow
aurora

If a Glance Could Be Enough

I recross. I circle. I turn back.
I mark my radius. I strain.
My collar tugs at a stake
in the paddock of the mind.
The links jangle
on the tether of memory.
If I could forget everything,
would I know that it was I
who forgot? Could I know
myself from my memory?
And how could I know
I'd forgotten anything unless
I could remember? And this I
which forgets, which remembers,
is no more than what it remembers,
what it forgets. Cut loose,
it drifts as waves against a rock,
as bubbles caught in an eddy,
as a swirl of random twigs,
a strewing of cast pebbles
enclosing upon nothing,
ground down as it is driven

watching a butterfly
dodging its way
in a meadow with the wildflowers –
a flared match,
a scrap of clipped persistence
flashing its message with twin flags
"I'm not hidden" –
or on a cliff top, facing the sea,
the wind coming up, riding the fiercest gusts,
after journeys on the farthest oceans,
it folds to a wedge

for rest, it clings,
a fragile voyager,
durably gaudy.

Perhaps a glance could be enough
if you could take a lifetime staring

as we settle our arrears
with heartbeat upon heartbeat,
breath on breath,
spending it out,
unwilling tenants
lodged in time

with one I knew and omihgodd
how she kept repeating that same omihgodd
to pace her days, in pain, absurdly gasping
omihgodd, snorting and fumbling round her room
from bed to chair to table back to chair to bed
and omihgodd her crumbling bones and failing heart,
arthritis, cataracts, a stroke, and omihgodd
one final wheeze and silence

but for the echoes endlessly repeating, part
of whatever it is of which we both are part,
this shifting aggregate
we can't possess and can't disown
who scramble daily for a pittance of a breath –
grass blades in a meadow
edging each other
thrusting to heaven
then cut down.

What aroma do we give, released?
What scent of harvest or sweet hay
to delight whose senses at our parting?

Rub out 'for ever.'

To remember
is a snare that tightens

and too much care
soon aborts the spirit.

In the cropped January light
of a late Sunday afternoon
beneath the sheepskin mottled clouds,
rain on my face,
I walked the hills and saw
the last leaf on a sycamore
swinging against the wind,
still twisting a precarious yellow,
raking the sky.

If a glance could be enough,
if you could take a lifetime staring –

with only the encumbrances of memory
to bind me to myself.

A Lamb

Yes, I saw a lamb where they've built a new housing estate, where cars are parked in garages, where streets have names like Fern Hill Crescent.

I saw a lamb where television aerials sprout from chimneypots, where young men gun their motorbikes, where mothers watch from windows between lace curtains.

I saw a lamb, I tell you, where lawns in front are neatly clipped, where cabbages and cauliflowers grow in back gardens, where doors and gates are newly painted.

I saw a lamb, there in the dusk, the evening fires just lit, a scent of coal-smoke on the air, the sky faintly bruised by the sunset.

Yes, I saw it. I was troubled. I wanted to ask someone, anyone, something, anything . . .

A man in a raincoat coming home from work but he was in a hurry. I went in at the next gate and rang the doorbell, and rang, but no one answered.

I noticed that the lights in the house were out. Someone shouted at me from an upstairs window next door, "They're on holiday. What do you want?" And I turned away because I wanted nothing

but a lamb in a green field.

Edge of Air

as the wind swept the sky
clear of cloud every twig
bare of leaf with my heart
just as clear just as light
broken free driven out
by the sheer edge of air

on the crest of a space
on a height to a far
other place beyond me
and that was within me
as I was far without
beyond where I was now

and I met and I saw
a strange face near to mine
but not strange whom I knew
and who spoke as to me
as one near whom he knew:

"How you look you look far
how you find never find
what you seek but have found
what there is and much more
than you thought or could seek
beyond here beyond you
beyond now as you are"

so I was was beyond
as the wind swept the sky
driven out by the sheer
by the sheer edge of air

Waves on the Shingle

glint flash of
sun blade on
hill crest in
dawn light

flake thin and
random flung
dart quick of
star bright

silver faint
wind drift of
moon disc in
cloud night

grain of rain
drumming down
heedless to
shut sight

wind from the sea,
   how you murmur, you murmur
stars in the night,
   how you quiver, you shiver
leaves in the dark,
   how you tremble, you tremble
waves on the shingle,
   remember, remember

It is there

it is there
in the crease
in the fold
in the grip
to be marked
in the shape
in the grain
in the print
who is blind
what he is
as he tightens
of his arm
all the strength
at his wrist

ready there
of his flesh
of his grasp
of his fist
to be read
of his bones
of his skin
of his thumb
to foresee
what he does
the cords
as he feels
of his will

of his voice
as he tries
is the roar
in his throat
on the words
as the thread
in his hand
as the line
in his palm

and the sound
in his ears
to cry out
of the breath
as he chokes
he would hear
of his heart
ravels out
of his life
is cut off

Witley Court Revisited

You used to be able to wander along
and watch it ruining
　　　feel it ruining
　　as it had been doing
　　as it would have gone on doing
for years and years, generations –
　　　　　trees and ivy growing up,
　　　　　roofs and walls tumbling in –
without much interference or help
except from the occasional vandal or souvenir hunter
doing their bit
with the birds and insects and stray sheep

until in the end
there'd have been a grass covered mound,
a few protruding stones, weathered smooth,
some clumped trees and bushes
and a presence –
　　　　　the presence
　　of something that had gone on quietly
　　in its own way
　　taking its inevitable course
at one with the wind, the rain and the seasons

until
the Department of the Environment got hold of it –
　　　I expect someone, somewhere, meant well
　　　and thought they'd preserve it,
　　　save it for the future –
　　　scraping off the moss,
　　　cutting down the creepers,
　　　propping up those chimneys
　　　that used to waver against the sky –

but you don't save something that's actually happening,
that's still going on,
by stopping it! –
                    the thickheads –
the last real ruin we had,
and they had to ruin it.

(1975)

A Reflecting Telescope

Grit in a bird's crop
(clenched, a sort of heart)
nourishes – and sand
(cliffs ground by breakers)
caresses wood (flowering
in undulations of grain) –
and diatoms of abrasive
(rotated under pressure)
hones glass
into a parabolic mirror
wherein spicules of light
may be coaxed from the dark
and resolved by an objective
into a moraine of stars,
each granule: a sun.

Never

It never went right –
there was always something:
she couldn't stand her father because he smoked a pipe,
her mother embarrassed her because she broke wind in public,
her older sister had the best room,
her younger brother was always top of his class at school,
her husband never got promoted as he should have done
and when he died prematurely, her pension was barely adequate
and then her daughter married someone she couldn't stand
and for years she's had this pain behind her left ear
    and something in her right leg and under her shoulderblades
    and a terrible itch in her crotch that wakens her at two in the morning
and a long list of foods (and medicines) that she can't stand (no end
    of people or things she can't stand)
and . . . and . . . and . . .   and now
she's got this peculiar sensation in her stomach that turns out to be a
    cancer but too far gone to be removed and they've sent her home
    to die
and quite literally she can't stand any more
and her sister-in-law is looking after her very patiently
    (particularly since she doesn't speak to her brother)
and she's seventy-nine
and the old gentleman next door (who used to do her shopping for
    her) has accidentally backed his car over a corner of her lawn . . .
it never went right –
there was always something.

The small change

The small change of love, the little coins –

a backward glance of the eye, a shopping note propped on the hall table, a joke (unspoken) shared in company, even a few words grunted at breakfast –

these are as necessary for the commerce of the heart

as the credit cards and banker's orders and overdrafts of passion

and like archaeologists we shall discover them where they have fallen, half buried in the silt of our affection, marked perhaps by the corrosion of time but soon repolished in memory,

irrefutable evidence, collectors' items, each with its date and face value, each with its weight and measure of perceptible happiness.

Remake

Remake the world?
Remake myself?
Troubles enough
rewriting this.

Keeping

Keeping and forgetting time,
his pulse to her pulse, rhythm and rhyme.

I am the Scythe

My arm has a crooked reach.
My smile is watered on a stone.
My song is a hiss.
My stroke, a swerve.
My bite, a flash in the sun.
To dance with me, you need both hands.
Rabbits and mice run from my kiss.
As I pass through the ranks of gold,
the proudest bows to my touch.
I part the stalk from the head,
the root from the ear.
I am the god of the harvest.
Remember me, when you slice your bread.

Scarcely I speak

(after the Sons' Wreck *of Egil Skallagrimson)*

Scarcely I speak these
surfaceless verses.
Slowly I summon
sounds to my mouth – though
few and forced and
far from my heart, so
wasted with weight of
what can't be forgotten.

Stunned out of silence, the
source of my voice is
hindrance and hurt. I am
helpless. No less a
despoiler than Death has
demanded a ransom – these
words that she wrestles
unwillingly from me. In

fury they're flung, like
foam from boulders the
bewildered surf batters and
bewails unavailing in
tides that return to their
trouble to struggle in
rhymes of the rending sea
riches of Ymir – that

giant whose jugular
jetted, who flooded the
deep with the drenching that
drained from his veins to
surge in this spattering
splendour of endings: the

roaring unrolling
cliff-raking of breakers.

Caught in a cross wind,
crimson leaves linger on
maple trees, mangled by
mid-winter. Singly, they
twist away, tumble, are
trodden down, fodder for
grave mounds and gathered in
grip of earth's stripping. So

first fell my father, then
fever reaped her who had
loosed me to life, and
later that dear one, who
years ago yielded his
youth to Hel's mouth. But be
wary of waiting – for
worst came the last. With one

blow, full abeam, I was
breached. The waves reached, still
greedy to grab, through the
gap they had sapped in the
hull of my household, my
heart's timbers parted by this
deed of undoing. With my
drowned son, I foundered.

Should I take shield against
shipwreck? hack down the
spume? or shock the surf's
onslaught? Once I fought
eleven and ended
each with my spear. If mere
courage was required, I'd
requite the sea's spite. But

no, no use, not even
nearly – however dearly the
will sets its way, it's soon
wasted. My joints quaver.
Time has trampled me with
truth. I'm no youth but a
dodderer – more of a danger to the
doorpost and to my cost. Thus,

beaten, I bowed my head and
believed grief would
deliver, not delay. I was
deceived – by the thief of
life. Breath lingered and
light. Enough of fight. The
pulse of this poem must be
praise for these days I've

gained – this grant, however
grudging, from Time's ledger.
Much or meagre, my
measure's not yet spent and
thronged with thought of
this: of all roots, his grew
straight to a sapling all could
see would be a great tree,

tall with sinewed timbers,
towering in its power. But
felled, and long before its
flower, who in need's hour was
firm against his father's
foes – now faced alone. Who knows,
until all's uttered, what's
unspoken? what trust broken?

Might is a maker of
men – but ended, our
names are as nothing if
no one remember some
deed of great doing while
daylight stayed for us and
most in the midst of my
mind I find him, my

brother, still at my back:
best of fellow guests and
bountiful at the battle's
banquet, lavish in his
cheer, no churl, no
cheapener with his reaping
axe but always spending to
attack. Now that's all past.

Few are the faithful and as
fleeting those I'd greet as
kin or count as
comrades. Friendship fades with
boredom in the bleach of age and
brittle bones grow fickle. Not
disdain but decay
depletes those nearest.

Crowds are a coward's
comfort and more hurt than
loneliness. I learn to
like men less and rightly
number most as nothing whose
one lord is money, who for
barter would betray their
brothers and boast of it.

Greed is a gallows where
good men may dangle and
gold, never a giver of true
gain or fame. I've seen
valour and virtue both
victims of riches and even
kings crumble when the
cash box jangles.

Silver can't satisfy or
sum what's gone. Can
surf be sued? or
settlement of debt be
had from hailstones? and
how could there be
reparation rated to my
wreck? or vengeance taken?

Brewer of breakers,
bitter's your liquor!
Froth is a ferment for
fools. You rule both
spume of wave-sickness and
shipwreck of drinkers –
bestower of barley and
bale of seafarers.

Mirth's not a mask I
manage. My face is a
grimace. My greeting, a
growl – and foul as my
manners, my mind. With
malice, I'm challenged and
abrupt in anger,
assess my oppressor.

Dissembler's delight, I
describe him: one-eyed,
rune-riddled, wrapt in
rhyme, many times a
stranger – who's stripped me
stark of pride, broken my
branch of life, beaten,
betrayed me: I name him.

Foe of the fearful and
friend of all fighters!
Awakener of worship and
wrestler with dread! I
tongue him this tribute, this
treasure of courage, this
utmost of utterance none
other may come to.

Great are his gifts, though
grudgingly given. I
tried them for truth and
proved their worth: a
fury at fraud and
never to fail to
name a knave and to
nail him, squarely.

More, what rust can't
ravish, he lavished. This
gift of all gifts that he
granted: the craft that
time can't tarnish or
tedium shrivel, to
carve as on crystal in
quarries of sorrow.

Nothing's left now but the
knot there's no dodging.
Few words are fitting and
fast comes the last. All
deeds must be done. No
dread of my ending
compels. I'll confront, not
concede, Hel's greed.

Time is

Time is a fisherman and in his net we're not the ones that get away
and time's the landlord, when he calls we must obey
and tallyman, not much is on the house, mostly you've got to pay
and referee, so mark your man, shoot when you can, there'll be no
    action replay
and irrelevant, whatever time the clock says, it's always now this
    moment that's today.
So help yourself! There's no room service. You'll not get it handed to
    you on a tray.
The best is to arrive, enjoy the scene, last out the night but not to
    want to stay,
for time's the wall at which the blindfold prisoner stands to wait for
    break of day.
Hang on to that, time's measure, for if you can't you'd better get
    down on your knees and pray,
for time's the croupier. He turns the wheel. We place our bets. And
    sometimes win. Who knows? You may. I may.
Though straight or gay, no one makes time. For all that he looks an
    easy lay,
and bent or straight, all get it. Because time rules. O.K. or not O.K.
and when the party's done, it's time that calls the cab, hands us our
    coat, opens the door and leads the way
whatever any one of us may say,
whatever song the band may choose to play,
however hard we join in on that chorus of
Delay, Delay, Delay.

You are

You are intent,
intensely sensed and densely
in yourself, not tense
but tensed and upon
an intention that you hold
not for but with
and of yourself
and that is towards
not what you are but what
you are bent upon, beyond
and that is beyond
even your intent, to which
you hold, that does not bend,
nor you, who are for the moment
neither less nor more than that
and in that, content.

Town and City

(1) February

A flurry of gulls
against the snow blotched hills.
You can't get further from the sea
or beat against more obstinate granite.
As refugees or the advance guard?
Either way, their extremity
must be severe to turn
for pillage or for refuge
even in these beleaguered days
on huddled Malvern.

(2) Old St. Andrews ("The Glover's Needle")

Second only to Salisbury as a spire
(though shorn of its church)
it hooks a distinctive spur
above the outline of the city:
a landmark
to the surrounding demolition
at public expense
after generations of "couldn't care"
and could do worse there,
pointing our attention
to the unravished sky
and not to Worcester.

Some Resonances and Speculations

thunder and lightning
in the galleries of the sky
in the theatre of the storm
an expression through a medium
from a build-up of tension
towards an accumulation of potential
unseen until expressed
in a pressure of decompression
and displayed in an inscription
across the blackboard of the night
making utterance of its urgency
declaring a transit of energy
along a line and through time
a graphic act, an elocution
demanding attention, alerting splendour

and in the gap between the flash and the thunderclap
we can count the distance as the pursued sound
encumbers the air with pain to escape from itself –
a collapsing tower of shattered drum-heads
a jettisoned mountain of crumbling anvils

but even the stroke of sight
isn't instant
though absolute
it can be measured
it has a measure
it becomes the measure
a divider to span the stars
to fathom the farthest vacuums
to calibrate the galaxies

in flung pulsations
of unwearied frequency

waves towards forever
light radiates greeting
and flickers of farewell
as epitaphs to stars that died
before we had eyes to see
or hands to wave across a room
who speak in waves, by waving

gestures of sight, of recognition
each quivering hand, articulate
beyond all straining tongues
except for what any man
may hammer his fist on a table
or force through incoherence
to alert even one ear against
all the deaf-mutes of the humdrum
it's no sinecure or penance
even talking to yourself
that self had better be someone
it takes effort even to listen
even to yourself, an intention
that consumes, that uses energy
must be directed as a blow-torch
to burn off the rust, to smelt inertia
or as fire in a kiln
fed by the up-draught of the heart
to anneal the ceramic of the will
into an instant of conception

by the intonation of a word
impelled from chords
struck by a force of air
expelled by effort
one lung-full of air
is all that any man has
until the next
and the next word

that falls to silence
gone as a stone into a pond
shattering the surface
but for the eddies widening outward
crest, trough, incline, decline
the shape of energy, its outline
a flowing contour that pulses forward
dependent on the element in which it moves

and waves come in towards a shore from storms far
out beyond our sight, from winds expended days
or years ago, and beat against the cliffs,
regathering, wearing down and falling back as
more waves come
        and every grain is shaped by the
fondling of those waves, is carved and polished,
every detail, by the gathering of attrition, in
the spendthrift ways of time,
        all the beaches,
holidays and picnics, every golden strand, the
children building castles, the lovers snuggled
in the dunes
        are the gift of waves from the toil
of winds in the munificence of time, from the
expenditure of the sun as it pours its radiance
to bathe the turning earth, creating heat,
convection, waves and storms

they say the sky is dark at night
not because the universe is infinite
but because it expands
the question was always there
and the answer, not the obvious one
perhaps not even the true one
but one answer
as the light pours away
down the insatiable sewers of darkness
gaping wider, the farther they go

so that every gleam, every syllable
becomes an event, an imperative

the least definition of a wavelength
or frequency of light to a retina
or amplitude of air to an ear
the recognition of a word
the registration of an outline
is always for the first time
always the last time

expending itself through the mantle of air
that clings to this globule of earth
as it swings on its tether of gravity
leaving no mark in the void
as it whirls towards where it came from
around an expiring sun
we can't even stare at, unguarded

we, who tremble
as spume on the wave-crests of time
hurtling forward, part of whatever
we can't get off or step outside of
for which we may be no more than a transient eddy
a gurgle down the plug hole
for the waste water of a bath tub we couldn't
        even begin to imagine
certainly not the punch-line, perhaps no more than
        the punctuation for the build-up of a joke
        we'd never see the point of, even if we could hear it

inscribing lines, smearing paint
muttering words, repeating rhythms
neither for something or for nothing
but because we must also transmit
whatever radiance is trapped within us

casting it out as if over a waterfall
down a torrent, into a whirlpool
that overflows through a chasm
along a gully, across moraines
into marshes, shallows, trickles
almost muffled to incoherence
but reaching at last to that sea
whose tides swell into clouds
that beat against the mountains of the future
and re-appear as springs, jetting from crannies
bubbling into the sunlight
voices from the heart-veins of granite
waves, pulsing from the rock

(1979)

Babylon

How many miles to Babylon?
    Three score and ten.
Can I get there by candle light?
    Yes and back again.
Can I get there by daylight?
    If the sun gets up on time.
Can I get there by star light?
    If they don't forget to shine.
Can I get there by electric light?
    Yes, if you've been switched on.
Can I get there by torch light?
    If your batteries last that long.
What do I need to get there?
    Take everything you've got.
Everything I've gathered?
    That isn't such a lot.
So tell me how to begin?
    But that's the easiest part.
Which isn't any answer.
    You start from where you start.
And if I'm at a crossroads?
    Try both ways at once.
They've taken down the sign-posts.
    Then try un-common sense.
But what shall I find if I get there?
    No one can tell you that.
Will it be worth my trouble?
    Tell us, if you get back.
How long could it possibly take me?
    Three score years and ten.
I don't want to waste a lifetime.
    You'll not get another again.
But I want to know what I'm in for.
    You'll not get to Babylon then.

Ballad
(in memory of old Camp 17 on the Abitibi, Iroquois Falls, Northern Ontario)

Jackpine "Chicot" Lumberhead
    was a forestry engineer.
Top of his class in College.
    This was his opening year.

Split pea soup for supper
    and wash it down with tea.
Before he goes to bed
    he has to take a pee.

"Oh don't go out there, Lumberhead"
    his buddy to him called,
"The stars are hidden tonight
    and the snow is deep and cold."

But he answered "There's a stove there
    and room for two or three.
They built it for our comfort.
    It's absolutely free."

"Oh don't go out there, Lumberhead!
    The snow covers the trees."
His buddy tried to save him.
    "You'll lose your way and freeze."

But he answered "I am faithful
    to the rules of the Company.
The Health Inspector's coming.
    He has put his trust in me."

He was not in for breakfast.
    No footprints could be found.
They dug down to the privy.
    They cleared the snow to the ground.

They hunted him with Indians,
    two snowmobiles and an aeroplane.
It was only fifty yards
    but they never saw him again.

So when the blizzard's blowing
    and you can't hold it any more –
don't go out to the privy!
    Take your leak beside the door.

Daft about

Daft about Sally –
in bed or out,
snogging at a party,
slanging me about.

Daft about Sally –
but not so daft as not to know
she'll see me when she wants to
and when she wants to, she'll go.

Daft about Sally –
who's daft enough to be
sometimes, when she fancies,
a bit daft about me.

Everyone was there

Everyone was there
even those who couldn't make it
because of distance
or the car breaking down
or work
or anything like that
even they
were with us
and knew
what I don't have to tell you
(but more of that later)
and everyone was high
really floating
with lots to eat and drink and smoke
and even crash out upstairs if you wanted to
and always someone else
you hadn't realized was there
suddenly appearing
and disappearing
with music and singing
and dancing and laughter
all at once and on top of each other
so you could hardly hear or move
(but could, just)
and even so-and-so
chatting up so-and-so again
and of course
a couple of people rather horribly pissed
and someone else being sick
(but outside)
and one girl having a quiet sob in a corner
(or it wouldn't have been believable)
but as I said
everyone was there

so there's nothing really to tell you
except
that if you weren't there
you should have been.

How I Did My Bit for Peace

I did my bit for peace one day
when Wiltshire swarmed with planes and tanks.
They sent me out to gather the hay
being too young to be put in the ranks.

I stacked my cart both wide and high
and started down the lane from the field.
The sun shone down from the summer sky
when I heard a crescendo of wheels behind.

It must have been a whole regiment
of motorized artillery.
The lane was long and narrow and bent
and try as they might they couldn't get by.

The drivers cursed me in prose and rhyme
and revved their engines to show their power
but I smiled at them and my horse took its time
and we held up the war for half an hour.

The Galvanised Dustman

If it's bring out your dead
or just a pain in the head
he'll take it away
and not tomorrow, today

for he's the one who can
there's no better than
he's a real dustman

for when you want him, he shows
and when you don't, he blows
it's no skin off his nose
he doesn't pass the buck
he doesn't trust to luck
no messing about
it's straight in and straight out
just leave it to him
he'll empty your bin
if no one else, he will
he's not over the hill

there's no dust on him
and no rust, not a glimm'
dipped in zinc
always in the pink
no need to panic
'cause he's all galvanic
all his bins are bright
all his lids fit tight
'cause he's anti-rust
like he's anti-dust
all polished and clean
any young girl's dream

so if it's bring out your dead
or just a pain in the head
he'll take it away
and not tomorrow, today

for he's the one who can
he's no "also ran"
he's a real dustman

and he's your Malvern man

You and I

You and I, old friend, between us, we should be able to design a
   better world.

First, we must get rid of the superfluous moisture, smooth down the
   more prominent mountains and equalise the temperature between
   the poles and the equator.

After that, it should be easy to remodel and redecorate. While I get
   hammer and chisel and mix the pigments, you can decide what it
   should be.

The only snag is that the shell is thin and under the pressure of our
   hands, the fledgling may hatch. I hear it pecking about inside,
   already.

Rain in Wales

Welsh hills are very beautiful
with no one else around.
The rain was raining steadily
when we found a lovely barn.

We were only sheltering from the rain
and it always rains in Wales

The hay was very comfy like
with nothing else to do
so just to pass the time we did
what any couple might do.

Just then the door swung open
and a farmer peered inside.
The hay was piled around us
but we couldn't really hide.

When I wake any morning
it's mostly rather late
so I get dressed very quickly
but never so quick as that.

He asked what we were doing
but I think he really knew
we were just out for a picnic
when the rain obscured the view.

We were only sheltering from the rain
and it always rains in Wales

What Makes the Weeds Grow Tall

So tell me what we've done
to make the weeds grow tall?
       Is it just the rain and sun,
       is it nothing else at all?
as the earth spins on its track
always going coming back,
       where Jack shall fancy Jill
       and Jill shall fancy Jack
until, until, until
       one day, Jack's tired of Jill.
Then alack, alack, alack
       if Jill's not tired of Jack
until she fancies Bill
       or maybe fancies Mac
who's always looking back
       and no one can keep track
for someone else again
       and then, and then, and then
and round and round it goes
       and no one really knows
       what makes the weeds grow tall
for no one knows at all
why Jack is after June
       (he'll tire of *her* quite soon)
or it might be Kate or Fran
       or Di or Sue or Ann.
So tell me what they've done
to deserve such endless fun
       as the earth spins on its course
for better and for worse
       till Jack shall find his Jill
(let's hope one day he will)
       and Jill shall find her Jack

(and be glad to have him back)
　　after the sun has shone
and the rain has rained its fill.
　　For it's nothing we have done
　　to make the weeds grow tall
(to make the weeds grow tall!)
　　and no one, no one, no one
　　looks after them at all.

Wulstan

This is the story that some
    of you may know
of Wulstan of Worcester – nine
    hundred years ago.
He was the Bishop of all
    of Worcestershire
and in those days to be a
    Bishop – that meant power.
He was a Saxon in a
    Saxon Kingdom
until one day there came
    the Norman, William.
William took the country by
    ancient right of war
as had the Saxons themselves
    long, long years before.
Then all the Saxon Bishops were
    replaced by Normans
except, strangely, Wulstan –
    he stayed on.
Was it merely because he was
    so holy and devout?
I can't quite accept the Normans
    being impressed by that.
Of course, there's the story of a
    miracle or two,
believed at the time, but for
    us it won't quite do.
And they could just be tales his
    friends had put about
to try to hide the fact that
    Wulstan – he sold out.
The Normans didn't trust any
    other Saxon cleric,

so why Wulstan? There's
    something strange about it.
And yet, and yet – the crux of
    it is this:
you can cover up a traitor but you
    can't quite fake success.
All of his life the praises
    never stop.
Worcester was proud as proud of
    its Saxon Bishop.
After his death, his tomb
    became a shrine.
Was that for selling out to the
    Norman Party Line?
No, not that. The truth's always
    simpler yet.
Wulstan, he held out for
    the best that he could get.
All of his people knew which
    side he was on
but somehow, somehow he fooled
    the Norman Barons.
How did he do it? Who knows?
    But Bishop Wulstan –
saint or whatever – must have
    been a crafty man.

A blind musician

A blind musician
who lingers by a spring
in the shadow of a hillside
and plays to what he hears
shall know clearly enough
that what overflows so freely
from the deep places of the earth
is not water but a song
from the throat of darkness –
a voice to refresh
not intrude upon silence.

As kelp

As kelp
strewn by the falling tide
folds dense on the uncovered rocks
so her endearments
cling to the least keepsake
of a departing lover –
as exposed
as quickly shrivelled
and as often by the hasty
trodden underfoot.

Love is

Love is a great door of oak,
studded with iron,
behind which is refuge against every storm,
that opens outwards
even before it is touched –

but, equally, can be
a dungeon gate
with jealousy, the hair trigger spring
to slam the bolt.

The dissipations

The dissipations of memory and the deceptions
of that inexhaustible tankard, always at the ready
to glut the heart with its indulgence,
would sweep us out of our depth on a fermenting tide
that has, suddenly, no mercy or counterfeit
and awakens us before dawn, nauseated, in anguish,
wanting only to forget.

The Unwavering Sun

Gnats churning in the stillness of a summer dusk
or showers of minnows swirling in a hollowed pool
or dancers turning in a flickering room
perceive no mockery in the unwavering sun
as it beams indifferently on their desires
but which, for all its heat,
cannot know one ember of the self-consuming fire
that makes their helpless pulses beat.

The seeking

The seeking of man for woman and of
    woman for man
throws both upon a fire that they
    mistake for love
as if such care for each other were
    any more than an incidental spark
cast from the flaring timbers of
    their splintered souls
to fuel the generations of mankind
    and thaw the chill, not of their lives
but of some unimagined fortress
    hall of loneliness
besieged on the farthest tongue of history.

It Can Happen

Love can be a small enamelled shell
picked up from the shingle at low tide

and then, it can happen, dropped and broken
or chipped away by too rough handling
or even crushed by greed for more

but also, the most terrible, misplaced
in a moment's lapse of care and then,
though you search for a lifetime
along the ocean strands of time,
it can happen, the same never found again.

It was

It was a good boat, never better,
and the sailing – winds, tides, harbours,
storms, discoveries – beyond telling
but now past salvage, good only for the axe.
Don't flinch. Every splinter
familiar as your breath, the wreckage
soon dried out, ready for kindling
to burn steadily enough on the nearest headland,
a clear mark to be seen far astern
on which to set a new bearing to steer
a new course with new companions
on a strange ship towards an unmarked horizon.

No

No, the sun doesn't fill the dawn with embers

and the stars aren't diamonds flung in
    handfuls across the sky

and the moon is a crust of frozen craters,
    not a phosphorescent bubble, not a pearl
    drenched in light

and my heart is not a furnace, but a pump and my
    thoughts are clear and detached, not unbroken
    horses without reins or bridles

and no, when you look into my eyes, it is not
    like waves against a shore, breaking. . .
    breaking always as if for the first time.

As the wind

As the wind, a sail
or a blazing hearth, a room
or the dawn, the world
or a song, each listening ear
or the rain, dry earth

or the tide, an estuary –
  flooding far inland at the springs,
  searching the farthest tributary,
  brimming the hidden inlets, the most
  secret pools, to every reach –

so you to me.

And I Think it Yours

That place
where a fold of hillside
scoops sun and shelter
from a mountain wind

or that
where a clear spring
pours out refreshment
never holding back

or that
where a steep track
veers unexpectedly
then opens on a crest

from where a traveller may see
far out beyond
which road to take –
all these

and all such places
have their names
but in the language of the heart
only one name

A Birth

As, at the end of winter,
the merest tip of green
declares survival

or, on fresh tinder,
the slightest eye of spark
proclaims light, warmth

or, at the gate of thought
the simplest word
releases utterance

so, a child may be
between its mother's thighs

by thrust of will
by pulse of need
by one despairing and triumphant cry.

The Ruin

Two lovers
driven by a summer storm
take refuge in the ruin of a tower
and with a kiss
would soon forget
those other lives undone
to shape their happiness.
Unseen above
in the fragment of an arch
a wild flower blooms
as it erodes the stone
to which it clings for root.

First loves

First loves
are unconsidered
never sought
but given
and even when reconsidered
are often sweetest
and most beyond regret

and so consider
lest you should ever lose
the unsought gift
of loving from the first
which being once lost
cannot be reconsidered

It is not

It is not the size of the peats
nor their number
nor anything particularly remarkable
about their shape or their quality
that sustains a fire

but it is their continued placing
without fuss and in due sequence
around the centre of the hearth
especially at morning and at night
so as not to starve or scatter or smother

so it is with our affection

decide to put it out if you choose
but don't let it die
for lack of a little ordinary care.

How much hurt

How much hurt can the heart?
How much drought can the earth?
How much rain can the flood?
How much wind can the sky?
How much dark can the night?
How much fire can the sun?
How much more can you want?
Would even that be enough?

If I take a stone

If I take a stone from the earth
and tighten my grip upon it,
however hard I strain,
it does not yield
and yet, let go,
it offers no resistance
but falls, is gone
back from where it came.

Then if I clutch at the air,
however far I reach
or long I try,
I cannot begin to grasp
what, for all my will,
cannot be shed
but envelops, insists,
enters me with every breath.

Even the sun

Even the sun
does not rise the same
proceeding and receding
in due succession through the year
and before each dawn was numbered
and the months described by name
men built great banks
and set up stones to mark
the turning and returning
of particular instants of the light

but whatever the predictions of a calendar
or alignments of a sunset may define
as each day turns to the next
and your eyes turn to mine
there is only one solstice
and one equinox
in the astronomy of our regard.

These rings

These rings that we exchange
renew themselves as the unwearied surf
that garlands but never binds
the coastline of an island
from which love ever sails
towards the horizon's circle
always farther
beyond which we cannot reach
and all of these
are emblems of our taking of each other
no more constricted
than is the earth
by the enfolding of the sea.

A Winter Wedding

Last autumn's heather
and the snowdrops yet to be
even by their absence
join to celebrate
both what outlasts
and what anticipates
as we two shall
look neither back nor forward
but to each other
on this brief day
and longest night for festival.

Your Hands, Their Touch

As in a sheltered inlet
the wind fallen suddenly, all hush,
with pulse of the waves on the naked shingle,
making back and forth, that sound,

so are your hands, their murmuring touch,
in long strokes, wakening tides, no rush,
to surge and carry us, lapped by delight,
in the stillness of one bed.

Beginnings

If I know you

tell me who I am.

Coal Mine

A July night half a mile deep

where crickets sing all day.

A Wedding Ring

Where I am is where you are

is where I am.

The Fodder

The fodder of everyday is never bested

passing like elephant shit mostly undigested.

New Year

When a fire is lit in the darkness

the dark is alight with fire.

What may be

That there are those who want to imagine it

is unimaginable.

For Shari

Enjoy. Love. Survive.

And send me a post card when you arrive.

From the Sanskrit

They find me crying and commiserate

but would I waste tears on less than joy?

Spaces

What might be said and then awaiting

what has been said.

A Marriage

They wanted for what they wanted

and were got by what they got.

Edinburgh

Familiarly of their sons and daughters:
    Vancouver, Hong Kong, Auckland, Rio –

"and you, away off down in England
    somewhere now?"

A stye

A stye

need not be an eyesore

Butterfly

A dab of splendour laced with acid –

no bird pecks twice.

Accounts

I don't spend my days

my days spend me.

A Last Poem

The merely unspoken

now beyond utterance

It is late afternoon and already dark

It is late afternoon and already dark.
I have been walking all day across open moorland.
I come to a forest.

It has been snowing for days.
Packed down on the road.
Drifted on the banks.
Clinging to the branches.
I hear only the grating of the boughs
under their frozen weight
and the crunch of my feet on the road
and the creak of the snow
as it settles itself in the drifts.

The air is dense with the cold
and the silence
and the exhaustion of the light

and every footprint disappears back under the snow
into an absence so complete
it is as if no memory had ever held it,
as if no man had ever pressed his weight,
had never trod, had never been
and never was – and least of all – there.

A wind from the north

A wind from the north
and north-east and by east
doesn't rest in the night
doesn't fade with the light
doesn't pause for the sun
doesn't stop till it's done
cares for nothing at all –
it'll thud at the roof
and scurry the wall
it'll plead at the window
and try at the door
it'll lean on the chimney
and twist on the floor
it'll find a way in
to unsettle your dreams
it'll crawl in the attic
and hollow the beams
it'll cram in the cupboard
and scrape in the flue
it'll snore in your pillow
and creep in your bed
it'll hunt in the churchyard
and pry up the dead –
and would loosen the bolts
and unbuckle the bars
of heaven itself
and shake down the stars.

Into the chasm

Into the chasm
into the void
into the vast and empty
last of every day
where we must stay
after the will has done
what can be done
then come what may
Into the unsounded deep
where we must drop
at the end of thought
and cause must stop
Into we know not where
or even, when we're there,
if we are there
Into we know not how
or then from now
Into that arbitrary truce
where all that we intend
and every choice must cease
Into that ritual of defeat
where every man must go
and be alone
where none may meet
Into surrender
abject and complete
that brings only a brief
and broken peace
Into that commonplace
of our extremity
we name as sleep

Hour of the Wolf

That hour –
hour of the wolf,
the hour to dawn –
      when only the hellebore is in flower
that hour –
      when every sweet is sickly,
      every freshness, sour
that hour –
      when you grip the battlements of an echoing tower and the
      stairs you have climbed have turned to salt beneath each
      step and fallen away within and memory is a sunken shaft
      and all desire a stone that drops and there is no sound come
      back within the hour
that hour –
      when you're flung beyond the stars through a gap in time
      and are given every choice to choose and have no power
that hour –
      when every pride must fawn
      and even love must cower –
that hour –
      when tears won't come when you want them and won't
      stop when you don't and your heart is adrift and your breath
      is clogged and you cannot sink or swim, you cannot float
      or drown, and there are no lids to hide the dark that gropes
      behind your eyes, the silence that deafens every thought,
      the sense that numbs the very chance to feel, the hope
      that crushes, the emptiness that bloats, the stillness that
      intrudes, the weariness that shatters rest, the absence that
      won't let you be, the nothingness unwritten, staring, the
      blank pages turning that devour
that hour –
hour of the wolf,
the hour to dawn.

A child lets go of its mother's hand

A child lets go of its mother's hand
as it takes one step, its first, and then another,
walking, running, slowly, faster, always closer
across a shimmering landscape of snow dusted ice
on which that approaching figure is no more
than one faint swirl of scarcely moving shadow
against an upward stain of melting light,

the beating feet stirring the powdered frost,
the face unfurling (as if in a mirror
that is the clearing memory of all I've known)

and always closer, always faster in its urgency
until upon me, calling out in greeting,
naming me by name

and at the resounding echo of that cry
I hear – as from a drum
that has fallen through a crevasse
into a glacier – far down,
the pulse of my own heart, beating again
as it melts free
in rhythm to each step, each forward step

and in the unfolding
and returning of my knowing,
I see my journey, where it goes
and the winter's going.

Wherever

Wherever you are,
to take the colours:
the colours of earth –

to take from the earth
a handful of colour:
a colour of earth –

to take the earth
from beneath your feet.

A Tight-Rope Act

Holding our breath
in apprehension,
we grasp life.

A Trapeze Act

Although she moves, she is not moved
while we are shaken from ourselves
and flung out into a whirling gap –
tracing inverted arches, falling upward,
swept to a hesitation in the void –
where our eyes are her momentum
and timing is the gravity of time.

Then breath and heart are halted in their hurling
by the ease of her grasp as she grips,
releases, tumbles, grips, releases, grips.

Gripping our seats, unmoving
in the grasp of her conviction,
we are moved and so dissemble
while she makes no pretence
of what she has imagined and in that
dares never waver, cannot shift from true

A Sun Dial

As a rim of shadow moves
across a numbered dial,
the gnomon pivots, fixed
on what's unseen by day,

to pace our moments only
and truly for so long
as the spun earth hold course
and the sun itself not waver.

Garioch Dead

Three hundred miles to the south,
a freezing rain, then snow and then a blizzard
stripped the ripening blossoms
and checked, for a moment, the advance of spring

as a tree
(of some considerable but no great age,
peculiar to the soil in which it grew,
by stroke of chance –
stirring a glacial wind across the continents
and dragging even the light down from the sky)
fell in the north.

Staples

At the supermarket checkout, a voice:
"all right love" but with what punctuation,
query, exclamation mark, comma,
capitals, intended or actual – even
if for me or just overheard, about
whom or whatever – is uncertain

yet clear against the tills, trolleys,
goods, feet, music, announcements, children,
those words as I go out to my car:

the free gift, bonus, surprise draw
I hadn't noticed was on offer,
collected, won, which asks
if it is and reassures that of course
it's "right" and "all right" and "all"

and that other word of renewal
I had managed to forget
to put down on the weekly shopping list
of everyday supplies.

Homage to Jean Tinguely

Design's the reassertion of
the possibility of choice of
the chance of the recovery of
the choosing of the unfolding of
the restarting of design of
the rearrangement of the chance of

a wishing of untangling
an unravelling of mangling
a tingling of insistence
a jingling of persistence
a tracery of mingling
a simplicity of jangling

that irregularly paces
that quivers as it races
that unstintedly reverses
that stops in anticipation
that alternates in motion
that trembles in precision

in sufficiency of instants.
at diversion of resistance.
into inconsistent stillness.
by coherence of wrangling.
for shaking of consistence.
with implicit resilience.

Great Aunt

Now scarcely
brought to mind
for thirty years
with whom I shared

five summer days
'ganging the roon'
your kin and mine
through the Borders,

Lanark, Lothian,
drunk with mostly
not much sleep
and tea and talk,

such talk
'guid crack'
as if excess
were timeless:

as chauffeur,
almost grandson,
briefly confidant
of you, my dear,

and even then
long widowed,
now long dead
great aunt,

here suddenly
in the particular
lift of a chin,
bob of a throat,

step of a girl
crossing the street
to meet her friends
this winter afternoon.

Even One Day

May these words be
as certain as this stone,
sun bleached, wave smooth,
I picked up once
as tally of that moment
when you splashed ashore
over the clattering shingle
of a steep sided inlet
where we'd sailed

remembering another
ship-weary voyager,
fate driven, wind opposed,
who returned there
to his waiting love:
so I to you – as if
after such broken years –
even one day apart.

The Elements

What holds the full weight of our trust,
can break our bones at the first clumsy step –

and what can satisfy our deepest thirst,
can drown us in its depth, if we fall in –

and what can fill our being with each breath,
can slip to nothing when we try to grasp –

and what can warm our bed and speed our pulse,
can brand our hearts for ever with its pain.

So, the mutations of love's alchemy, these elements
can bruise and suffocate, elude and scar

while, hidden in the seeking of each other,
we forget and yet uncover who we are.

The Platitudes

They are everywhere that man is to be found, though skilled in camouflage and evasion. Put out something sweet, even a few crumbs at the back door and they'll soon appear.

Of the many species, all are so much alike that no one bothers to distinguish. Most die off at the first sign of rough weather but as soon as the sun shines, are as plentiful as before.

Sometimes hunted as a nuisance or even as vermin, there's no evidence they are capable of lasting harm. For sport, they are much too gullible. For the table, lack both substance and flavour.

But don't despise them. They have their place in the natural order. And some day, in bad times or when you are old, you may be glad of their company, their eagerness to please, even what brief nourishment they can offer.

A Place Called Gefryn
(Bede: 'quae vocatur Adgefryn')

There is a place
between a river and steep hills
where once men built
in wood, not stone,
a palace for a king
and where, one winter evening,
remarked on by a nameless man,
through smoke and clamour of an echoing hall,
a bird flew from the darkness into light
then back to dark, gone
as those timber walls
now sunk to earth
in that almost forgotten place
where you may stand alone
and see how green the meadow is,
how smooth, unmarked,
and it is good
they built in wood,
not stone.

Something So Singular

Foraging for it, that word,
how can there not be,
for something so singular, so emphatic

but not alien, not eccentric
to wish to speak of what others before,
uncountable, by whom I am shaped,
surely might have had occasion
to desire means to declare

or has it lapsed, a dialect term,
something eroded from the vernacular
before lexicographers could record?

or is it that those who also knew
had no craving for even a syllable
of what they could know without saying
and certainly not from anything said?

or were they so famished for speech?

as if utterance was prepackaged
to expedite to recipient,
with invoice, carriage charges, insurance,
request to sign for receipt?

and not this hunger to acclaim,
make manifest celebration
of whatever it is that is ours
unimaginable to others –

however unlikely to have happened,
however commonplace in occurrence –

and so perhaps after all, rightly
without that word, one particular
though there are words and no famine,
not one adequate for it.

(1986)

A Riddle for Jill

Two images, two words, even two
    syllables express
my meaning and fond hope, no
    more or less:

one, ranging with summer sweetness
    to a secret place –
the other, from buried darkness
    into air and space –

the first, to gather nourishment
    in all men's sight
and then, where warmth and
    riches may be brought to light.

A Racing Walker

If you define what's not unnatural
and persevere in that most strictly
you'll soon cross the frontier
into that single-minded kingdom
where strides a racing walker
who is consumed by the commitment not to . . .
not to do what would be merely natural –
who makes both mockery of what he doesn't
and veneration of his refusal of the easy answer –
who is the self-mortifying saint of travellers,
ascetic of movement, clown of urgency,
even a sort of hero of the ungainly –
and commands our amazement
by the ferocity of his intransigence.

A Clown

Urchin and dotard,
he is sly, then innocent.

His effrontery, self-defeating.
His simplicity, a contrivance.

Pretending mischief,
he effects laughter

and confounds himself
to delight us.

The Slater

Not trapped in rigid box
like the crab
or encumbered by megalomania
like the lobster
or immobile
like the barnacle
or in pursuit of futility
like the prawn or the waterflea,

the only crustacean
to grasp where the future lay
and get its feet on dry land,
it has gone on steadily since
from arctic to equator
recycling the left-overs:
dead plant material, animal remains,
dung, bacteria, fungi,
partial even to paper –
its only inefficiency: copper
(compensated by reprocess
of its own waste products) –

a surviving pioneer
for 200 million years resisting change
(not a lot to improve)
and if the meek shall inherit the earth
that's of no concern to the slater
with every reason to be confident
that of all God's creatures
it well might
not by being humble
but by getting it right.

As from a Kiln

These our familiar
and daily recognitions
are not glazed
as eyes may be
by waste of age,
lapse of attention,
distractions of event

but as seeming casual
strokes of pigment
may be sealed
and fused into clarities
which cannot ever then
blur in the least detail,
ever fade their tint.

At MacDiarmid's Grave

Who was a granite of volcanic crystals,
mottled from ancestral source,
might yet awake from unaccustomed silence
for one last scorning of all agreement
that his name should be inscribed
on such a bland and sedimentary
and alien stone.

On the Somme

"Nothing was spared"
said the guide
"and no one needed
the full cost
of this monument."

Almost Lost Poem

Clearing through
old papers and letters
for the bonfire when
a folded card drops
out inscribed:
I LOVE YOU MADLY!
BUT CAN I HAVE
MY LIGHTER BACK?

Takings

As sea . . . rain
earth . . . dust
fire . . . stubble
silence . . . us.

By the Tweed

Who called me "Tuppenny" and took
me fishing, tried to teach
how to pierce worms, minnows
"so they dinna die too quick"
or rip throat, guts from fish,
 not scornful but "whit's wrang?
ye're queerways, there's nay harum"

and there was none in him,
gone to the kirkyard now
with all the life he "heyked"
from that flashing river
where I'm still snagged
floundering on the bank and he
the one that's got away for ever.

A Voltige Act

A man runs and leaps into the air
and lands upon a horse that seems to chase
itself for nothing, to nowhere
in circled invocation, ever back in place.
The man's hands are empty and the horse's back is bare.
The tribute of our clapping fills the tented space
as he curves in acrobatics while we stare.
Though never equal, they must keep in pace.
One is the master, one the slave and yet they share
for a moment, and with us, the embrace
of their commitment and the care
of their unnatural and headlong grace.

Mornese

Through sloping vineyards
of a mountain village,
a young man takes us
to his father's grave –

talking of home,
of children, family
as if to the one
whose name is there –

then reaches down
in silence for a moment,
resting his open hand
upon that earth.

Homage to Cid Corman

As surely as

a shadow's absence.

Yes (1)

Remarkable how today is as remarkable

as every day.

Yes (2)

Every time and always each time

always the last time until next time.

Homage to Edwin Morgan

Perhaps everything happens eventually

in any event nothing happens perhaps.

Beneath

That old mother

to tuck us in at the last.

All the Blue: From the
Director's Book of Josiah Spode

To procure all the blue
from monoxide of cobalt –
the most rich, fine, solid
and fixed of any colour
on porcelain or flintware –

combine plaster and borax
with partly purified ore
in quantities as directed,
the materials very fine,
exceedingly mixed together,

after which set them
in a reverberatory furnace
the fire to be increased
until the mixture is perceived
to be in a state of fusion;

the same degree of heat
to be continued some hours
then hastily slackened.
You will find a blue calx
at the top of the crucible

but as a large proportion
of the colour will persist
in ore sunk to the bottom,
it will be necessary
to pursue the same method

with the residue and then –
although the exact duration
and quantity of heat
is impossible to state
for it varies directly

with the body of ore,
the size of furnace
and strength of fire –
without doubt it will yield
the remainder of the blue.

To Tell Us

fallen for a local lass
my isolation threatened
dare I say, I dare
in better mind than before
though complicated
all measure of juggling
suffering a kind of siege
and not tell even a tenth
the harassment, confusion
but we persist
to retain a sort of sanity
when all is possible and right
here, there or wherever
as the pressure eases
these few acres, so rich
harvest mice and red squirrel
only yards from our door
a juvenile goshawk, an eagle owl
haymaking for neighbours
kestrel following for voles
her eyes, a real companion
quicker than mine, we marry
early next Friday
no guests as such
though if anyone of good will
turn up, whisky and brown ale
maybe some buns, cake
and Sicilian Marsala await

To the Tune of Annie Laurie

Come to Bonnie Scotland
where blows by loch and glen
not just the flowering heather
about each but and ben.

By roadside etc

Discarded fast-food carton
and plastic throw-away
beside the rusting Export
deck out each mossy brae.

By roadside etc

No need for pipes and tartan
to host a welcome here
where our traditional litter
grows richer every year.

By roadside, park or field,
by every wall or hedge
there see how proudly gathers
our national heritage!

One Hundred Years On

The laird, the dominie, the minister
take pride that each are secondary to none
and most years summer's nearly over
before between the clouds we glimpse the sun.

The makar like the gowk can still be heard
even in rhyme, if not to such concision,
and, having nothing much to celebrate,
claiming whatever honour in derision.

Trees are for cutting down, bawbees for getting,
river and moorland there for hook and gun
and we contend on principle for principles
as cheerfully as we have ever done.

Information

With an hour or two to spare,
I stopped once in Langholm
to enquire for Information
at the Office near the Square

where I was courteously told
that Mr Grieve had moved away
when young ". . . though some say
often back for a visit when old

and certainly, yes, in the end
buried here. No, I didn't know
him personally and so
only an opinion but understand

he was never one to shirk
stirring a quarrel, while deemed
to be very highly esteemed
in his own field of work."

'The Gates of Eden'
(Map reference: NY 360 895)

No secret. You can even buy
a postcard of the view
from those who live near by
which clearly proves it true,

where I came on them by chance
and in Scotland after all,
remarking, at a glance,
no angel, terrible

as the word of God narrates,
to stop me going through
those long imagined gates.
Then suddenly I knew

how muddled I had got
and quickly turned about.
If they're an exit,
what fool would venture out?

The Scotch Asphodel (Tofieldia palustris)

The name's nothing
extravagant
for such a flower
while yet I grant
(even in our Elysium)
'a sub-arctic plant'.

"A Handkerchief with a Moral Purpose . . . A Brisk Aid to Order"
for Ian

To raise more than
a passing lustre
with puff or feathered
mop or bluster
of mere squall or
cannonade, needs
a real duster.

Calvinism

Can I expect
to be surely
of the Elect?
By concern for
the question, be
assured, you're not
assuredly not.

Either way
(after Bridget Riley)

True enough that
"Happiness is
not important . . ."
while equally
unhappiness
is, unhappily,
no guarantee.

Tea leaves
for Hamish

Hard to read what
they tell, sometimes.
Life? Death? A lot
of money? Love
perhaps? Or not?
Well, there's always
more in the pot.

Sky Lights

Are mostly small,
tend to leak, don't
in fact light the
sky, though seldom
have bars, need no
curtains and do
look to the stars.

T'time in the Caucasus
for Eddie

What more could one
conceive than T'
b' lieve yourself
T' b' blessed with
T' bliss of a
T' rip T' see
Tbilisi?

A Dictionary

Vacuum cleaner
of expression
gone into reverse?
Don't mock.
Perhaps just the
ultimate
minimalist baroque?

Dark Ages carving of a creature apparently swallowing its tail

By keeping grip
on what's behind
and giving a nip
just to remind
the latest part,
my ending's firmly
in my start.

Poetics (Genesis I, v.3)

Pedantic it
may be or trite
but I've remarked
no text on "dark
verse" and surely
God's quoted as
"Let there be light"?

The Parthenon

What the Goths missed or forgot

completed by a Scot.

No Answer

The craving to decode silence

speaks for itself.

Morningside Road

Safely up where none may gather round

is the mustering stone for Flodden.

With Thanks and Homage to That Critic

Who advised it was of great importance
for all kinds of sake, in these days
of book deluge, to keep out of the salt
swamps of literature and live
on your own rocky island with a lake
and a spring on it, though why so many
should have a pure taste in words yet
false taste in art was a phenomenon
which puzzled not a little;

and of the moderns, to keep to Z– ,
while Y–'s "X–" was, so far as he knew,
the greatest the century had produced
but to cast aside W– as shallow and
to give up V– , if not able, as you would
sea bathing until strong enough, and never
to read bad poems or write poetry yourself,
there being perhaps rather too much
than too little in the world already.

The Poetry Reading Poem

The next poem is called.
Was written at.
Is dedicated to.
Was published in.
Is concerned with.
Was inspired by.

This poem contains.
Describes. Expresses.
Means.

This poem is.
This poem was.

This poem might.

Going South

I sometimes have occasion
to take the train south

where the farther I go
the more my heart rises

until trekking about London
become positively cheerful

at the sight of all the lemmings
choking themselves together

that might be otherwise
clogging up Scotland.

For whose delight

For whose delight
do we perform these feats

under the spangled big-top
of the turning sphere,

thronging the arena
with our dreams and needs,

jumping through flaming hoops,
striding on wires across the air,

spurred by a cracking whip, a sugar lump,
of fear, desire

when we hear no cheers
or laughter from out there

in the banked darkness
where the audience should be?

Nowhere

had been scribbled on the signs
we followed as we travelled
to where we supposed was somewhere
by a wavering road that led us

down a narrowing reach of land
 to docks and cranes and slagheaps
terraced houses and allotments
then a bridge across to an island

with sand dunes and a foreshore
swept by the wind continuously
where we walked on tidal shingle
with views of surf and mountains

and sky and sea unbounded
to find ourselves at last
not anywhere or elsewhere
or nowhere but simply there.

The Daughter of Alasdair Ruadh

when forbidden to make songs
both indoors and out
began to make them
half in and half out.

Comic Relief

it's called, this day
as I go to work,
to earn my bread,
no relief in that

and the comedy is
'dell'Arte' in
this intent to relieve
where I find

myself on the stage
with supporting cast,
even props,
well rehearsed,

ad lib, no script
in the long running show
of the sick, the helpless,
the lost, and

to climax the act:
a frail old dear
of far more years
than she can recall

with some misery
of the nether parts
which presupposes
my presence to ease,

lying carefully draped
in a pose on a bed
with as much of decorum
as can, to reveal

355

all the crannies
and apertures, portals
of privacy, shame,
even love

where my fingers
must juggle
and pry, in contortion
to aid, as we play

our parts,
my Harlequin
to her Columbine,
and she wails

"can't you give . . .
give me something
. . . so that
I can die?"

Buzzard

An india ink of wings
inscribing arcs
upon a whitewashed sky

as ideogram for
no more than "You
may be. I am."

A Cairn

As by barren trackway
on a mountain crest
with view of scree and corrie,
ridge and col,
a traveller might pause,
take bearings, cast
in tribute to record:
'A man came here, went on,
left common token, shared
with those who went before
and shall come after.'

Perhaps

Perhaps the llama we saw once
tethered outside a travelling fair
somewhere along the coast of Normandy
found the sand-dunes and holiday makers
as unremitting in amazement
as any prodigy from afar

even after all the miles and years
since first taken from its home
amid the distilled air and comfortable peaks
of a mountain valley in Peru
still to be glimpsed in the astringency
and altitude of its stare.

A Cat

fastidious at each step
is nimble in mischance
then fearful of descent

– a peacock in its grooming

obsessed by novelty is
unwearied in waiting
then restless at a whim

– a serpent in its gait

feigning indifference is
desolate when thwarted
then dawdles with its prey

– an introvert in pleasure

scorning to be commanded is
servile in its begging
then gives of love unasked

– an extrovert in hate.

There are words

for a particular size of stone about the size of your fist
for water only just enough to cover something
for little walks which an invalid could be expected to take

for a rocky hillocky bit of land still capable of cultivation for the
    most part
for a small triangular piece of land that can be ploughed only on
    one side
for land from which two crops have been taken in succession

for the left hand side of a furrow
for half of a pair
for the night after tomorrow night

which have been recorded in word lists
compiled on the outer islands with spoken examples
from old persons who still had their wits
in a language not even my grandparents understood;

and shall our descendants some day
be curious to know the words we have,
though I have not found them, giving examples
and idiom of use, explaining the context

for the sort of attention needed driving on a motor-way
for the attention driving slowly on a winding country road
for driving to and from work as you have done perhaps too often

for land approved for development but still standing idle
for land that attracts subsidy provided it stands idle
for land that has been re-zoned and is suddenly valuable

for the time you get for the smallest coin
for the simultaneous programme on the other channel
for a duplicate of a duplicate

for delight in remarking on small details
for the enjoyment of exploring dictionaries
for the indulgence of finding words?

A Poem Containing

containing the word: launderette –
the words: finest equipment –
the words: oily overalls, horse tack and muddy
    sports gear you must not (repeat underlined
    must not) attempt to wash in these machines –
the words: load drum, amount detergent, add
    appropriate, desired wash, select cycle, coin
    in slot, proper amount, push slide, add before
    Rinse Light ON, again after Rinse Light OFF,
    not complete until Lid Light OUT (will not open
    until Lid Locked Light is also) –
then by pressing the words (it distinctly says
    pressing the words) High, Low, Permanent Press
    as required, ensure you follow in sequence the
    words to pre-set, then by pressing the word
    Start and re-pressing if need be –
each word as required, in sequence, expressing,
    resetting –
in words and with words: a launderette,
    containing a poem

Though we must have coals (1813)

(1) *In contempt of evils*

Though we must have coals and men
must be found to dig them, in contempt
of evils that embitter and shorten their lives,
it is not necessary
that we should view with total indifference
the condition of those who are toiling
and suffering for our advantage, where
immoderate labour and noxious atmosphere
 has marked each countenance
with signs of disease and decay,
mostly half naked, blackened all over
with dirt and altogether so miserably
disfigured and abused that they look
like a fallen race, and
though the strength of a man is required
in excavating the working, women
can drive the horses and are thus sacrificed
where a man is not required
as a matter of economy and in consequence
the most abominable profligacy prevails
among them, so changed in appearance
by the filthiness of their occupation
as to lose every quality that is graceful
in women, to become a set of coarse
licentious wretches, scorning all kind of restraint,
yielding themselves up with shameless audacity
to the most detestable sensuality
in those dismal dungeons, where
if a man and a woman meet
and are excited by passion at the moment,
they indulge it in the darkness
without pausing to enquire

if it be father and daughter,
or brother and sister, and though
their abominations are confined during the day
to the dark recesses of the mines, at night
they are cast up from the pits
like a pestilence to contaminate the town
and thus, though we must have coals,
as I have said, surely something can be done
and ought to he for the redemption
of these wretches, though it should wring
a few pounds from the hard economy
of their service that takes
not the smallest account of human life
where we came once upon a chamber lit
by an unusual quantity of light showing
the black roof and walls and haggard faces
of a party of men and girls, met together
in that infernal place, with the sound
of their voices mingling together
in a general expression of mirth,
roaring with laughter at a conversation
which outraged all decency, resembling
as it appeared, a band of devils.

(2) *The office required of them*

Among those broken down by poverty
or brutalised by vice, the moral affections
become cold and dull, and thus
there are multitudes of wretches
who for bread or gin are ready
to sell their children into misery, which
on a first introduction to the mine

struggle and scream with terror
though there are to be found persons
brutal enough to force them into compliance
so that after a few trials they become tame
and spiritless and yield themselves up
without noise or resistance
to any kind of slavery that it pleases
their master to impose, with few
more than eight years and many
considerably less, in strength
barely sufficient to perform the office
required of them which is to open the door
as the horses pass through and who
at this duty are compelled to linger
in solitude and darkness, so that
in wintertime they never see daylight
except on a Sunday for it has been discovered
that they can serve for thirteen hours a day
without perishing, condemned to this
with as little consideration
as is felt for the hinges and pulleys
of the doors at which they attend
where, when I first saw one open,
did not perceive by what means
until, looking behind, I beheld
a miserable little creature standing there
without light, silent and motionless,
resembling in the abjectness of its condition,
some reptile peculiar to the place.

When I Write to You: The Diapason Closing

not a very civilized being but
when I write to you, have to be myself
and in that enough's too much
like hell on a jam butty, meanwhile
and how mean it can be, fit for nothing
with internal upsets, piles, bad weather
in the knees, chained to the treadmill,
unable to look sideways and clearly
at times not knowing what I am doing

in this stinking town, of poor parents,
father blown up in the Somme, an invalid,
mother dead early, had to set to work
to put up with the mess, never succeeded,
tried to get out, failed, trampled
on well meant offers, foolishly slaved
at the hopeless, less and less
my own master, with hate and contempt
from the silted depths of my soul
by the wretched externals outwitted

dreaming the other night of a pamphlet
still on my shelf, crumpled and tattered,
the last sheet as if black carbon paper,
being eaten and messed about with
by a crowd of small creatures
like ants and yet also something
like very small house flies
and I couldn't stop them

though think something left in me
besides piss, shit, semen, spit,
phlegm, spew but no time for theory,
the diapason closing in gangrene,

heart ache and malice, blank foolery
confusion, with that something above us
drizzling obscenity as we glissade
down the inevitable slope

the way ahead obvious enough,
just not able to follow or discover
a condition of mind which allows
but to hell with . . . while you,
do you drink much, pray, curse,
enjoy life, feed well? tell me
if you have time or patience,
if I have, if there be such
and the final cadence delay

so no need for concern
or about my verses, as sooner or later
all will come to light, however
memory is a queer bird, a dodo
and thinking to avoid self pity
at times whooshed into something like,
though no such thing as a new year and
the heart thuds away in time to a rhythm
nobody's yet written down

Impellings

As from a fleece, twisting together

where imperatives of wind disperse
the fall of leaves – and more
than half a century of rings are since
inscribed within those trees that shroud
stone lions sentinel above a roar
of cars – only grass renews unchanged
amid the litter by the railed off sundial
'silken as a dove's wing, time'
where first steps lifted forward

near that remembered haven, walled
and sunlit garden of my grandparents,
a sea mark shrouded far astern until,
at random past that door, found open,
with young couple and their infant son
just moving in, had sight again
down passage to that same unchanged
held place, made present and thus shed
to him and those unknown, come after me

according to the interval, according to the context

by shipyards and that venerable well
where history was compiled and I
first walked to school then later came
to stay with friends, midwinter festival,
by chance and choice, to call on one
whose resonance of words I knew,
thought dead or exiled, telling there
of his oldest friend, I never met, whose son
in time I did, to become thus mine

in the south where – at summer gathering
by resting place of one who shaped
from another tongue, fresh cadences – I met
the mother of that son, exiled, estranged,
from a former age who wrote of hills
where by vagrancies of time I came to walk
by another also venerated well
'found cold spring water . . . bathed my eyes . . .
had quite forgotten how far one might see'

take hold anywhere and all shall follow

'. . . who come, then go, and must
we know not from nor where . . .'
in words compiled of one who spoke
unmarked by name 'as bird
that flits from dark to dark
through hall in winter lit by flame
where men hold court . . . and know
only in mind of others do we stay,
are held to linger briefly, fade'

where they came once and built
in wood, not stone, a hall
between a river and steep hills
where you may also come, then go,
to stand alone in that almost
forgotten place, and find no trace
of mould or rubble, know how good
the silence, deep the air,
how sheer the meadow is, unmarked

one gulp of air is all we have

bees, honeysuckle, sound and scent
in the ruin of a mill house at Rhos Goch,
dust in my throat, a drifting afternoon,
remembering the day by day of one,
three generations past, recording tales
he heard repeated of the miller who
sleeping in the mill trough at midsummer
'often saw the fairies dancing
by moonlight' where I stood

and dust, soon harvest, hum of a car,
long roads through Périgord to Ribérac
where as a boy I had always longed to go,
then to laze in the square, amazed,
drinking a 'citron', scent and savour,
to be where he was born who made his songs
in an older tongue less spoken now,
transmuted yet by others, lingering
on other tongues, paced syllables

impelled by riches, not poverty

with a generation lapsed to the day
since 'given your address' you wrote
in soon familiar script, then came
at my reply, bring that 'Njala'
of 'bare style . . . more full' or 'glad
that you fell ill since it kept you
here' up the Gatineau where we walked
years afterwards in snow or along the Wye
with 'hard times also... mostly good

just hard to see sometimes just how'
or counterplying 'what no confessor
will ever hear us say . . . enjoyed

myself all the time that I was there'
who are moving now and yet remain
your self 'to a smaller house
eleven miles away' or near
'remembering the good times gone'
your hand 'and ever gone to stay'

articulate beyond mere sequence

imaged in words, as news from nowhere,
awakening to what might be, in a dream
of where a dustman 'while the sun
flashed back from him at every step
as if clad in golden armour' strolls
toward us on some casual morning
'with that somewhat haughty mien
great beauty is apt to give' to bring
discarded things to whatever lasting place

and from beyond the curve of the world
out of a storm of light and spray
Columba's boat steers to us and that island,
burial place of kings, who comes a stranger
to the land that he made his, claimed him,
watched by two lads, dumbfoundered,
sprawled on the machair– in the pigments
of that painting which still hangs
within a stroll of where I came to birth

in frequencies beyond prediction

listening to a retired prospector
near Hudson Bay–huddled by the stove

columned icicles from eaves to sill–remark
it was his uncle who had hired the coach
by which the famous rebel had escaped – thus
to pre-empt one side, placate the other,
maybe save confederation – with the money
and connivance of his opponent: which
is not a detail in the history books

and in the Mojave Desert, near high summer,
up some back canyon, engine flooding,
wouldn't run less than full throttle – so
nothing for it but to dismantle carburettor,
never done before, no manual, hardly guessing
even the problem, then reassemble, found:
obstruction in the needle valve – just one
brass shaving, hair thin, glittering, no more
than half length of a finger nail

granting momentum to each particular

where an ash tree reaches out
its branches with an eagle
its roots coiled with a serpent
and a squirrel runs between
to provoke, make variation
by shuttling motion, restless
as the unwearied flick
to keep a spindle turning
thread winding on a shaft

so the spiral chains reduplicate,
reshuffle origins, divide,
rejoin, each ply unwinding
propagates, transmits beginnings
with change as subtle, unremitting

as tracings in a patch of sand
inscribed afresh each day
by the shifting cycles
and cross currents of the tide

continuously transformed, always conserved

who was tormented by all he could not say
or do, among other things to gather
all the Titians, Tintorettos, Veroneses
into one great gallery of marble and serpentine
and get them all perfectly reproduced
so that everyone who wanted could have copies
and then go himself to draw all the subjects
of Turner's 19,000 sketches of Switzerland
and Italy and further elaborate or complete

and to get everyone in the world a dinner
who hadn't one and find out why they hadn't
and then hang all the knaves responsible,
not that he had any personal animosity
but it would be good for them and even better
for the world though sometimes he despaired
and just wanted to rearrange and relabel
his entire mineral collection or even
be perfectly quiet and not even think

down through the eye of the millstone

taken by a stroke three weeks later
which left him unable to speak or write
except for the occasional syllable –
impossible to understand in spite of effort –

otherwise lay, had bowels and bladder emptied,
squeezed her hand, took sips of liquid,
sometimes waved one arm at the ward
or opened his eyes and shook his fist
until heart and breath faded out

and at the crematorium in the middle
of several miles of derelict expanse,
there was a pile of rubbish lying outside
including floral sprays with violet ribbons
still wrapped in their plastic covers
abandoned from a previous funeral
that the wind suddenly tumbled across
the car park towards us and which no one
appeared to notice or find remarkable

exacting a means for, by contrivance

and outside the town where the camp had been
there is nothing to mark the place
except a tall stone, a plaque, a few words,
the dates and several acres in the forest
of harrowed and bleached earth where nothing
is allowed to grow, a place cared for
but not with love, that nothing
not the least blade of grass might ever
again be where such things had once been

and in a patch of neglected woodland
between farms, the undergrowth so thick
he could scarcely walk, after thirty years
where his comrades had died, buried
in unmarked graves, their enemies also,
fighting for three days without sleep
or food, for a few yards of ground, now

dense with brambles and wild blackcurrants
such as he had never seen, like grapes

through what we seek, what comes to hand

met, begging near Tollcross, no coat,
summer jacket 'grew up, children's homes'
on street now . . . four months 'sleep
where I can . . . bus shelters, doorways . . .
'until shifted on . . .' where the sheddings
of affluence are disposed by a wind
that slashes across the Meadows as if
direct from the stars, and where the mark
of each foot is dark against the frost

and on a shimmering screen: vagaries
of snowflakes on the wind, men cheering
at shipyard gates, with image of a man,
his tatar profile, crashing into rubble, who
'did nothing by halves', shifted history,
laughed once at irony, 'sat down to chess
unwillingly' and before dying spoke again
'somewhat sadly' of an old comrade from whom
he had, by much necessity, parted

who cling and yet relinquish

'we found him crawling along the track
who told how he met the other unexpectedly
both with guns at the ready, both had fired,
both fell, he wounded in the leg had hidden
behind a tree, tried to reload, but the ball
jammed half way, or would have fired again

at the son whom he watched dig a grave,
lay his father in with weapon and blanket
then cover with dirt and so get away...

. . . in a land very good to many poor people
with hunting and trapping, wild duck,
all kind of fish in the creeks and lakes,
berries, nuts, even vines in the woods
which we cleared bit by bit, at first
growing wheat and corn between the stumps
and after the rocky hillsides we came from,
the earth so rich, perhaps no wonder
that each wanted it for themselves'

in a propagation of waves

morning, already heat haze, watching
an Indian woman, Tumamait or Shamash,
down from the hills near Santa Ynez
within glitter of the Pacific surf –
the scorched air thick with scent
of anise, eucalyptus, sage –
her eyes, under tatar eyelids, dark
as wells without reflections, caverns
into a past and distance beyond us

and at dusk, blurred by falling snow,
five of them from off the tops,
largest of creatures in this land,
only a few paces from our door,
in winter coats, some still with antlers,
as in cave paintings, charcoaled, ruddy,
massive in shoulder, turning their great heads,
not cautious but aloof, part with the storm,
their eyes unseen upon us

gripping upon itself, compact of detail

the song patterns of many birds
'much too rapid in variation
for the human ear to distinguish'
and certain butterflies 'transparent scales
with opaque particles to scatter the light
creating the same blue as the sky overhead'
and under volcanic pressure and temperature
in the deepest rifts of the earth
'living organisms that thrive'

and by the shore of an open bay
watching the crests of the long rollers
from the full reach of the Atlantic
as they move in from over the horizon
in unwearied sequence to some rhythm
familiar beyond definition, to remember
the eyes of a man by the road somewhere
in the southern bush who said, when asked
how many years he'd lived, just 'much'

steering by where we come from

after day's travel, equatorial sun,
rinsing beneath a waterfall to glimpse
a rainbow there inside the shimmer
within a handsbreadth of our hands;
or again, toward Iona, sailing
south of Mull, between the squalls,
snow on our decks at Easter, the refraction
of three quite separate and concentric arcs
in company with him, my shipmate then

geologist, surveyor, traveller, who
through mountains on earth's farther side,
after day's toil, wandered some steps
to watch the sunset, slipped: three days
to reach the body, frozen at that height,
so heaped a cairn, in the Gilgit Valley
ringed by peaks, his resting place
in that dry air, such clarity and where
are no rainbows, who has need of none

in a filament of utterance, a shape of energy

guitar chords, a voice, the beguilement
and of asking 'the miles to Dundee'
from an entry off the main square,
winter approaching, the street traders
putting away their stalls, and I
know the song, though cannot sing it
of great lords and wandering makers
of verse and music, and 'cannot well tell'
for a moment where it is I might be

then I toss a coin into the open case
at his feet and salute him, amazed, who
stinks of booze, sweat, tobacco, travels
the north with his van, dog, sleeping bag,
five strings and a capo, is from Glasgow
'with no high Duke of Scotland, no bonnie
rich lassie' though no less partaking
'how far it might be on the road
and the distance, the miles to Dundee'

with plough-share equally to ridge and furrow

repeating 'please' tric-trac 'are we . . .
a long way?' who had no tears,
never smiled, was always asking 'a long way . . .
and from?' but from where, who knows,
tric-trac, he called her Jeanne
as she called herself, across the frontiers,
adjusting his watch every morning, the train
forward, the sun put back, telling her
'rest against me, sleep'

and wherever from, was no matter –
she said 'Montmartre', or how met
or what became of her – it was always
a long way and long time, to the kettledrum
of the gaps between the tracks, the rattle
of sand in an hour glass, the repetition
of droplets falling in a cavern, breaking
the silence, weeping through rock,
dissolving away the mountain

amid a plankton of expiring suns

who marvelled at this propensity
to suppose ourselves possessed of distinct
and uninterrupted existence throughout
the course of our lives where memory
alone acquaints us with the continuance
of the succession of our perceptions
and is the source of this notion
of personal identity which it does not
so much produce as discover to us

and confessed that he allowed others
might be different in this particular
of their being but for his part, when

he entered intimately into what is called
himself, always stumbled upon some perception,
never caught himself without a perception,
never could observe anything but
each perception and were all removed
should have been entirely annihilated

in a flowing contour pulsing forward

'for the wind blaws whaur it will
and ye hear the souch o it'
at interval and by continuance
bringing rain, drought, snow, haar
then clear sky and by night, frost
with stars, as it crests and trembles
the spin-drift blaa: sheep's wool
snagged on whin, briar, dyke,
wavering evidences that cling

in traces to be gathered, carded,
spun, rewoven by such as need –
packmen, drovers, vagrant singers,
disbanded men from far-off wars –
by contrivance patching garments,
shelter against that wind, who track,
are driven, those upland roads
'but whaur it is coming frae
and whaur it is gaein til'

defining the explicit from the possible

with tremor of hand or mannerism
shaping each imprint   'better is clay

compact, well worked   a stylus cut
incising words   a tablet marked
fired and sealed   than boast of kin
than funeral rite'   out of the rubble,
unknown scribe,   name broken off,
transcription errors   'our breath spent
beyond the dust   to speak for us'

holding and found as marks
on certain rocks of foot prints seen
only as shadows yet tenacious
in the sunlight that flames, sustains
undiminished by distance or as pulse
we finger at our wrist where time may
vanish in the gap between each beat:
so a shuttle through warp, a tremor
fluctuant, carried forward, unbroken

to remember that one day we shall not

as a dunnock, scarcely fledged,
strayed from heed of parents,
perched on an upper ledge, quivers
and flares its wings, tensed and eager
to be loosed, then projects itself
out exulting on the air
where a sparrowhawk registers, locks
upon, impelled also and by desire,
curving in flight to meet

so, winged and finned, lifting
from their cradles, balanced on flame,
a plume following, stately, the exemplars
of our devising, yearning on course,
ascend through cloud beyond our sight

to make revelation in a ripple
of brightness, the sound following
only after a pause, as if an echo
returning from the unheard

the reach of draw proportional to length of fibre

hand scarcely on tiller, a light breeze
abeam, starboard tack, leaving harbour,
bearing south west in the early sun,
until, resolving out of haze, a headland
wine dark on the horizon, named
and famed in words, transfixing history
where one displaced by war, misfortune,
yearned to return, so we, retracing,
laying a course to find a landfall

and holding course, beneath port bow,
breakers out from beyond a cliff base,
tightening sail, as a squall unnoticed
from open sea to west heels us over
with heavy swell, the breakers nearer,
going about, almost not, then clearing
eye of the wind, boat trembling forward
through spindled foam, shrouds singing,
weight thrust against the tiller

ply against counterply, keeping the tension

the sun at zenith, no shelter, walking
below sea level on former mud flats –
the grained surface, a drum head
of fissured parchment, veined with salt –

each footprint breaking crystals
and in the silence between each tread
another sound, of the ground itself
shrinking, expanding, as if in anguish
on a rack, in the crescendo heat

for lack of what is condensed
across distance, then clustered, thrust
against peaks, to be released down
corrie, strath, in flood over banks,
assailing eye, ear, and above that rush:
tremor of a withy, stripped of leaf,
half submerged, vibrating in the onslaught
as if tormented, guttering, a supple bow,
tensed and tongued in utterance

sometimes fearful with splendour

her face alight, a young girl, fingertips
on ivory keys, rising, falling,
the music driving forward, gathering
to a pitch, toward a gap of stillness
under the dome of a concert hall
with orchestra assembled, converging,
every movement, her each breath
as we hold ours, feeling a halt
in our throats, a flare of sound

while the prow of a warship lifts,
drops upon the swell, dividing forward,
rimmed by foam, making its course,
assembled with others, converging,
strained to a pitch, alert, until
in a moment, throbbing out of stillness
'orange streak . . . ball of light . . . a roar . . .

my fingers numb . . . then rush of heat . . .
couldn't breathe . . . saw men on fire . . .'

so might any voice, any phrase

hearing, three hours after dark 'a sighing,
whistling wind' then from south, a rumbling
'as if several trains at once . . . looked up . . .
saw it explode . . . engine apart spinning down . . .
the streets, light as day' with next door
vaporized into a crater, another house
just wreckage clogged with corpses,
the fragments, litter, branding the forests,
mountains, some still being found

and over the north, on clear nights, said
to be the result of magnetic storms blown
across space from the sun, flickering
in shadows against the stars, said
to be angels fighting with each other,
their wounds bleeding, wavering down,
searing certain marks said to be found
on rocky hilltops, as they battle soundlessly,
out of heaven, with Lucifer, falling

and not a word but sound till heard

with an owl sounding in the dark
above a lapping millpond, wildflowers
on a kitchen table, a last butterfly
drowsy by a windowsill, the tea things
washed and put away, her eyes
lit by the open hearth, the others gone

and no more to he done, he turned
to find himself at last and without words
reaching out one hand, was gripped by hers

or a drum, pipe music, in an open square
with sunshine, cheering crowds, a drifting haze,
dancing 'The Willow Tree', their limbs and feet
unwearied, lifted forward, every breath
seeming their last, near blind, shed
from themselves but never from each other,
needing no utterance beyond that pulse
as if of beating waves to carry them
and him toward a distant shore.

Also

Scratched on the walls
of the border tower
the escaped guards
had also marked
their days of endurance.

Bass Rock

With winds that are
so sheer they'd pry
the blue from the sky
and leave no scar.

Not Sand

Not dribble of sand through neck of a glass
but the rattle of scree beneath the tread of a man
as he makes his traverse, as he climbs
between sheer heights in a resonant place and hears
no sound but the pipes of the wind
and the drum of each breath
and the shedding away of stones at every step.

Gone

As a landscape can be ravaged,
even the balance of the sky
shifted on the horizon's brim
at the falling of one tree,
so a city quavers, is depopulated
by a familiar face, now gone.

National Trust

We wander round, amazed.
Bed where a czar once slept.
Stuffed bear. Victorian stays.
Embroidered screen. All kept.

Ten generations, more,
Have gathered all that's here.
Bronze pins. Chinese armour.
Mantraps. A Zulu spear.

Grandeur and minutiae.
Then exit. Buy a card.
Acquiring is what's easy.
Relinquishing, what's hard.

After

After the red wines and the white,
or spiced or resinous, and after
the coffee from Colombia or Kenya,
liqueurs or rarest Malts, and after
all such, to find myself
after long climb beside a mountain burn
and there, amid the birch and rowan,
where it falls over the granite boulders,
to bow my head and kneel
and taste again.

Wreaths

Is this where a hostage was shot? where
a protester died under the treads of a tank? where
a student set himself on fire against tyranny? No

this is where a passer-by, walking home with friends,
was set about and knifed, on a drunken whim
and for the swagger of it.

An Òran (The Song)

The music of her voice
was of islands beyond the sunset
and harpers from when the world was young

but what the words said was
"Even on a north slope of gravelled stone
I would find a way to make a living for my love."

Near Sloc Dubh, South Uist

The roof beams have fed the flame,

the walls bowed to the wind

and the pasture made welcome the heather.

Where the drove road scarred the hill

is only a caress of shadow, nearly healed.

Even the old don't weep any more

or the children go to bed hungry.

Silence inhabits the glen.

Remembering is our tomorrow.

Forgetting, what won't come again.

When I said

When I said that what stayed with me
the most from a visit to his country
was, "By a river in the forest
at sunset, just listening,
especially to a family of baboons
settling for night in the trees,
all their chatter and stir . . ."

he said, as we walked by the shore,
"Yes, while for me
when I go back, it will be . . ."
lifting his head, with around us,
the flap and scold of the gulls.

In Memoriam Norman MacCaig

No one now to interrupt
the questioner from the floor

to interrupt the poet
droning on the platform

to interrupt the comfortable
onrush of the universe:

"Speak up. Can't make out
a word you're saying."

Definitions

If by not telling all,
the truth's confused
or by your silence,
others are accused,

you're not a knave
but just a Waldegrave,
not dishonourable,
just a Lyell.

(1996)

For you, once enemy

For you, once enemy
to all I was or might be –
always to windward
with better rig or bearing,
always with right of way –
these words are raised
as signal flags
to your final passage
with recognition
that I must at the last
sail in your wake
where all are comrades,
even shipmates,
on that setting tide.

Whin

A familiar of hillside,
heather, bracken, thistle –
without thorns, its leaves:
tough, slim, sharpened
and evergreen – its blossom:
yellow, of delicate scent,
yielding only to persistence
for pollination, nectar –

and of no usefulness,
even as fuel, burning poorly,
except perhaps
to plug gap in hedge
or dyke, or in extremity
as fodder, well crushed,
if all else fail,

it thrives where much
does not, is rarely
disturbed and never
in need of encouragement
and may it be
as it mostly is, always
somewhere in flower.

December Leaves

If a sparrow trying to escape a hawk
doesn't usually sing or a child laugh
as a sniper's bullet enters its mother's head,
can I find words for a beech leaf as it drifts
across a garden while a man drives past
who sold that gun? or remark on the colour
of that leaf while in a mountain pass refugees
crouch in the wind and the snow begins to gather
on the bodies of those already fallen?

Or perhaps it is the words that find us,
that drift, gather, descend, enter the head,
that don't sing or blow away, that we try
to escape, as another gun is sold, another
straggler dies, another bullet enters another head,
another sparrow falls or leaf casts its shadow
across a garden or under the wheels
of a receding car, and another snowflake
makes white the frozen silence?

To all the Gods

Usual format, carvings, but
'Dibus deabusque omnibus'?
set up by you, Frumentius,
no especial rank, auxiliary
on western flank, north
of Solway, far from home.

With intention, strategy,
ecumenical? or cautious,
covering bets? or free-thinker,
tongue-in-cheek? or?
but no answers and,
if there were, irrelevant:

it's results that count
as you, a soldier, knew,
not private thoughts
or motives. Did you
make it at last? get home?
come out ahead? Only

one certainty: your name,
inscription have survived
and here on your altar where
I'd gladly join my hand,
make offering to whatever
Gods or Goddesses required.

Lifetimes

A lifetime away. New voices, faces,
tongues in the streets, and I
marvel at what brought them, need
or greed, compulsion, even hope,
all familiar enough; and thus we are
not altogether strangers, belonging
to the same absence, sharing
in what also took me, left me
even from myself sometimes estranged.

When I envy an old friend
who's never lived anywhere else,
knowing one place that knows him
as its own, he grins, "Don't be misled.
Though never shifted, didn't need to.
All done for me. Here's gone.
Elsewhere's arrived. What was, isn't.
What is, won't be. No one belongs.
We're all misplaced now."

A Good Warfare

Thank you for your excellent letter,
very like yourself, most letters
are not like men at all but like other letters,
though my time occupied with various forms of
nothing, a poor wanderer on this earth,
the faculty of blundering growing upon me,
having a constant succession of visitors
of all varieties, with much wear to mind
and body, yet many whom I love
for that activity in their friendship
of heart and intellect, contending for reality
against shadows which is always a good warfare,

for many speculate on religion,
not with the desire of arriving at truth
but of finding arguments for opinion,
inflicting desolation and paralysis – though He is
indeed far above all doctrines, Whose thoughts
are not as ours, and the cry of a child
will produce a greater movement in almost any mind
than twenty pages of unanswerable logic –

but that God should be omnipotent love
and yet the world be a vast cauldron
of violence, pollution, misery, is a riddle,
and the seeming triumph of darkness over light,
a riddle, we have our being in the midst
of what encloses us as a net
on every hand, and among the many marvels
in man's character and condition,
few greater than this, that he should be able
to contemplate his situation without astonishment,
which is indeed, a mighty riddle, God's riddle,
and none can solve it but God

whom I desire to know as really –
and far more – as I know any man, for
it is not by thoughts that I am to be comforted.
I desire and expect an actual putting forth
of His Hand, a direct breathing of His love.
I should like to be able to receive
all the sorrows and pains of life, as it were,
by the kiss of God. Dear friend, I find
that I had entirely forgotten
who it was that I was writing to . . .

(from various letters and writings by
Thomas Erskine of Linlathen: 1788-1870)

Erskine of Linlathen

In the guise of a Lowland laird
of the old school, speaking of Plato,
Greek verbs, family, Calvinism,
the strict doctrine of his youth
and on one occasion in his garden,
of the awful silence of God,
how it sometimes became oppressive,
the heart longing to hear in answer
to its cry 'some audible word . . .

but has not always been . . . I
had one revelation and only
a memory now and not of anything
did not know . . . but a joy, for which
one might bear any sorrow, that He
had broken silence . . .' in the cool
of the summer evening, touching
his companion's arm quickly
the once, and then walking on.

The Real News

". . . Bald limestone in early spring,
now much greener. Rain almost every day.
Ireland set to dissolve. Grey skies.
All the more reason to hug the bright ones.
What is it about Africa, I can't shake off?
Two years now since I've seen someone casually
dance down a street. How are you? Here's
raw from last evening: a gorgeous moth,
black and red, finest and strangest ever.

Sometimes just want to shout: Thanks. Or
the camomile tea has gone to my head? Paradise:
a small livelihood, all my books in order
together in a house, absence of relatives,
an open notebook. While this place: turning
into a blue cheese, starting in bathroom
and working out. But looking back or forward,
it's a bad habit. Stop. Here's my son
with the real news: *Dinner's ready . . .*"

The Ballad of Rillington Place

They hanged Tim Evans,
hanged him by the neck till he was dead –
     oh, yes –
on the verdict of a jury
and the sentence of a judge
who said
         "And may God
have mercy on your soul."

The police had questioned him,
had got him to confess –
     oh, yes –
that he'd killed his wife and daughter
in a quarrel over debts,
they said –
       and may be
          – and maybe not –
it was all quite fairly got.

So they wrote it out for him
who couldn't read or write –
     oh, yes –
and he signed, but after
to his mother and his priest
he said
         "I never
done it . . . Christie done it."

Though he didn't know that Christie
whom he'd thought of as a friend –
     oh, yes –
had murdered many women and,
convicted in the end, years later
even said

"I confess
it was me killed Evans' wife".

But the jury didn't know
of his habits at the time –
          oh, yes –
so they took Christie's word
as a witness in the case
and said
                    "Thus we find
the prisoner guilty as charged."

So the law took its course
and too late to dig him up –
                    – though they did –
     oh, yes –
to give him Christian burial
as if, for good behaviour, it
was said
                    "We remit
that much of your sentence."

Later on, it's true, he got
a free Pardon from the Queen
          oh, yes –
but the courts even yet
don't admit to a mistake –
          oh, no –
or the judges or police.
"A dead man can't appeal"
                    – that's in law –
they've said
                    And may God
have mercy . . .
                    oh, yes, maybe God.

THERE IS a visitation of summer, most potent in northern
countries, which comes when September is ending, a trembling of
the light, a transparence of the air, which can drop without warning
into the bedsitting room of a maiden old lady without surviving
family living on the most meagre of pensions

to awaken memories of a dangerous kind, set the imagination to
work, undo a lifetime of resolve, and against which even such a
veteran of the impossible can find herself helpless and weeping as
she has not done since her first day at school.

"WHY IS the sky dark at night?" an astronomer asked, years ago,
for if the universe was infinite and unchanging and the stars shining
undiminished, by now the sky should be so choked with light that we
would be dazzled, as he was by the question,

while today we are told that the universe is finite but expanding, so
that the increasing emptiness dissipates the radiance, and thus we
are also overwhelmed, but by the answer, that it is only by the stars
receding at such unimaginable speeds that there is darkness enough
for us to see them.

(with homage to Heinrich Olbers)

BURNING JUNIPER on the fire and, as the scent fills the room,
there's the presence of a time not now and a place not here

so immediate that it's as if the answer to some first and final question
had been revealed and was to be found only in what is lost at every
moment.

THEY ARE EVERYWHERE that man is to be found, though
skilled in camouflage and evasion. If easy targets when spotted and
vulnerable to hostile conditions, the platitudes have never been
threatened by extinction for they recover quickly and exterminated in
one place soon reappear in another.

Yet don't despise them. They have their place in the natural order and
in bad times, or when you are old, you may be glad of their company,
their willingness to please, even what brief sustenance they can offer.

NOT ONLY as achieved objects but as functional practicalities,
perhaps certain writings like favourite shoes, the most comfortable
since worn the longest, may be repaired as needed, first the soles and
then the uppers, changing colour, stitching, style of laces, certainly
shape

so that in the end only the feet that fit into them appear – but only
appear to be – the same.

A VERY INGENIOUS MECHANISM, keeping time to within half
a second a week, the limit of such device when not running in a
vacuum: the hands driven by an electric motor which raises a gravity
arm which in turn falls to drive a pendulum, which, by its position,
determines that period of swing during which the motor is made
to run faster so that over the whole period the rate is most precisely
varied,

and thus, though pendulum and movement are never actually
connected, yet the latter drives the former and the former controls
the latter.

(with homage to Alexander Steuart and the Royal Museum of Scotland)

A SPARROW has found a crust and a crow is after it, harrying the smaller bird which dodges neatly, until the larger bird gives up or appears to, perching on a branch, pretending it doesn't care, far enough away to hope to persuade the sparrow to relax but still near enough to pounce,

while the sparrow takes its time, enjoying the crust, fluffing its feathers, flicking its tail, making a show, also pretending, as if the crow weren't there.

IT'S A STUBBORN BEAST, crouches, shows a yellow tooth, won't be hurried, shies at sudden approach, poking with a stick is no good, a titbit in front of its nose may help, other ploys

but it's mostly patience, expectation, sometimes pretending to turn your back, for the mind has its own necessities, and above all: will start when it's ready.

THIS FEAR, not of oblivion but of the ever-approaching nearness of, with always less time and for all that's yet unfinished and undone, as if there ever could be that much time

until there isn't so much time, as if there ever was that much, and then with almost no time left, scarce time enough for anything, and then just not.

ESTUARIES, neither lakes nor seas, rivers or bays, they receive and open out, subside and fill, are shallow, deep, cluttered then cleansed, predictable yet shifting, never quite afresh or quite relinquished,

and in the consistency of their insistence upon change, while alien to monotony, threaten no surprise.

AS A STONE SKITTERING across a pond, as sounding into a well, as
a whet for honing, as carved and kept as charm or set as monument,
or with others, found or cut, assembled as boundary, barrier, shelter
against the sticks and stones of . . .

or to strike as with iron from, or stand with back against, or rest our
head upon, or be as ballast, as foundation, corner, cap, head, or mill,
or inscribed upon, even to be cast as a first, as a last, or to get blood
from, having the look of, a heart of, a face of, to be turned into, to be
raised up, to be remaining, to be unturned.

STARTED . . . and so begun, have already said too much to guess
where this may lead, as if a knotted cord I wind into my hand and
follow into a maze, finding amazement, what is meant, as meaning,

and yet tensed in my intention, not pretending or dissembling,
listening to the words, assembled, gathered, understanding what may
stand, may not go back or falter, but go forward in due sequence to
arrive, from where it started . . . as this does, and has.

THIS CRAVING to save – something at least, though it be the least,
of what is sensed so intently here as present in each moment, all
that's given only as what's shed, what's gone yet we would grasp:

now hereafter as a net of words cast over and around what is, by its
insistence, once perceived, an absence – how strong it is.

SURPRISED IN A MIRROR, not by my father's face as if my age but by glimpse of that lad he was, that I was once, not unaware but as yet unwary, eager for all that was to come,

never thinking that some day I'd look, surprised, into a mirror and see that former self, both his and mine, remote yet near, as if untarnished, still present as shared presence, not just in the mirror but surprised in me.

AS RECENTLY AS my grandfather's youth, a sighting hardly caused comment but the world has changed much since then and I did not expect to see one for myself, walking up from the foreshore carrying her tail.

You may scorn it as a conceit and say "Only a girl in a wet suit with a surf board under her arm" but she was glistening from the waves and her long red hair was matted with salt spray and even a mermaid must adapt to the times.

CLUTTER of memories I won't reread, intentions long faded, unwanted hopes, ideas out of fashion, resolves I've never used: the attics and cellars of the mind long overdue for a clear-out

but the dealers aren't interested, even the jumble sale doesn't shift them. Or is there a resource centre, to recycle, repair, rewrite? Must all go to the tip?

AT THE UNIVERSITY luncheon, the old poet sitting opposite, who has been listening carefully to all my talk about poetry, suddenly leans across, "Yes . . .

over your shoulder, beyond the wall of the library, I can just see the hills."

"DID YOU REALLY meet him once?" my children ask and I answer truthfully "For an afternoon when I was young, we talked together" knowing him then as someone who had enriched the world, who even called me friend

while if we'd met when he was young and I the same, might have argued, disagreed, even parted bitterly, not understanding all that I do now, and so could have more truly said, "Oh, yes, we really did meet, once."

THE INSCRIPTION STATES "replica of stone on which the kings of Scots were crowned", that stone of destiny which was taken away, then retrieved, then taken away again, then returned but elsewhere and only on loan, although the taken stone itself, so we are told, is probably a reproduction

as are the postcards on sale or glossy prints you can take for yourself, as I have done, now also destined, if in other ways, for these further words inscribed and perhaps only the gloss, even this gloss, is what it seems, acclaims what's real.

LAST CURTAIN DOWN, the company dispersing, contract at an end, with taxi at the stage door waiting to take me to my lodgings for the night

and though I know my lines, every detail of my part, cannot bring to mind, remember anything of where, when my first morning had begun, I must have come.

JUST AS I DISCOVER corners, rooms, even a whole wing which I had never used or even known were there,

to notice that the floors and walls are bare, windows boarded up, a demolition order on the door.

LAPPINGS OF DAY as each dawn shifts its coming sooner, to summer's highest tide, then back to winter's ebb,

revealing mud flats of the night exposed where we may venture, fearful perhaps but curious to find what the glare of too much light may have concealed.

A LONG BEAT up the sound toward the narrows, with winds funnelling down between the mountains, tide setting against, darkness coming on, and already a long day behind

but no other passage and what did you expect, an easy run?

AN IDIOT CHILD once took a man to show him a pit in the forest where bodies of hostages had been thrown and while they looked, a rat disturbed a shoe so that it appeared as if one of the corpses was waving its foot to them.

The child wanted to laugh but knew just enough not to, while the man, not wanting to laugh but knowing altogether too much, in what way could he?

HEARD ONCE, price of a drink, near empty bar, half a lifetime away, the tunes gone, like him, but not that grip of stained fingers, sweat on coiled veins, ballooned cheeks, clamped mouth, tensed neck, sagged eyes

which maybe saw us, maybe not, their intent not elsewhere but all there, on what he knew, was about, whether anyone heard or not, playing, as they say, for all he was worth.

FOR MONTHS, DETERMINED to ask a girl he saw each day, spoke with, to come for afternoon tea at his lodging, and always failing, until even the resolve failed, turning back to shadows, self regard, long walks alone

but also, for a few moments, perhaps longer, the great telescope to his will, scanning out into that beyond always beyond, as if falling into a dust of suns, resolving out of the darkness, where his self was of no consequence, even to himself.

WHEN I SAID to him that it was our human understanding which
varied and those expressions we devised for it, while that reality
which was beyond us had to remain unshifted,

he told me that we had progressed beyond such simplicities, that it
was no longer possible to conceive of anything beyond the statement
of it, that the only absolute was in the word.

WHILE LOOKING for some missing papers, he comes across the
remains of a small notebook. It appears to be the start of a sort of
journal but undated and undoubtedly in his handwriting although he
cannot recall writing it. He starts to read: "While looking for some
missing papers . . . 'and so on, down to' . . . although I cannot recall
writing it. When I turned the page . . ."

but at that point the writing comes to the bottom of the sheet and
he feels his hand begin to tremble as he cannot bring himself to turn
that page.

IN THE CORNER OF a railway station he notices a young couple
sleeping, their heads on their rucksacks, while the commuters hurry
past and the taxis sound nearby. They appear to be students and he
remembers his own youth: the hitch-hiking, the overnight buses,
the post war cafés, his digs, the girls for whom he yearned, his
incoherence, his shame, even the occasional moments of camaraderie
or happiness, piercing him even yet by their intensity and brevity.

Search though he may, he can find nothing durable for which he
might have nostalgia, until it comes to him: their ability to sleep,
curled up oblivious, while the world crashes forward about their ears.

HE HEARS THAT an old friend is seriously ill in hospital, and not expected to recover. They had parted painfully some years before. This might be the last chance to sort it out, even heal. He is apprehensive as he comes down the ward toward the bed

but at once, they are talking over old times as if the gap of years and whatever happened, had never been. As visiting time comes toward an end, he remembers what had been on his mind and starts "I wanted to say . . . all that about" . . . but his friend laughs, brushes it aside, even scoffs, and he finds himself trapped in the same frustration and resentment that had so poisoned him before.

ANYWHERE THEY CAN BE FOUND – a railway foyer, a post office, a shopping centre – he is in the habit of picking up the torn fragments of discarded prints beside the Instant Photograph booths. Later, he reassembles the aborted portraits, rather as one might eavesdrop on retracted confessions.

Ignoring those rejected because of bad centring or other obvious technical faults to concentrate on those sufficiently realised, he speculates on what it is in the images that decided each of those pairs of eyes to deny so vehemently what the camera had recorded.

AN OLD MAN SITTING on a bench in a city park is suddenly aware in his mind of someone he loved half a century ago and that this awareness has been prompted by a woman who has just walked past. He looks after her and begins to be persuaded that it is her again, old and grey, but with the same way of walking, the same angle of head, the same he could not explain what.

She sits on an adjacent bench, turning slightly in his direction, not appearing to see him. He watches her surreptitiously, now able to distinguish her profile. The more he considers, the more convinced he becomes

but is not absolutely certain. Eventually she gets up, glances back once, then moves off. He starts to follow, then hesitates, unable to shake off the conviction while doubting it, not sure if he is afraid that it is her, or afraid that it is not.

The worst is that he cannot be sure, and that he fears to find out, and in the humiliations and the impossibilities and the tenacity of his obsession, relives all that they had, or failed to have, together.

MIGHT A SHAPE of words be realised or contrived upon the principle of an asymmetric and rotary pendulum with flail arm where the long term pattern depends largely upon the initial impetus

but which becomes particularised because of non-linear effects built into the design, with ability to confound recurrence, never settling to a steady state and always possible with surprise?

THE SEA is calm as he swims out from the shore and the water clear in the sunshine. Dipping his head, he can see his shadow stretched out on the sand beneath, moving exactly with each movement he makes. Fascinated, he pauses, scarcely moving, yet enough to prevent himself from sinking.

Thus he becomes aware of his life, that it is exactly like this exertion to float, an effort almost without effort, no more than enough to prevent his body from rejoining that shadow from which, though he might swim to the limit of his strength, he can never finally escape.

"IT'S BECAUSE I love you so much," he said, "care about you, can't stop thinking of you, wanting to look after you, make sure you're safe, because

I can't bear not knowing where you are, who you're with, what you're doing, all the time, everywhere, and only because I love you, can't help loving you so much."

SCARCELY a year old, she looks out from a photograph and laughs, instinctively and wholeheartedly, perhaps at the young man holding the camera,

who may himself appear one day on another photograph, taken by her, of himself as an old man who also laughs, if with fragmented heart, enjoying the absurdity of possibility and the resilience of paradox.

ALWAYS SO SURE that she'd survive him to give his wheelchair a final push, deriding his concern, blowing cigarette smoke in his face, never walking if she could ride, indulging every whim, then flouncing out of his life,

that now, standing by her grave and given the last laugh, it's as if some final betrayal, missing only the bitter affection of her scorn.

THE PITCH OF A VOICE overheard, the way someone settles onto a seat in front of him in a cafe, even the tap of a heel on a pavement and he is possessed by memories he believed forgotten, didn't even want to return to: their last conversation, specific phrases, his state of mind, her insistence. He finds nothing to add to it, nothing to retract, as if watching a film which runs toward its inevitable end.

Yet throughout, he is clearly aware of that first flare of brightness which brought them together, as if the match which ignited it all had remained intact in the ashes of the bonfire.

WANDERING ONTO A BEACH at low tide, he starts to walk, seeing only an edge of scalloped sand extending into the distance, without shadow or interruption, under the diffused light of a winter sky. He feels no hunger or cold and it is as if he could go on like this for ever, into a distance always further, and he thinks of nothing

except the most intolerable of clarities: to dread everything closing in when it is the emptiness of the world which baffles.

DECIDING to end it all, he writes a last letter to his children, then realises that, under the pressure of the moment, he may have misspelled a word. Irritated by the uncertainty, he looks it up in a dictionary and, old habits being what they are, cannot resist allowing his attention to wander from the original word which had in fact been correct.

In so doing, he comes upon another which he realises was the image he had been looking for as the key to something be had been trying to write, for which he had had high hopes but had abandoned. He begins to make notes on the back of the letter, fearful that the inspiration might escape, that he might not be able to go on after all.

PERHAPS by tracing back, relating himself to some landmark, he might understand where he is now and so he searches through old journals and diaries until he comes to an entry he had forgotten: "Perhaps by tracing back . . ."

then, tearing up all he has written, he is filled with hope once more as he buys a new notebook or constructs one from loose sheets or even cuts the used sections from an old one not yet filled as if the blank pages were what he sought, could make possible, might answer the questions he has not yet inscribed on them.

A YOUNG MOTHER is alone with her four year old daughter on Christmas Eve. She's angry with the child who won't do as she's told and threatens, if the child doesn't behave, that her still-wrapped presents will go into the dustbin. The child is still defiant and the mother, though they cost her more than she could afford, throws them out in a fury,

and the daughter, years later, remembers nothing of the incident. Such conflicts were a familiar part of the every day. But what does remain is the frightening experience of her mother sobbing in a corner of the settee, for once oblivious to all the mischief the child could devise.

A BOY IS AMAZED to see his father home from work in the afternoon with a bandaged finger. An accident, not serious. A week later, the boy even sees the stitches, just before their removal. Then his father is once more gone during the week.

But that scar, though fading over the years, persists. No one else seems to remark on it: a narrowing streak, merely an absence of pigment, eventually hardly more than a crease. Long after his father's death, when that now grown boy tries to remember him, it is as if nothing else were so eloquent of his father or so particular to himself.

SHE SAID, "My father never encouraged me. My mother never gave me any affection. I was always alone against the world and laughter, a luxury. You had the fortune of a happy childhood."

But he replied, "Not at all. They taught you well. I was never prepared for life and am still struggling to learn what you absorbed so naturally from the cradle."

IT WAS AS IF she couldn't know herself. Only other persons could do that. When she searched for her image, there was always the reminder: one green eye, one brown. Her mother had tried to reassure that it made her attractive, interesting, that it was an asset, not a defect,

which wasn't what troubled, or even the lack of symmetry, but that when she looked in the mirror, she was always reversed, with her green right eye on the left, her brown on the right. Only others saw her as she was. Only others might make the affirmation, "You are." For her, it was always the reflection, "Am I?"

A MAN WAKES and hears his wife moving back and forth in the next room. Getting up to join her, he is distracted by the flapping of the curtain by the open window and glances out into the street.

Thanks to the darkness outside and the light in the next room, he sees the outline of her figure reflected in a window opposite. He stares, unable to tear himself from that image, as if it was finally able to clarify what had always made an illusion of their nearness.

EVERY EVENING a mother makes up another episode of the same story for her son. The next morning, he retells it to his grandmother who in turn can't resist relaying his account to her daughter, and also his detailed speculation as to what might happen: how the princess might escape from the castle, who she might meet in the forest.

The boy begins to realise the role of his grandmother but says nothing, scarcely able to contain himself with delight, certainly not able to decide which is the more wonderful: the continued uncertainty as to how it may develop or the recognition of his own fantasies given substance by the voice of another.

"IT'S BEST WE DON'T know anything about each other" he decided at their first meeting when it became obvious that they would become lovers. "But aren't you curious?" she asked. "My personal situation, where I live, what I do?" He put his finger to her lips. "Not a word. The less we know, the less chance of hurting each other. Not even a telephone number." So they would meet in a cafe and only then decide where to go, perhaps for a few hours, perhaps days, always somewhere different.

When it was time to part, they would arrange their next meeting, with only one fear: that if by chance one of them was unable to keep the rendezvous . . .

READING ANOTHER MAN'S autobiography, he wonders how much has been improved by memory, even fabricated, or what significant details just not recorded. If he were to attempt the same account, would the result he more honest or more misleading, deliberate or otherwise?

A few days later he receives a note from his sister – "I thought you might like to have this" – enclosing a letter written to her half a century ago. As he reads, he can hardly recognise the young man it reveals: in harmony with himself and the world, even generous to others. Yet his memory of those days is totally different: of someone inarticulate, indecisive and, at the same time, intolerably conceited.

GOING TO SCHOOL alone one day, he found himself unable to cross a street against the wind and was even thrust back by the gusts, until his hands gripped some railings by a bus stop, unable to go forward but holding on,

so now, a lifetime later, he knows again that panic of being swept back, unable to do no more than clutch, hold on somehow to what is now no more than a resolve not to retreat further.

CHECKING her account of what had happened, where she had been, what she had been doing, he realised that she had not deceived him but once having needed reassurance, it was as if he always needed more. He knew that all she asked was to be trusted, that he was closing a trap on himself.

When at last, in desperation, feeling the doors shutting about her, she found herself forced to tell him a lie, it was done so plausibly that for once he completely believed her. From that moment, she began to hate him. If he had plied her with further interrogations, the burden of deceit would have been easier, they would have been together in what was happening. Now she was alone and with the knowledge that she had become a cheat, even a skilful one.

TAKEN SEVERELY ILL, he is conscious only at brief intervals, enough to know that the diagnosis is as uncertain as the outcome and well beyond any treatment

until, one afternoon, he recovers enough to know that he is recovering, would live and not die, which seems a matter of great indifference except for the novelty. He finds himself weeping, in amazement at the gift of it, as if no more related to him than the pattern of clouds he can glimpse through a corner of the window.

A WOMAN GOES to visit her bedridden mother who takes something from a bedside drawer. "I want to be sure you have it after I'm gone. I know how much it meant to you when you were young." It is a small brass frog. The woman tries to control her panic as not only had she always thought it inexpressibly ugly but that era of her childhood had been far from happy. Once again, she will have to dissemble and as ever the effort will be flawed by saying too much. As she hesitates

the mother misjudges, "I knew you'd be affected. No need to say anything", and closes her eyes on the pillow, exhausted. Then the woman feels an immense love and gratitude, such as she had rarely felt, that her silence should have been so misunderstood.

A MAN STANDS WAVING goodbye to his grandson as a train pulls out of a station, the same from which he left when he had come to visit his own grandfather at the same age, now a lifetime away. Indeed, he has no articulate memory of his grandfather who died shortly after, and certainly none of that last goodbye. This had always been a sorrow, that so poignant a moment should he gone for ever.

But as he walks up into the town, he feels no loss at the realisation that his own grandson might scarcely remember, perhaps not at all, and so becomes aware of his grandfather in another way, more intense than any memory, more intense even than the image of that little boy waving to him through the still receding window.

AFTER MANY YEARS away, he finds himself in a taxi being taken from the airport toward the street where he grew up and where his parents still live. When he first made the decision to return, it was with as much elation as for any journey, but nearing the familiar suburb, not greatly changed, and recognising landmarks, he becomes uneasy and decides to walk the last few hundred yards.

Pausing outside the corner shop where he used to buy sweets, he notices that he is sweating, though the day is cold and overcast. The extent of his mistake becomes clear: that it is possible to become weary of being away without the least desire to return.

A WOMAN HAS devoted her life to her family. One evening at the table as her husband talks of his day at work and the children of their friends at school, she picks up her half finished meal and turns it over on its face, carefully pressing it down onto the tablecloth.

The children stare open mouthed. Her husband finally gasps, "What are you doing?" She smiles at him sadly, shaking her head. "You understand nothing. It wasn't me who did that. The woman who did that, by doing it, no longer exists."

MANY YEARS since she'd mocked his clumsy advances and he'd resolved to protect himself, even have revenge, sometimes exacting it from other women. Now, encountered again by chance, his desire for her returned, though he was no longer a fumbling boy. He joked of his rash behaviour and then, "I was so young."

but she interrupted him, "So was I, though had quite forgotten. How silly we were!" and as she laughed, his anger returned, and then relief: he was safe again.

SOMEWHERE BETWEEN the Danube and the Vistula, a man returns for the first time to the town where he was born, of which he has only a few confused memories. On the wall of what appears to he a synagogue but is only a replica, he finds the list of those deported who never returned. He himself at the last moment had been sent to friends in the country, who were able to get him over the frontier and he had grown up with strangers. He searches down the list for his parents and his grandparents

whose names are there as expected but so is his own. Momentarily shocked by the error, as he walks back to the railway station, he is overtaken by a strange peace. That child he was has now rejoined them and the alien he has become is free at last to live this other life that chance has given.

AWAKENING at her side, he rehearses past miseries, incompatibilities, things said in recent argument. Their separation is inevitable. He imagines the division of the furniture, the crockery being carried away by the removal men and even starts to go over those things he would never agree to part with.

It's then that the alarm rings. They get up, breakfast in silence. He studies her face across the table and sees, above the rim of the cup as she drinks her coffee, a half smile that might be taken as a glimmer of affection. Or just the satisfaction of a good night's sleep?

A MAN STOPS his car in a village square to look through a gate into the playground of a school. Everything is as it was, shrunk but intact and on a wall nearby he looks for a name he once scratched there. But how to find it, amid so many, circled sometimes by a heart or linked under a date?

Yet it had to be there and the face of that schoolgirl remains strangely clear, as much part of him as the nag of a broken bone, long healed but never letting him forget. He wonders what would have been the course of his life if, one evening on their way home from school, he had found the courage to put his hand in hers.

YOU WON'T FIND THE NAME in any dictionary but it is known to all who spend their days struggling across the more desolate wastes of human affliction, those rare instances, which the inexperienced can easily miss and the most hardened sceptic not totally discount, when something is actually achieved

and there is that transient brightness of a minute blossom almost invisible in the undergrowth, uniquely recognisable by such as persist in the quest, but unlisted in any index or encyclopaedia of the possible.

HE HAD REHEARSED what he would say, even the intonation. Then, as once on stage knowing that it was his cue, he had a moment of panic, unable to remember what he was expected to say but opening his mouth to speak,

so once again the words came, articulate and from where he did not know, but unlike that former time, not at all what he had prepared, and she had replied as if expecting them, already familiar with the script.

AT LEAST ONCE, having seen what was needed and the possibility, worked out the means, structure, I took down part of a wall, rearranged the stones, put in posts, hinges:

a gate, aligned and balanced so that, as contrived, it closed exactly, the snib dropping into place as if only natural, meant to be, the same "Why not?", the same "What more?"

AN EVENING OF CONVERSATION by the Loire, the words ranging, our thoughts also, sometimes falling silent, scarcely listening to each other, the river idling past and as I speculate on the shallows, sandbanks, levels, tidal movement, seeming lack of definition, he remarks

". . . the last great untamed river in Europe." And then – as the talk eddies on to other rivers, absent friends, Cendrars and his "Transiberien", the permutations of language, birds' names, migrations, even the virtues of occasionally losing one's way – I begin to see what he means.

IN MY DREAM, the real one that dreams of me, it's always the same house. I could tell you the town, street, number. You could go there yourself. I could go. Where I was once, and go again in my dream, and where I can't understand

why I moved out, away, on, or why I'm back as if summoned and always with this reproach as to why I've been gone so long, why so careless as to leave and where I can't find the answer to that familiar and returning question of "Was I not what you dreamed? Not all you desired?"

MY CLOTHES FIT. They recognise me at work. The bank accepts my signature. Even my wife and family keep up the pretence.

But I know I've been replaced by this other that I didn't choose, that I don't recognise, that I can't evict, that has learned to play me so well that even I begin to be convinced by the part.

A BIRD trapped against the inside of one of the windows refused to give up the struggle until frightened by my efforts to help was distracted from the obvious and so found another window which was open:

thus each of us achieved what we desired but neither of us how we had intended.

HE EXPLAINED "With age, there's a lot of wear and tear on the self-winding mechanism and that's why it needs attention more often to keep it going"

and as I walk home, I give myself a shake and look at my old watch and wonder how much more effort it will take to keep us going and for how long.

SEARCHING THROUGH an art gallery, I came upon a canvas of worthies assembled in conference, entirely filling the end wall of one room, each figure lifesize but so blackened by age and neglect that hardly a face could be distinguished

except on one side in a doorway, where someone was glancing in. With curiosity? complicity? late in arriving? Or like me, just looking for the friend he had arranged to meet somewhere in the building?

AS IT HAPPENED, several lifetimes ago, I was employed to escort an elderly man to a distant city. He was said to be in need of supervision, while amiable enough, and we travelled overnight by train, sharing the same compartment. When he was settled asleep in his bunk, I climbed into mine

and the night slid past the window. Then I woke, to find him out of his bed and leaning over mine. "Tell me," he whispered. "Please tell me. I need to know. Where are we?"

HE WAS SOMEONE who, during the most important years of his existence, had been a sort of outlaw from life so that his ability to feel much for others had withered, acquiring only that insight which age sometimes brings and a tolerance so often the child of indifference,

knowing few of those troubles which are brought upon us by those we love, for the most banal of reasons: he had no one to love.

THE ONLY NAME he remembered from his childhood was that of Mavis, two or three years older, who often organised play in the street. One day, she instructed him and another lad of the same age to help her dramatise the story of Joan of Arc. As Joan died heroically in the imaginary bonfire, the two boys were supposed to kneel and murmur, "We've burned a saint"

but all they could repeat was "We've burned Mavis" and even that was scarcely audible amid their laughter. Fury and exasperation tested Joan's sanctity to the point of tears. But those rough soldiers did not relent, though one of them at least felt some pangs afterwards, if not to the extent of being fully able to regret his share in her torment.

WALKING in the country, even following a path marked on a map, he could never rid himself of the impression that it was most precisely there, beyond the limit set for going back or diversion for the night, that something – he could not specify what – awaited.

Then, far from becoming weaker over the years, this senseless anticipation grew more intense as he became less and less able to walk anywhere.

HE HAD DESIRED HER, realised it was impossible, even ridiculous, even persuaded himself she cared nothing for him and that he had blanked her out of his life

then, by chance, finding himself in the same room, could not resist catching her eye and was back where he had been before in shared awareness of how much was absurd and awareness of how much was real.

HOME AGAIN for the first time, having started a new life elsewhere, she became aware of what appeared to be a change in her parents. True, her mother still nagged her about not eating enough and her father about going to bed too late. These were familiar, almost endearing

but she found herself obsessed and irritated by what she did not remember: her father snoring in his chair in the afternoon, the noise her mother made drinking tea. Yet they had not changed. It was she who had and in trivial ways. As if the effort to escape had trapped her in what she most despised.

STANDING HERE in this circled pattern where they have been set by men and for whatever purpose, the stones will stand after we have gone – though some have fallen – as we read in the guide-book what little is known about them and how much is not,

where we also stand, adding our pattern to theirs, and our words, for our own purposes, then falling silent, silenced by their silence, by our need to understand and our understanding that we can't.

THE WORST was – that although the pain of their separation, like her love, had long ago receded, so that she scarcely even remembered the name of that other who had taken him from her –

the bitterness of her jealousy remained as suffocating as ever.

UNIMAGINABLE that she could have imagined us, these centuries later, staring at her in a photograph: exposed and naked, preserved by the peat, no sign of injury or restraint, with only the left side of her head shaved. Making distinction? And her eyes covered. To shut out this world? See beyond into another?

As we would see into hers but are shut out, divided also, by this need to discern, lay bare, imagine, what is beyond us, unimaginable.

A SPIRITED LADY, whose marriage had never been consummated and who refused to ever throw out a milk bottle or believe her husband was terminally ill, when he finally died was found in his bed trying to warm up the corpse which had to be pried out of her arms,

then carried his ashes everywhere and when arrested for shoplifting ("It was only a present for my psychiatrist") unscrewed the top of the jar and threw the contents over the attending policeman.

THE GIRLS working in the radar control room could hear the
comments of the fighter pilots on the radios which were often
obscene in the excitement of combat which upset the commanding
officer of the unit but didn't trouble the girls

but what did upset them was sometimes when a plane was hit and
caught fire and the pilot could not get the canopy free to bail out, his
screams as he burned to death.

RETARDED since birth, mother schizophrenic, father alcoholic
and dead of a stroke when he was five, reared in a variety of foster
homes, then most of his life a farm labourer until the old farmer died
and the new owner had no more use for him, now diabetic with leg
ulcers and retinal damage, he sits all day in his caravan watching the
television and is going blind in his remaining eye

and one morning, a spring day with birds singing outside, I hear him
ask "Why . . . ?" and start to go on about arteries and metabolism
and genetic inheritance until I realise that he can't make sense of
anything I am saying and neither can I.

WHEN I POINTED OUT that for her to bring her life to an end
or ask me to do it, whatever her suffering, was against one of the
fundamentals of her belief,

she replied, after a pause, "Oh, God understands even if his priest
doesn't."

A SNOWSTORM, and we build a snowman and snowoman side by side in the garden. They stand awkwardly, as if something were expected of them.

Next morning, there's a thaw. The children point, "Look! They're trying to kiss." And indeed they have begun to lean, almost touch, as if not quite sure how to comfort each other.

AT CERTAIN MOMENTS of the year there is a particular splendour of the evening horizon, as if from massed tapers in the chancel of an otherwise darkened cathedral

into which we have wandered or been summoned without explanation, able to glimpse the movements of the celebrants only as shadows on the vaulting, as we try to guess our part, if we have one, in the ritual.

IF YOU ASK what it's all about, this reshuffling words, I can only relate how someone once told me he'd heard by chance verses of mine sung, without attribution, in a club in London, though he couldn't recall by whom or even when

or how, buried in a time capsule under a cairn in Australia, there are other words, if the ink hasn't faded or the paper crumbled, which may survive human history but also perhaps never again be read.

WANDERING INTO the streets of a strange town while waiting for a train, came upon a local museum which turned out to be a converted chapel and where someone, I don't know why, was playing a piano, if not well, with great feeling

and the tune "abide with me" though it was mid-day and not "eventide", and with those words, once so familiar, the boundaries began to dissolve, and soon my eyes, so that indeed the "darkness deepened" despite the sunshine, and if I sought no "help of the helpless" yet I was helpless, carried elsewhere, and by what I could no longer help.

HE WISHES to remember his early childhood but the more he tries, the more anything tangible eludes. Only one detail remains

of a Christmas Day, his father trying to amuse him with a conjuring trick and after several failed attempts finally succeeding, then looking to him in triumph for a rewarding smile that he was unable to give, and now never could.

LEAVING HIMSELF behind had become a pattern, and mostly without choice except that he appeared to allow it to go on. Now, almost erased, trying to recover something, he can remember little of the process, how, when, where, other than as if a plug left open, a rent in the fabric not repaired, so that he scattered himself as he went.

Even trying to retrace, the landmarks had became unfamiliar as if he had forgotten the route. Or had never paid attention? Or was this his destiny, this replacement of who he had been by this other, now mostly an absence? Grateful and hungry for any fragment it might gather afresh.

HE REPORTED in his journal how, being guided through unknown country by a band of Indians, he could not escape watching them ambush and massacre a group of Inuit and saw a girl actually pinned to the ground with a spear through her lower body, still fully conscious and struggling to get away

until he persuaded one of the Indians not to leave her in agony and was much struck by the fact that, as the war club was raised over her head, she could not resist lifting her arm to protect herself.

A MEMOIR, opened at random, and in another language, of a village in the Haut-Doubs near the Swiss border, and it's an early summer evening, 1906. A schoolboy, Michel, fancies a classmate, Judith, and wanders past her house, dawdles. She comes out. "Where are you going?" "For a walk." "You wanted to see me?" He nods.

She goes on, "You're being silly, why didn't you come in?" "Didn't dare. I'd no excuse." "You can always find that. Go on, have you finished your homework?" "Yes." "I haven't. You can help me."

The text continues "La phrase resta en suspens, mais les yeux parlaient." The phrase remained in suspense, but the eyes spoke. The words hung in the air, but the look expressed.

The sentence lingered, the glance implied. So many possible translations, so many possible meanings, and with all their lives to unravel.

REMARKING to us ". . . that only in the familiar is there renewal.
Thus, awakening this morning: light on ceiling, wardrobe mirror,
clothes at foot of bed, flowers in a jar, window curtains, glimpse
of rooftops. I never tire of their shapes and colours, depending on
viewpoint, time of day, mood,

yet often lacking focus without someone in the pattern, perhaps
turned away, even preoccupied with other detail. And if my
utterance, this composition, seems only a whisper, it is the voice of a
confidant. Lean closer. What I have to reveal is for us alone."

IT CAN HAPPEN at any time, always when he doesn't expect it, as
if a chink has opened, a cloud or curtain parted, and he glimpses
something through the gap, something belonging to him, that was
once part of him but which has detached itself, the loss of which he
has only just recognised.

Then, over-anxious to reclaim, he fumbles and the opportunity is
gone. Yet he remembers the experience, even the familiarity and
resolves that the next time it presents itself he'll be prepared, that he
won't panic, that it won't escape him again.

YOU CAN STILL SEE IT THERE – where there is no smoke any
more, not even ashes, the ovens swept clean, only a slit in the wall
between the slides of the measuring bar against which the prisoner
stood willingly, even eagerly, for record of his height, even of his
existence –

a discreet opening, unremarkable and convenient, behind which, in
the next room, was the revolver with the silencer, held at the level of
the base of his head, to avoid disturbance.

The Kid

for Hamish Whyte

credited with
so many, when
asked the reason
why he'd shot one
man, is said to have
explained, "His gun
jammed, mine didn't."

William McTaggart

On the sands of west Kintyre,
legs apart, slightly bent, facing
the surf, in a photograph, his son
holding the canvas against gusts
'first in my own rather than second
in any other' – no need to sign –
of which the best, he judged
were those few which had cost him
after much labour, the least

'never hurry, then, when everything
is as you chose, stop' – by power
to create space – the primer showing
as tinted ground with touches
of muted colour only in places
but those the right ones 'and
where harpies wait, though powerless
without aid, so do not lend yourself'
who held – to paint the wind.

A Bit Part: from Chekhov

not even a walk-on – a voice from behind a backdrop – not
even words – but calling something–summons? greeting?
directions? – and Cherbutykin: "That's Skvortsov, the second,
shouting from the boat"

before the duel, before the Baron is killed, off stage, a fool
anyway – who wasn't meant to be killed, just frightened,
grazed – but however careful, a bullet is a bullet – and
Skvortsov

must have had to deal with the body, tell the family, sort it
out – and Cherbutykin, later: "What does it matter?" – and
Olga: "If only we knew, if only . . ." – what isn't in the script

or of what happened to Skvortsov – after the curtain – who
remembers, if nothing else, as no one else – being there,
unseen, unable to see, listening for his cue, ready

to call out in the silence – to make it matter, understandable,
what Cherbutykin would say – and then, whoever – and so
on – and perhaps even Olga – what only Skvortsov – alone in
the dark – only he knew – he knows.

This Rigmarole of Going On

As pedlars or mendicants.
jugglers or fools,

where could we get to?
whom might we impress?

moving on or staying,
escaping or in quest,

what else have we –
improvise, rehearse –

but irony in laughter,
in desperation, jest?

★

While the years drain away
and each poem, shaped
from a sediment of words
is, however briefly,
a sort of stopper
for that plug hole, time.

★

There's also luck.
That once Norwegian
who fled his kingdom without fight,
Eric Haraldson –
who'd remember him
except for his nickname, Bloodaxe?

85th Birthday Greetings
in Terms of a Public Monument

No plinth
where you'd be set
or pigeons
on your head
yet.

Nothing

Ferai un vèrs de dreit nient
  – William of Aquitaine, c 1100

A poem about nothing
defines by its achieving,
unhindered by mere something
to which the words might cling.

A nothing to he said.
An absence in my head.
This nothing that I find.
This clarity of mind.

The nothing that is me.
The nothing I will be.
The nothing that I was.
This prodigy of cause

with neither bounds nor base,
that existing, leaves no trace.
Nothing's the only thing that's sure.
How else to make a poem pure?

For André Breton One Hundred Years from his Birth [1896-1996]

"Je cherche l'or du temps"

that the working of the mind might not just understand itself but in the real expression reveal its workings surely though how can we if only in dreams even derangement when to explain a joke without erasing is impossible and if the most potent the most fleeting and the most naked the most powerful where the embrace of poetry like love so long as it last is proof against all evasion upon the misery of the world if all this and the disordered sheets for it happens as in a bed the polarity to engender and if they tell me what's inscribed on your grave who was never that where else to find words for the gold of each moment where there's always the marvel of a shovel to the wind in the sands of the dream and always an arrow let loose as a star in the pelt of the night that the working of the mind

[This includes phrases adapted from the *Surrealist Manifesto*, the phrase that Breton is said to have most cherished from his favourite poem, the words on his gravestone, as well as a few other expressions, all variously transmuted but without apology.]

Islands

I

He told me he worked on the mainland and was only home every few weeks, and so never learned to get over his sea-sickness, but did know what to do crossing on the ferry. Leaving the island he would eat on board, knowing conditions would improve as they went but never ate going the other way and advised me not to, almost certain to lose what you'd paid for.

II

There are few trees and those stunted from wind and salt spray but with enough driftwood for roof timbers and peat for fuel, little need. The post came regularly, weather permitting, and when the postman was ill or off duty, it was delivered by a neighbour who was used to the conditions. She knew everyone but refused to deliver to one crofter who lived in a sheltered spot, who had even put a fence around the adjacent ground to keep off the sheep and deer. The trees had grown taller than her, than the house, as tall as on the mainland, threatening her with shadows blotting out the light.

III

Talking with an old fisherman, I remarked on the number of men lost at sea as recorded on the stones in the graveyard, some quite recent, and he nodded, that it was often dangerous but they always took great care and had great respect for the sea. "We only get drowned once in a while."

IV

One evening we saw agitation in the water by the shore of the loch
and went closer. A group of seals had come into the shallows from
the skerry and were splashing and leaping about for no apparent
reason. I remarked on it to our host who said it was not unusual.
"Having a party. No different to us. Like to enjoy themselves when
they can."

V

When I asked "Don't you get lonely?" after hearing that he often
spent weeks by himself between the mountains and the sea, he
smiled, "With all this space to look at and the silence to listen to?"

The Words

. . . no by breid alane but by ilka wurd . . .

There's this need to make utterance   be heard, even understood
as I shape these words for you   gone into that silence from where
I still hear your words   as once you heard mine.

Did you believe   I wished only to believe
with you   and to believe we understood
each other?   who have shared the bread and the wine
as we have the air and the sun   and now these years
from childhood to this age   come at last to me also

and if your words   those we have from our forefathers
for that bread and that wine   are no longer those
I can use, I must believe   you also believe
they are only words   if necessary
in face of those questions   of that beyond where I would reach

with these, the given words   we find on our tongues
from which we can't escape   that I would not disown,
the familiar and necessary words   I received from you,
the unanswerable words   we share and always shall.

A Perception of Ferns

from unseen source
conceived to generate
what's now revealed
flowering invisibly
then manifest
by shoots asserting
what was concealed
with fronds unfolding
for the eye to reach
inverted searchings
of wavering crosiers
finding reflection
by reflecting on
as shadowed light
so spores are shed
dispersions made
from unseen source
conceived to generate
what's now revealed
flowering invisibly
then manifest
by shoots asserting
what was concealed
with fronds unfolding
for the eye to reach
inverted searchings
of wavering crosiers
finding reflection
by reflecting on
as shadowed light
so spores are shed
dispersions made
from unseen source
conceived to generate

what's now revealed
flowering invisibly
then manifest
by shoots asserting
what was concealed
with fronds unfolding
for the eye to reach
inverted searchings
of wavering crosiers
finding reflection
by reflecting on
as shadowed light
so spores are shed
dispersions made
from unseen source
conceived to generate
what's now revealed
flowering invisibly
then manifest
by shoots asserting
what was concealed
with fronds unfolding
for the eye to reach
inverted searchings
of wavering crosiers
finding reflection
by reflecting on
as shadowed light
so spores are shed
dispersions made
from unseen source
conceived to generate
what's now revealed
flowering invisibly

The Nicing

"Have a nice day!" she says,
as she has been taught,
and it is nice of her
to think of it and I think
I should be nicer to her
than my thought inclines
and wonder if the offer
of a day, especially a nice one,
is for me to choose or whether
it has been allocated,
as reward for buying enough
or inducement to buy more . . .
which is, for a nice day, I agree,
not very nice of me.

A letter from

A letter from a dead man,
what urgence could that lend?
which starts:
           "Received yours . . .
thanks for all the news . . .
and wishes . . . too bad that . . ."

Nothing significant
beyond what he might intend?
going on:
           "We're pleased . . .
the parcel safely . . . so in due time,
all does arrive . . . I had the . . ."

Written while still alive,
so why hope it could portend
to more than:
             "Our recent news is . . .
came and went . . . our plans are . . .
no space for more . . . it's sad that . . ."?

A letter from a dead man,
how could I want that it should end?
which does:
           "Now having autumn sunshine
mixed with cold . . . We're glad that . . .
greet everyone there for us . . .
all our love . . . Dad."

Or So We Are Told

(1)
Nightingales sing at night because they sing nearly all the time and
we just don't notice them during the day when other birds and
sounds clutter our ears but do after dark

when there's silence enough to hear them.

(2)
A most curious effect can be observed if a fragment of rock crystal,
ground down so that the undersurface comes to a point (which is
then rounded off) is balanced on the wet surface of a piece of
window glass which is then slanted (the least inclination is sufficient),

whereupon the fragment has a tendency to tumble and a rotary
movement begins, the whirling sometimes becoming so accelerated
that the eye can no longer distinguish its shape.

A Little Kindling for John Christie

In ignorance
not a glimmer, then
words struck, clinging
as if by insistence
fanned, as marks remarked,
a grit of light
alighting, lighting,
falling upon tinder, calling,
kindling
an ignition
of recognition
as end, beginning,
singed, flared,
consumed, singing.

We celebrate

for Edwin Morgan

We celebrate your name
as no mere eddy
but niagara of invention –

not swords to ploughshares, rather
claymores to pipe organs! –
and as alchemist translating

not just to gold or new from old
but words into wonder
wonder into words.

All Those Good Fellows

(Field Marshall Earl Douglas Haig)

"It could not have been done without
all those good fellows who time and again
formed up their companies in darkness
to lead their men forward in the grey of morning
so often to certain death" –

at his command who still rides
on the castle esplanade, scarcely a mile
from where he was born, eyes fixed
toward the south and his own headstone
without distinction
from those uncountable beyond

who was not without sadness or care
but without doubt
as to what had to be done and was done
and could not have been done without
all those good fellows who time and again
formed up in darkness and in the grey of morning
went forward to certain death.

(partly from various expressions in his diaries and in a letter)

Sureties

'... by inscrutable providence for sik end
as His eternal wisdom ...'

Those fathers, setting forth 'the plaine
Confessioun of sik Doctrine' with remonstrance
'to ... the Inhabitants of Scotland ...
to seill the assurance of His promise', in expectance
lived as they died
with that assurance.

Fallen at Rullion Green, hoisted aloft
in Grassmarket, exposed in Greyfriars, in defiance
of all authority except His word of promise, they –
by noose, starvation, musket, sword or lance –
died as they lived
by that assurance.

With power themselves over 'the Thrie Estatis',
they showed to Thomas Aikenside no tolerance
and astonished Europe with their zeal
for burning witches, in their vigilance
living while others died
from that assurance.

Some doubted, quavered in their souls.
Fraser of Brea was one who, even in the manse
knew agonies, his preaching all a sham, until
by trust in that 'eternal wisdom', simple compliance,
found rest before he died
in that assurance.

Campbell of Row, declared a heretic
for seeming to give that 'rest' undue importance,
came to believe at last 'that the true peace'
was of itself, with creeds mostly encumbrance,

and lived as he would die
with that assurance.

Others, like Hume, framed cogent reason
'against superstition', while resolute to advance
all 'Human Understanding', never indifferent
to that 'Enquiry', thinking no more or less mischance
in death than life and facing
both with assurance.

Or Maclean of Glasgow who, with new confession
as 'Manifesto' of 'materialism', swore his allegiance
against 'slavery of wages', asserted 'freedom
as awareness of necessity' and took his stance
in life, not death, unbroken
for that assurance.

So now, of their many sons, this one – convinced
no more of 'Doctrine', if words have relevance
to life or death, or questions, answers, then
we're part of what continues, even what they began –
must also find, at no great distance,
what rest or providence I can
in that assurance.

Refractories / The efficiency of . . .

The efficiency of coke ovens, blast furnaces, electric furnaces and
open-hearth furnaces, depends to a large extent on the refractory
nature of the materials used in their construction

and thus, recognising our former general ignorance of such
refractories, a programme of research is presented

for the investigation of the fundamental mechanical, physical and
chemical properties, particularly the softening temperatures,
with or without load –

the thermal conductivity of retorts, oven walls, baffles and the like,
the radiation of heat, influence of texture,

volume changes, permanent or not, after contraction or after
expansion, the penetration of vapour, molten slag, fluxing
agents, flue dust, vibration at various temperatures,

also cracking, fissuring and cognate phenomena, the extent of silica
conversion, what conditions favour this,

and to what extent it is advisable or any advantage in precalcining all
or any proportion of the various materials so as to relieve the
work to be done in the kiln in the subsequent firing and a critical
evaluation of alleged furnace temperatures,

including methods for increasing the plasticity of the clays used, with
an auxiliary investigation on the measurement of the complex
property known as the plasticity of clay –

and although the various operations and processes employed have
been largely stabilised by a process of trial and error

447

none-the-less some of the fundamental operations want revision so
as to make reasonably sure that important essentials have not
been overlooked.

A Lady of Pleasure, The Netherbow, Seventeen Hundred and Something

"This drunken bundle of iniquity,
about fifty years of age, lusty and tall,
who has followed the old trade
since she was about thirteen, can boast
of being the natural daughter of a late
worthy Baronet who was a brave General
in the war before last, but
being a disgrace to her relations
who are among the best in Scotland,

she was sent to the north where she continued
her business successfully for a long time
before returning. She regards neither decency
nor decorum and would as willingly lie
with a chimney sweep as with a Lord,
and of a desire so undiminished
would think nothing of a company of Grenadiers
at the one encounter. Take her all in all,
she is an abandoned piece."

Better than was

Better than was
    though something of a totterer
in this shaking season
    where I go on with courage
if to prate upon rubble
    on a scurvy splenetic day
lumped with lies and insistencies
    finding a great giddiness in the head
as much cooler of making
    with the constant cant of puppies
all in a matter of nothing
    yet afraid of disobliging
which puts me quite out of method
    but piss take their frolics

and on a foolish errand of old pretensions
    have come down proud stomach
which vexes me to the pluck
    though uttering gives me ease
even a curiosity to reckon
    but must talk of things as they happen.
You desire a style so melancholy?
    Would keep a little to possibilities.
Walking is a strange remedy
    And God send it holds.

(from phrases in Swift's 'Journal to Stella')

From the Equator to the Pole:
A Figure for the Earth

Further study has confirmed
that meridian arcs in low or middle ranges
cannot distinguish between errors in the radius vector
and errors in the flattening

and that there is distinct evidence
of a cause, deep-seated,
which distorts the geoid in certain latitudes
which must be further investigated
before we can be sure
that the meridian sections are even sensibly ellipses.

Thus, before we can state what, if any,
is most fit to be adopted as a figure for the earth,
these preliminary results show
that the existing estimates
have been computed to a degree of accuracy
beyond what can ever be justified
and we may never know to a millimetre
the distance from the equator to the pole.

(adapted from A.R. Hinks,
The Geographical Journal, Vol. LXIX, No.6, 1927)

Herein described

From the town where the river
is full of rocks, shelves
and great falls in the water,
I continued through narrow lanes
toward hills they call fells
until I came beside a great lake
of standing water which does not
ebb and flow as does the tide,
neither does it run
so as to be perceivable
but seems to drift
and wave about with the wind . . .

whence I rode on
in view of that same lake,
though sometimes lost
by reason of great hills interposing
to hinder any sight but of clouds,
and so gained by degree to the side of
one of those hills or fells,
about the middle, for looking down,
it was at least a mile
and looking upward,
I was as far from the top,

walled in on both sides
by those inaccessible
high rocky barren hills
which seem to hang over one's head
in some places and appear
very terrible, of a height
from which many little springs
and currents of water
from sides and clefts

do bubble up and trickle down
and as they meet with stones
or rocks to obstruct their passage,
come with more violence
which gives a pleasing sound
and murmuring voice . . .

herein described for such
as might be inquisitive
after such places wherein I went.

(from passages in 'The Journal of Celia Fiennes', 1698)

Though I Have Met with Hardship

(letter from New South Wales, 1852)

"This is a most beautiful country, all green
to the very tops of the hills, where we arrived
after a good passage but not a quick one.
98 days sailing and then three weeks in quarantine.
Seven persons died on the voyage, two with consumption,
and about 40 of the children, including
I am sorry to relate to you, our youngest lassie, Janet.

Though we had plenty of water and good victuals,
there were too many aboard, 950 emigrants as well as 60 crew,
and a great number took the ship fever.
Nobody that has got any serious trouble about them
need think they will stand this voyage
and I would not advise any man with a weak family
to come out by the Government ships
because of the want of room and foul air,
but it was the cold and bowel complaint
that destroyed all the children.

Every word I put here is true
as I have got to meet with death, and so, dear brother,
I hope you will make up your mind to come,
you and Donald Macleod and John, the sooner the better,
before your family gets any more in number, for children
are a great trouble and sadness on the voyage.

Give my love to our mother if she is still alive
and tell her that we are as well off as she would wish
though I have met with hardship since I left,
and that I will send her what will do her good
if I be alive for another year, and give our kind love
to all our friends and acquaintances and to Donald Mackay

of Arscaig and his family and I wish they were here
and not on the black muir of Arscaig."

*(adapted from an original letter to her great grandfather
in the possession of Joan Michael of Ullapool)*

Jeffrey to Cockburn 28 June 1832

". . . odd how strangely I felt
as I walked home to my lodgings
alone last night after all was over,
our cause won, instead of being elated
or relieved . . . could not help feeling
a deep depression or sadness, and
rather think I dropped a tear or two
as I paused to interrogate . . ."
there in the midsummer darkness

under the trees of the city square
". . . and cannot very well explain
but a sense somewhat of the littleness
and vanity even of those great contentions
was uppermost in my mind . . . and
have had ever since a most intense
longing to get home as I hunger
and thirst for another view
of the lochs and hills of my own . . ."

Do not be deterred

Do not be deterred
by dread of the extravagant,
for the possibilities of existence
run so deeply
there's scarcely any concept too extraordinary

with certainly something very peculiar,
indeed anomalous,
about the jaws of the Coccosteus
the use of which in the economy of the animal
is as yet unknown,
               despite my find
of a near perfect specimen
which I have most carefully examined

revealing a group of teeth in the molar position
acting on a similar group in the intermaxillary
plus two other opposing groups at the symphysis
set at a right angle to the former

thus uniting in the one orifice
both vertical and transverse mouth.

(From Hugh Miller: *The Old Red Sandstone*, 1841.)

How in Sundry Sorts They Were Shattered

We came full in their face from the hillside,
where it was very hot on both sides with fearful cries,
the day darkening with smoke overhead, arrows flying
so thick and so uncertainly landing that nowhere
was there any surety of escape, quite against nature
with horror to make any man forget conceit for himself

where we encompassed them
as a web to catch a swarm of bees and where for a time
they stood very brave and bragging, shaking their weapons
but when they were once turned it was a wonder to see
how soon and in sundry sorts they were shattered,

letting fall their pikes like a wood of staves,
or rushes in a chamber, so thick in places
as to be unpassable for horse or man, with helmets,
swords, bucklers, daggers, armoured jackets,
and all things else that either were of any weight
or might be hindrance to their flight.

So began a pitiful sight of the straggled corpses
from the fallow fields of Inveresk
almost to the gates of Edinburgh itself –
the most so little differing in their apparel
that few of their great men were spared,
without ring or brooch or any semblance of show
to distinguish the gentleman from the lout,
the lackey from the laird –
the bodies scattered in clusters, as widely
as a man might note from a distance
sheep or cattle settling for night in a pasture.

(Adapted from various passages in
William Patten's 'An Expedition into Scotland', 1547)

In reference to our being

In reference to our being
    and its end, if such be knowable –
under that awe of truth
    proper to those who enquire what is, not speculate what ought –
where all forms are, in shape of words,
    as intellect separate from spirit
and having liberty to think
    (indeed, obligation)
men of differing beliefs may come to recognise in each other
    that impress by which they converge,
although indeed a line may well be drawn somewhere
    in regard to doctrine
and yet one which wider perception reveals
    is joined upon itself
and continually shifts
    to enclose a narrower circle
until becoming a mere point
    even that vanishes.

(adapted from passages in the writings
of John Mcleaod Campbell)

(March, 2001)

James Young Simpson: If it is our mission . . .

"If it is our mission
to alleviate suffering
as well as to preserve life
there should be no conscientious restraint

and if God has benevolently given us means
to mitigate the agony
it is His evident intention
that we should employ it

which requires no special kind or instrument –
even the perfume is not unpleasant
with ten to twenty inspirations being enough
sometimes fewer
so that sleep speedily follows –

and on one of the first occasions
after the influence had passed off
it was a matter of no small difficulty
to persuade the astonished mother
that the baby presented to her
was her own living child."

(from the writings of James Young Simpson in 1848)

from lazy blue flowers

(Preliminary draft 11 June 2004)

from lazy blue flowers that develop
into lobular pods with elliptical seeds
producing, when crushed, a yellowish oil
with characteristic smell, not totally disagreeable
having large variations in viscosity
and the peculiarity of absorbing oxygen
on exposure to air, eventually yielding
a compact, elastic mass, capable of being combined with
a great variety of substances, such as
wood flour, ground cork, pine resins, gum arabic
tallow, gutta percha, varnish, others, plus pigments
– including lamp black, white lead, iron oxides, prussian blue
– into paste called "kiver", to be applied to fabrics
such as hessian, canvas, linen, even cotton,
making it waterproof, flexible and of much resilience
and when dried, capable of being polished or printed on
in a variety of ways for table, wall or floor
each worker employing their own particular standards
as experience taught them, by creative industry
– so that what seems impossible to one
may be common daily practice with another –
flexibility of process being very desirable
even for this building around us, dedicated
to the practice of science and the arts
to give an impetus of advantage to the town
where all of this has been derived
by progression of effort over many years
from lazy blue flowers that develop
into lobular pods with elliptical seeds
producing, when crushed, a yellowish oil . . .

1. A Zig-Zag Wake

Marking, adjusting course
               inscribed by time
against tidal current, vagaries of wind
               each shift, each tack
as furrow that divides
               that calls to us, that signals
what was from what might be
               as image and reflection
glimpsed far astern
               that we reflect upon

or through a window, over shoulder
               as once, yawning awake
not quite yet dawn, coming into Dijon
               rain puddles in the gutters
velvet drizzle, charcoal light
               with passers-by, their feet, each stride
each impact mirrored, shimmering
               and droplets, breaking surfaces
each pulse, a wavering
               as the bus jolts forward, nearing halt
to reach a station, make connection
               in time, on time, through time
by arrival to make welcome
               then depart

even as boy, a war time crossing
               mid Atlantic spray
keeping lookout
               as the cruiser's prow uplifted, fell
through twists of foam
               each lurch, a shudder, nausea
slicing each crest
               until the Kintyre hills through overcast
then shelter, entrance, coming up the Clyde
               willing to partake

or elsewhere through enchainments of the years
         after tedium, hitch-hiking, fatigue
traversing filament of road, going north
         massed palisades of trees, broken by swamps
rare clearing, stumps of forest fires, sometimes a lake
         a litany of darkening green
to where he found himself no stranger, everyone being strange
         where he longed to stay
where no one stayed
         as if by inertia, by momentum trapped?
and was that mistake?

         so earlier, walking hilltops
stumbling to utter
         yearning to apprehend
realised too late
         all those words he'd gathered, failed to hold
all that's shed, that dissipates, that seeps
         though he wedged, contrived
what eludes all fury to retrieve
         as if a hull: strakes, gunnels to an utmost strung
all urgence to defy
         wrung out
as that day on Skye, scrambling through heather
         snaking, sodden
by exertion to assuage, to dull
         what he clung to
all he could not, would not ever finally erase, deny
         that loss
to uncoil, to shed that slough, that froth
         he'd never slake, retake
which must be enough
         recoiling on himself, itself
in quest to forsake
         veering towards and from
to shape
         a zigzag wake.

2. To Meet and Hear Upon the Way

"Forsake your leaving,
                    stay.
                    The homing of your quest is done.
                                        Do not
betray.
            Daybreak may never come.
                        What's near is here.
                                        Outreach it if
you need.
            It makes no claim
                        or wall.
                                Merely this ache
                                        to satisfy, infold.
All's told.
            The script is clear.
                        Let the wind rage.
                                    Drought, forest fire,
earthquake or flood
                dust, tedium, the abrasions of the road
                                        are far.
Why grasp or rake
            at hope or fear?
                        Why turn the page?
                                    Wish to remake?
There's no mistake
            or wavering
                    only as if with pigments –
                                        lucent or
opaque –
            the colours sometimes drift:
                            lake-scarlet,
                                    madder (light or

deep),
      crimson, geranium,
            as the light varies, shifts.
                      So any phrase
or word
      murmured, then heard
            may quaver, resonate
                  of what we are,
what is
      and not what was
            or may.
            Tell me you hear
                  that you do know
that it is so.
      Do not forsake.
            Say yes, not no."

3. Sheddings

"sun-baked"

. . . out of the mud, the clay, the river – shaped, sun-baked –
their tablets have survived – impressed, incised –

each imprint, marking words –
signalling syllables – a story told

of how the familiar pain returned –
the bruise, unease that would not heal –

thinking he might rewrite the scripted code,
grasp water, gather up the wind,

and Siduri knew she could do no more
than wish him well in his folly, point his way,

but when he returned at last it was by another road –
voiding his footprints – as if he had forgotten her . . .

"reshape"

. . . who went, who would
        reshape, reshake the dice . . .

"flakes"

saluting:
        "Tout bouge!"
said Tinguely, ". . . nothing's fixed . . .
don't be intimidated . . . make design
open to what's possible . . . contrive
not to predict . . ."

as flakes
that scatter from an anvil
may reveal, surprise
with patterns, chimings
that drift, that resonate,

who shed his words
                    ". . . all shifts . . .
don't freeze the moment . . ."

                                        "making / taking"

. . . making a transit,
    taking in the sights . . .

                                              "faked"

. . . not to be faked: old diary found,
date, number, name, street, door, and stench
of one I knew – on as good a day as any, good a place –
with herring gulls screaming above, the sun diffused,

up broken stairs to find
sprawled flat on back, eyes fixed,
lips gaping, mustard pale,
empty of breath –
                    and jest of it
that after so long arriving
such drama to depart –

whose voice was "ohmihgod" to pace each day, absurdly gasping,
snorting, fumbling, bed to chair to table back to bed, and
"ohmihgod", those crumbling bones and failing heart, arthritis,
cataracts, a stroke and "ohmihgod" one final wheeze then silence

but for the echoes in my ears repeating,
needing no gloss, no shaping pen . . .

                                                    "break"

. . . break, break,
    reject . . .

★   ★   ★   ★

                                                    "caked"

. . . till caked with silt of years,
accretions of desire,
dust of regret –
to linger, weary,
swerve, digress

                                                    "naked"

. . . strip down,
plunge in, rinse free, be rid –
thrust to an utterance beyond mere choice –
with one full breath inhaled, expelled,
all moorings loosened, cut,
escaping harbour walls,
naked as once . . .

"forsaken"

. . . then for what's used
    and thrown away –
the old and rumpled
    and the strayed,
the pale and crumpled
    and the torn,
the chipped and battered
    and the worn,
the rusty and forsaken
    and unwanted –
may some sort of grace
    be granted
and a gathering place . . .

"keepsake"

. . . who went
with only the treasons of memory
    as keepsake . . .

13 June 2004

The going

"The going is harder"
he advised me
"as one gets older."
I didn't believe him.
After all, he was old
and the old are like that.

Now I find it easier
if only to believe him.
Much easier. And the going
not downhill, as advertised.
No descent beckons.
One doesn't get "past it".
The real climb
comes toward the end.

For an Old Friend, Beyond the Grave

You firmly held, to your parting breath
that the spirit lives on after death

while my bet was for oblivion where
by definition none may be aware

and thus it seems your wager's best
implying as it does this final jest

that in heaven above or hell below
if you've got it right we both shall know

but with no shared laugh or rueful grin
if both unknowing I should win

National Poetry Day

"Transform your life with poetry"
the card said, and briefly I fussed
that this overestimated the effect
until I remembered how it had thrust
several old friends,
plus near and dear,
into distress and penury,
how even I, without the dust
of its magic, might have achieved
peace of mind, even success,
so maybe the advice is just,
a sort of timely
Health Warning from the Ministry
of Benevolence
at the Scottish Book Trust.

Observed at N.E. Corner of
Bank Street and Royal Mile

Hmm . . . there it is,
not obviously tomb:
the presence on a pedestal
of more than lifesize
human male
who ponders
ponderously (as I do here),
draped in a sheet
discreetly, toga I presume,
as metaphor and emblem for
some classic mode
appropriate to whom?

With right hand balancing
upon his knee
an unmarked something:
building slab or doorstep?
mystery box (no obvious lid)?
Brobdingnagian domino?
if book, unreadable.
Certainly weighty, poised
in a pose above four letters
H U M E:

our David,
I assume,
just sitting there,
who thinks.
To make us think?
Well, it does
make you think,
wonder at least.
Yes, hmmm . . .

The Great Grand-Daughter of Sine Reisedeach Reports to her Cousin in Australia

The red deer are fenced off
to protect the trees,
which grow dense,
shutting out the light, the view.
Wool and meat come from elsewhere,
like everything, and the sheep
are only kept to attract subsidy,
like the poets. No one dies,
just passes away but not at home.
Everything is available,
even counselling. Many islands
are not islands any more. The young
have instant access and complain
it is not instant enough
while the old, as ever,
just complain.

Five Resonances / Echoes from Apollinaire

A trumpet sounds
across the far shadows of thought
but those battles are past
and the memories
in unmarked graves.
Or could it be the trick
of some forgotten enemy,
setting another ambush?

Love swallows wise and stupid
with one flash of the eye,
quick as the tongue of a toad
gulping a fly.

The mouse of time
nibbles away my days.
I set a trap of words
and wait
            but hope
is feeble bait.

I was on my way to be buried.
There was no coffin
and no mourners.
Even you had stayed away
but suddenly after all those years
I heard your voice again
speaking my name
clearly, which was strange,
even for a dream,
since it meant nothing.

I've swept the leaves.
Autumn's done. Remember
we'll not see each other
ever again. What more?
Or less? The wind stirs.
We wait. Don't forget.

These Transits
All That's Given
What's Here

where even the sun might weary

as if an alchemy

erasing and compounding

through the surf of time

resounding as on a shore

surprising us with moments

realised only in parting

we try but cannot grasp

between what was and will be

pacing each fall of leaf

across the tidal years

may waken our delight

can yet confound what might.

could outreach our sight.

each day alike, unlike

we would but can't inhabit

in exile from where we are

entrusting us with absence

Since

Go on, you don't mean
twenty?
I don't believe.
How could?

Perhaps moments?
lifetimes?

Since I was,
you were,
and we,
in the plural,
met, past tense,
historic,
and years.

That many?

But seriously,
you're probably right.

Serious stuff,
time.

July 2003

Not to Forget

that not to forget
is not necessarily to remember
or rather to remember
is more than just not to forget

for though we may forget
to remember it is impossible
(though we may attempt it)
to remember to forget

what? which is not just
a twist of words (if forgettable)
but expressive of distinctions
because to remember can be a choice,

an intention later accomplished
while to forget will have happened
when we realise it, when perhaps
we try to remember and cannot

if not necessarily irrevocably
as a memory may return,
wanted or regretted,
perhaps unforgettable

or, after forgetting,
just remembered again.

Do you . . .

(after Jacques Charpentreau)

Do you see who dodges away,
disappearing into the blue?
That is life, on its way,
    dancing beyond you.

Do you feel a breath tease
your cheek, stir the grass, lift the dew?
That is time, like the breeze,
    having fun with you.

Do you hear singing, a choir
of echoing voices, promising anew?
Relax. That is only desire
    playing tricks with you.

Do you sense at your elbow
an old friend but can't guess who?
That is death, faithful shadow,
    laughing with you.

Into Harbour

My voyage over,
you can lash me fast
to my final mooring
and nail to the mast:
"Don't disturb. Enjoying
a good kip at last."

Some Afterwords

A poem, once made, must speak for itself. The hopes, ideas, difficulties or circumstances of its maker may be of curiosity but are in the end, irrelevant.

Most persons, however, are curious about other people and in our response to a poem we often experience, even intensely, something that is akin to what is called in other contexts 'personality'. There is the understandable conviction that this sense of a 'person' speaking to us in the poem must have connection with the person who assembled the words.

Yet other experience tells us that this connection is not straightforward, that a poem in which we may take delight or which we may find engaging, may be written by someone we find unpleasant or even tedious. And there is the sense in which all poems are fictions, even when the 'I' of the poem may appear to be that of the maker. Thus what a writer may say about his connection with what he has written needs to be read with caution.

I am aware of a lack of consistency over the course of time in regard to my own ideas about the construction of poems, even, in the words of the Catechism, of that 'chief end'. Some were written for my own interest, at least initially. Others specifically for a public context. Others to complement set rhythms or patterns, or constructed from or upon the words of other men or women. Some are based on single images, some on the relationships of a multiplicity. Some, which I would not wish to disown, jests and ballads, are more appropriate to the spoken occasion than the printed page. Some, now mostly fallen away, were written in the mistaken notion that I might impress or inform the world.

I have often had the wish that I might have been born into another age and had the fortune to be court poet, *makar* or *skald*, to a minor chief or lord, called upon to provide poems for particular occasions, to celebrate, to mourn, even to castigate or to jest, finding voice for public and private experience, in a context which could be defined. What context there is for a poet today, at least in what is known as 'the West', seems mostly bound up with the words 'literature' and 'culture', much annexed by universities and arts councils. Committees decide who shall receive grants, examination papers are even set and there are obviously those who are able to relate their poems to such a context.

There is also the point of view expressed by a recent commentator: '. . . that every poet's task is ultimately and essentially, if not mythopoeic, at any rate religious; and that it is dangerous for any poet to think otherwise.' We must make our choices as best we can.

I have in the past committed to print, sometimes rashly in retrospect, and to notebooks for my own use, various speculations as to what I thought poetry, even my own, was 'about'. A few quotations may give a background of intention if not always of result, which may be of curiosity and can be ignored if not.

'. . . the form of a poem must be of positive use – and it may be that it functions more in the making than in the result . . . Where certain words, or in certain places, are "given", then the final result is not entirely dependent on our choice, except for that initial design . . . The "free form" suggests nothing . . . it is a much harder "form" in which to write something that is verbally and conceptually interesting.'

'. . . the most rigorous distinction between Fancy and Imagination . . . between Fable and Vision, need not deny that one may open upon the other.'

'Recurrence, Resonance, Reassertion, Refrain – yet with Variety, Variation – these are all words that carry something of what makes verse characteristic – the mind takes pleasure in these – "To get into the rhythm of something" . . . is to get into harmony with it – these are also terms to do with the activity of living our lives – so equally they are terms we use in thinking about poetry and its structure . . .'

'. . . in writing [a poem] . . . when we speak of something, we affect it . . . The very language we use is not "mine" but only "ours" . . . as what is "said" is shaped by meanings which are in the pattern . . . which perhaps we discover as much as create.'

'. . . clarity and concision; but these are dead without cogency, and it is the cogency of an individual in a living situation which provides the greatest urgency. I would like to write poems which combine astonishment that a poem should be so, with astonishment that anyone might suppose that it could be otherwise.'

From an appreciation of another poet: '. . . many pleasures, but chiefly these: the conviction of direct knowledge of physical experience and: an unfailing devotion to the poem as a construction of words to be both said and heard.'

'. . . many sorts of interest which a poem may have but without an essential grain of delight in language and in the possibilities of utterance, I believe that it [the writing and reading] is all in vain.'

Gael Turnbull, 1992.

Author's Notes to the poems

Saga poems (p.51 et seq): These are free interpretations based on existing translations. 'Bjarni': from the *Weaponfirthers' Saga*. 'Gunnar' and 'Valgard' from *Njal's Saga*. 'Gudrun': from the *Laxdaela Saga*. 'The Author': from an incident in the *Greenlanders' Saga*.

'An Irish Monk on Lindisfarne, About 650 AD' (p.63): Lindisfarne, now Holy Island, is off the coast of Northumberland and connected to the mainland at low tide. Irish monks, by way of Iona in Scotland, founded a monastery there in 635 AD. 'Dryshod' is not exactly accurate but you can walk across.

'At Mareta' (p.125): The name is a convenient fiction, if not the place.

'Twenty Words, Twenty Days' (p.133-152): The days, of no prior significance, happened to be those from 17 November to 6 December, 1963. The word for each day was picked from a large dictionary by an entirely random method. The subtitle of the original publication was: 'A Sketchbook & A Morula'. The word *maieutic*, which occurred, expressed one of the things I had hoped to achieve.

'I, Maksoud' (p.179): It is of course impossible to know the exact number of man-hours involved but it would have been in the range of the average working life of one man in 1540 AD. Maksoud (or Maqsud) was probably the master weaver who supervised the work.

'Riel' (p.181): Louis Riel was the leader of the Métis in the troubles in the west of Canada in 1870 and 1885 as settlers moved in to displace the mostly French speaking and fur trading population. He was eventually hanged for rebellion at Regina in 1886.

'John Bunyan: Of Grace' (p.182-3): Most of the phrases and images are from his spiritual autobiography *Grace Abounding*.

'An Invocation' (p.201-203): This is one casting or occurrence, as valid as any other, of a more extended construction which consists of 28 substantives and 112 modifying phrases, with multiple possibilities which may be used, with variation of pronouns, as love poem, as divination etc., even as threnody. [The author prepared this version, previously titled 'A Word / A Phrase', and published as such in *Scantlings* (1970), for his Canadian Selected Poems, *While Breath Persist*, in 1992.]

'Residues' (pp.222-245): The word to be understood in the sense both of 'the left overs' and 'what survives'. 'Down the Sluice of Time': no overall formal verbal structure. 'Thronging the Heart': though the effect may be subliminal, constructed on a system of pairs of words or phrases, recurring at alternating intervals of 3 and 5, back and forth between each 'side' or 'strand' and the other, and linking back upon itself in a continuous band.

'The Borders Revisited' (p.248): Since I composed this, Nisbet has apparently moved, or been moved, an eighth of a mile nearer the Jedburgh/Kelso road.

'The Last Fool: Berkeley Churchyard' (p.251): He was employed by the Duke of Suffolk. There are more lines to his epitaph but this gives the gist.

'It is There' (p.259): Composed for the programme of an original musical based on the Macbeth story: *The Real McCoy* by John Cooper.

'Scarcely I Speak' (pp.265-271): Egil's poem 'Sonatorrek' was composed about 980 AD in Iceland, in Old Norse, though was probably not written down until several generations later. His favourite son had been drowned in a sailing accident. He had lost another son and both his parents by illness and his brother in battle. *Hel* was the Goddess of Death. *Ymir* was the primeval giant from whose blood the sea was made. The God of the Sea was also the God of Brewing. The 'one eyed stranger' is, of course, Odin, who was Egil's personal God and also the God and giver of poetry. This version is based on other translations and follows the 'argument' of the original, stanza by stanza. It was not merely permissible to seek retribution for injury but a positive moral duty.

From the Language of the Heart (pp.292-305): These [. . .] were originally composed as if translations from previously undiscovered texts, and owe something, if tenuously, to Fr. Alan Macdonald's *Gaelic Words and Phrases from South Uist*.

Spaces (pp.306-313): The visual 'space' is, of course, merely a typographical indicator of what is more strictly a pause or hesitation, even a temporary dislocation of attention.

Texturalist Poems (pp.361-365, 447-459 & elsewhere): a reweaving of an existing text into another texture, previously only implicit. All the words and phrases, except for minor adjustments and connectives, are 'as given', then re-patterned. 'Coals' (p.361-3): from 'A Voyage Round Great Britain' by Richard Daniell. 'To Tell Us': from a series of letters from a friend. 'Josiah Spode' (p.339-40): from quotations in 'Spode's Willow Pattern & Other Designs after the Chinese' by Robert Copeland.

Editorial Notes

General note

Titles have been standardised in this edition, following the rule that only the first word should have an initial capital when the title is also the first line of the poem, or when the title repeats the initial words of the poem. Free-standing titles follow normal titling conventions. Wherever possible the poems have been presented in their original sequence, and in their place of first publication. Where a later revision has been used, that fact is noted on the following pages, and the source given.

Trio

'Socrates', p.26: revision from *A Gathering of Poems* (1983).

'Love Poem 1' p.32: revision in manuscript dating from ca. mid-1970s. The revision was simply titled 'I walk away', presumably because it was intended to be republished without its companion poem here. In view of the fact that the two poems are printed together in this edition, we have retained the original titling.

'Inscription for a Mirror', p.34: revision from *A Libation* (1963).

'Ballade', p.35: revision from *A Gathering of Poems*. The original title of this poem was 'Oh Yes'.

'Industrial Valley', p.39: line 7 of the original version has a comma after the word "chisel", which we have read as a typographical error.

'A Song', p.42: revision from *A Gathering of Poems*.

The Knot in the Wood

'Thanks', p.43: revision from *While Breath Persist* (1992).

'In Memory of George Orwell', p.45: revision from *A Gathering of Poems* (1983).

'The Sensualist', p.47: revision from *A Trampoline* (1968).

'He may wander far', p.47; 'A Dying Man', p.48; 'And what if', p.49: revisions from *A Gathering of Poems*.

Bjarni

'Bjarni, Spike-Helgi's Son', p.51; 'Gunnar, from his burial mound', p.54; 'Valgard, called the guileful . . .', p.55; 'Gudrun', pp.59-61; 'The Author. . .', p.62; 'An Irish Monk on Lindisfarne . . .', pp.63-5; 'Suzanne Bloch in a Billiard Room', p.67: revisions from *A Gathering of Poems* (1983).

Libation

'A Libation', p.68; 'Black Spruce, Northern Ontario', p.70: revisions from *A Trampoline*.
'You Said I Should' p.71: revision from *A Gathering of Poems* (1983).

Uncollected (1949-1960)

'A Chorus (of sorts) for Tess', p.81; this early poem (the date of composition is uncertain) is an early version of what was eventually to become 'Suzanne Bloch in a Billiard Room' (see p. 67). The original is offered here as an example of how Gael Turnbull's poems could change over time. See also 'If a Glance Could Be Enough' (p.253-5) and 'Transits' (p.460-467) for another such development.

With Hey, Ho . . .

A Round', p.86: revision from later, undated manuscript.
'Now That April's Here', p.88: revision from *While Breath Persist* (1992).

To You I Write

'They have taken', p.91: revision from *A Gathering of Poems* (1983).
'I Look Into', pp.118-9; 'You and I', p.120: revisions from *A Trampoline* (1968).

A Very Particular Hill

'A Hill', pp.122-3: revision from *A Trampoline* (1968).
'At Mareta', pp.125-6: revision from *A Gathering of Poems* (1983).
'The Mind Turns', p.127: revision from *A Trampoline*.
'A Western', p.128: revision from *Scantlings* (1970).
'At the Mineshaft . . .', p.129; 'Death Valley', p.130; 'George Fox, From His Journals', pp.131-2: revisions from *A Gathering of Poems*. The original title of this last poem was 'George Fox (1624-1691), from his Journals'.

Twenty Words, Twenty Days, p.133-152: text from *A Gathering of Poems* (1983). Comparisons were also made with the versions published in *A Trampoline*, *While Breath Persist* and *Etruscan Reader 1* (excerpts only in the latter case) when arriving at the layout used here.

Briefly

'The Ever-Presence', p.155: This poem was reformatted as a 'Spaces'-style poem for publication in *While Breath Persist* (1992). The variant printed here is taken from a still later manuscript and is carved on the headstone of the author's grave.

'Not piecework', p.156: revision from *A Gathering of Poems* (1983).
'Two Jibes', p.157: The first of these two poems is a revised version from *Scantlings* (1970); the second was republished in *A Gathering of Poems* (1983) as 'A Jibe'.
'Rightly', p.158: revision from *Scantlings*.

A Trampoline
'The Sierra Nevada' (p.173): revision from *A Gathering of Poems* (1983).
'For a Friend' (p.174): an earlier version, titled 'A Confession', published in the *Beloit Poetry Journal*, carries a dedication to William Carlos Williams.
'By Auction in a Marquee in the Grounds', pp.177-8: revision from *A Gathering of Poems*.

I, Maksoud
'I, Maksoud', and 'A sea-stone', p.179; 'For a Jazz Pianist', p.180; 'John Bunyan of Grace', p.182: revisions from *A Gathering of Poems* (1983).
'Walls', pp.185-191: revision from *Scantlings* (1970).

Scantlings
'Six Country Pieces', pp.197-8: originally 'Seven from Stifford's Bridge'; this revision is from *A Gathering of Poems* (1983).
'Cigolando', p.200: revised version from *A Gathering of Poems*.
'For Us: An Invocation and Processional', pp.201-203: originally 'A Word / A Phrase'; this substantially shortened version is taken from *While Breath Persist* (1992). Notes in the author's files specifically state that this version should replace the original in any subsequent compilation of his work.

Finger Cymbals
'A Meagre Song', p.208; 'Amber Toad', pp.213-4: revisions from *A Gathering of Poems*.

A Random Sapling
'A random sapling', p,219: revision from *A Gathering of Poems*.
'A Regret', p.219: revision from a later manuscript, published posthumously in *Chapman*.

Residues
'Down the Sluice of Time', pp.222-241: revision from *While Breath Persist* (1992).
'Thronging the Heart', pp.242-245: revision from *Etruscan Reader 1* (1997).

If a Glance Could Be Enough

'There's more', p.247: Orignally titled 'These Dances'; this revision is from *A Gathering of Poems* (1983).

'Aurora', p.252: this poem was later published without its title as part of *A Winter Journey* (1987). The title is retained here in view of the fact that the poems in *A Winter Journey*, whenever republished elsewhere, were given titles by the author.

Uncollected (1971-1980)

'Some Resonances and Speculations' (p.275-9): This sequence was written for the opening of an exhibition of paintings by Melville Hardiment in Saffron Walden, in 1979.

Rain in Wales

'Wulstan' (p.290-1) first appeared in a single-poem publication in 1975 but we felt it belonged here rather than on its own at an earlier point in the collection.

From the Language of the Heart

'It Can Happen' and 'It was', p.295; 'No', p.296; "As the wind', p.297; 'And I Think It Yours', p.298; 'It is not', p.301: all are revisions from *For Whose Delight* (1995). 'Your Hands, Their Touch', p.305, was officially first published in *For Whose Delight* but had previously been included by the author as a holograph poem in the 1985 limited signed edition of *From the Language of the Heart*. The sequence of the poems here is as in the 1985 Gnomon Press edition, with the holograph poem at the end. This edition carried the subtitle 'Some Imitations from the Gaelic of Sine Reisedeach'.

A Winter Journey

The complete book has been excluded in accordance with the author's wishes – his dissatisfaction with the volume is recorded several times in papers found in his files. The five poems rescued from it here (pp.314-8), in addition to 'Aurora' (p.252), are three poems with titles, later republished in *While Breath Persist* (1992), and two untitled poems later republished in *Etruscan Reader 1* (1997). We have taken the republication of these poems to indicate the author's wish to preserve them, notwithstanding his negative feelings concerning the book from which they are drawn.

Uncollected (1981-1990)

'A Tight-Rope Act' p.319; 'A Trapeze Act', p.320: both poems, and three others – later collected in *While Breath Persist* and *For Whose Delight* – were printed in the limited-edition collection, *Circus* (1984), with prints by Pamela Scott.

While Breath Persist
'A Clown' p.331; A Voltige Act', p.335: these poems first appeared in the limited-edition *Circus* (1984), with prints by Pamela Scott.
'The Slater', p.332: revision from *For Whose Delight* (1995). The poem was titled 'The Woodlouse' in *While Breath Persist* (1992).
'As from a Kiln', p.333: this poem appeared in the 'From the Language of the Heart' section of *While Breath Persist* but does not appear in either of the two published collections of that name.
'At MacDiarmid's Grave', p.333: this is the title used in *For Whose Delight*. The original title is 'Langholm: MacDiarmid's Grave'.

For Whose Delight
'For whose delight', p.353: this poem first appeared in the limited-edition *Circus* (1984), with prints by Pamela Scott.
'Though we must have coals', p.361: the first of these two poems appeared under the same main title, but with the addition of the year 1813, in *While Breath Persist* (1992).
'Impellings', pp.366-383: revised text on pp.366-376 (up to 'in a filament...') drawn from the anthology *A State of Independence* (ed. Tony Frazer, Stride, Exeter, 1998); the remainder is unchanged.

A Rattle of Scree
'Definitions', p.389: revision from an later, undated typescript.

Might a Shape of Words
'Wandering onto a beach', p.412: there is a minor revision in the second paragraph – authority is an amendment in the author's hand in a copy of the book.

Uncollected Transmutations
The first twenty-two of these poems (pp.421-430) were collected by the author in 2003 in a pamphlet titled *At Least Once*, printed privately as "a supplement to *Transmutations* and *Might a Shape of Words*".

Uncollected (1990-1999)
'A Perception of Ferns, p.439: this poem was composed as an installation piece, each phrase being placed around a pool in the Kibble Palace, in Glasgow's Botanic Gardens. The text was printed in mirror image so

that it could only be read through the reflections in the pool. The form of the poem is of course driven by its intended location. Most of the author's performance and installation works have been excluded from this collection – as being too difficult to represent on the page – but we have made an exception for this poem, which was also printed in the form of a tiny pamphlet, with folding pages, by Essence Press in 2003.

from lazy blue flowers (p.459): The poem was commissioned by Litfest Lancaster as part of a project to renovate the Storey Institute as the Creative Industries Centre and was published in a booklet *The Storey's Story* in 2004, which was dedicated to Gael Turnbull. The author's accompanying note to the poem reads: 'This text is derived from a variety of sources, using the original expressions as far as practical, including some by Thomas Storey himself.' It was the last poem he wrote.

'Transits' pp.460-467. This poem was left incomplete at the author's death; the version of Part 3 presented here has been extracted from the enclosures to a letter to Peter Makin, dated 13 June 2004, after comparison with other typescripts in the author's files. Notes in the author's hand indicate that at least one further 'stanza' was required to complete this third section, and that a further 'stanza' – presumably still unwritten, as no trace of it appears in the author's files – was to have been inserted at the point on p.466 where the asterisks appear. The text also uses re-uses part of the poem 'If a Glance Could Be Enough', which can be found on pp.253-5. A further note in the author's letter to Peter Makin clearly indicates that the "tag-words" – those to the right, before each section, were to be removed in a final published version. However, we have opted to retain them here, in view of the fact that the poem as a whole was still unfinished at the time of the author's death.

Index of Titles

Title	Page	Title	Page
A Beast	90	A Regret	219
A bird	422	A Riddle for Jill	330
A Birth	299	A Round	86
A Bit Part: from Chekhov	432	A scar closes a wound	79
A blind musician	292	A Sea Story	204
A blindfold	158	A sea-stone	179
A boy is amazed	413	A snowstorm	427
A Breath of Autumn	116	A Song	42
A Cairn	357	A song	156
A Case	171	A Song	185
A Cat	358	A sparrow	401
A child lets go of its mother's hand	318	A spirited lady	425
A Chorus (of sorts) for Tess	81	A stye	311
A Clown	331	A Sun Dial	321
A Dictionary	348	A textured mist	221
A Dying Man	48	A Tight-Rope Act	319
A Fish-hook	69	A Trapeze Act	320
A Fragment of Truth	166	A very ingenious mechanism	400
A Girl	199	A Voice, Voices, Speaking	104
A Good Warfare	394	A Voltige Act	335
A Handkerchief with a Moral . . .	346	A Wedding Ring	307
A Hill	122	A Well Known Road	113
A kite	176	A Western	128
A Lady of Pleasure, The Netherbow	448	A Wild Joy	168
A Lamb	256	A wind from the north	315
A Landscape and a Kind of Man	36	A Winter Wedding	304
A Last Poem	313	A woman goes	417
A letter from	441	A woman has	418
A Letter, of Sorts	92	A young mother	413
A Libation	68	Accounts	312
A Little Kindling for John Christie	443	After	386
A long beat	405	After Catullus	184
A man stands waving	417	After many years	418
A man stops	420	All right	109
A man wakes	414	All the Blue: From the Director's	
A Marriage	310	Book of Josiah Spode	339
A Meagre Song	208	All Those Good Fellows	444
A memoir	429	Almost Lost Poem	334
A Painting of Beatrice Sforza	66	Also	384
A Perception of Ferns	439	Always so sure	411
A Place Called Gefryn	328	Amber Toad	213
A Poem Containing	360	An Accident	169
A Poem is a Pearl	41	An Actress	175
A Portrait	76	An Apology	80
A Racing Walker	331	An evening of conversation	421
A random sapling	219	An idiot child	406
A Reflecting Telescope	261	An Irish Monk on Lindisfarne	63

An old man sitting	409	Counsel	34
An Òran (The Song)	387	Daft about	282
And I Think it Yours	298	Dandelion Seeds	209
And what I thought	89	Dark Ages carving of a creature . . .	348
And what if	49	Dawn over the City	46
Anywhere they can be found	408	Death Valley	130
As a stone skittering	402	December Leaves	391
As from a Kiln	333	Deciding	412
As it happened	423	Definitions	389
As kelp	292	Derelict, City Morgue	73
As recently as	403	Did you really	404
As the wind	297	Didn't ask	158
Aspects	31	Do not be deterred	455
At certain moments	427	Do you . . .	477
At least once	421	Don't Know Blues	110
At MacDiarmid's Grave	333	Done speaking	153
At Mareta	125	Driving (A Litany)	84
At the Mineshaft of a Ghost Town	129	Edge of Air	257
At the university	404	Edinburgh	311
At Witley Court	207	Edinburgh	350
Aurora	252	85th Birthday Greetings	434
Awakening	419	Either way (after Bridget Riley)	347
Awakening	416	Enough	43
Babylon	280	Epitaph	37
Ballad	281	Erskine of Linlathen	395
Ballade	35	Estuaries	401
Bass Rock	384	Even One Day	325
Be So	155	Even the Sun	303
Beginnings	306	Every evening	414
Beneath	338	Everyone was there	283
Better than was	449	Excavation	40
Bjarni Spike Helgi's Son	51	First loves	300
Black Spruce, Northern Ontario	70	Five Resonances / Echoes	472
Boys in the Street	46	Five/Four Time	206
Briefly	153	For a Chinese Flute	215
Burning juniper	399	For a Friend	174
Butterfly	312	For a Jazz Pianist	180
Buzzard	356	For an Anniversary	117
By Auction in a Marquee	177	For an Old Friend, Beyond the Grave	469
By the Tweed	335	For André Breton 100 Years . . .	435
Calvinism	346	For Gaston	82
Checking	416	For months, determined	406
Cigolando	200	For Shari	309
Citizen	31	For Us: An Invocation and	
Clutter	403	a Processional	201
Coal Mine	306	For Whose Delight	353
Comic Relief	355	For You, Once Enemy	389
Conundrum Blues	83	*from lazy blue flowers*	459
Could it be	249	From the Equator to the Pole	450

From the Sanskrit	309	In Reference to our Being	457
Garioch Dead	321	In the corner of	407
George Fox, from his Journals	131	In the silence	199
Going South	352	Industrial Valley	39
Going to school	415	Information	344
Gone	385	Inscription for a Mirror	34
Great Aunt	324	Into Harbour	478
Gudrun, old and blind, to Bolli	59	Into the chasm	316
Gunnar, from his burial mound	54	Inventory	200
Happiest	221	Is there anything left	107
He and She	117	Islands	436
He explained	422	It Can Happen	295
He had desired her	424	It can happen	430
He had rehearsed	421	It is late afternoon and already dark	314
He hears that	408	It is not	301
He may wander far	47	It is there	259
He reported	429	It was	295
He was someone	423	It was as if	414
He wishes	428	It's a stubborn beast	401
Heard once	406	It's because	410
Herein described	451	It's been	250
Homage to Cid Corman	336	It's best we don't	415
Homage to Edwin Morgan	338	It's dark	193
Homage to Jean Follain	160	James Young Simpson	458
Homage to Jean Tinguely	323	Jeffrey to Cockburn 28 June 1832	454
Home again	424	John Bunyan: of Grace	182
Hommage à Cythera	183	June Nineteenth – Rosenbergs	
Hour of the Wolf	317	executed – Riots in East Berlin	74
How Could I Not	220	Just as I discover	405
How far?	112	Keeping	264
How I Did My Bit for Peace	284	Knarsdale	246
How in Sundry Sorts . . .	456	La Sainte Face (a painting by Rouault)	124
How much hurt	301	Lake	211
However	154	Lappings of day	405
I am the Scythe	264	Last curtain down	405
I look into	118	Learning to Breathe	167
I would speak of him	114	Leaving himself	428
I, Maksoud	179	Les Toits	163
I'm sorry	111	Lifetimes	393
If a Glance Could Be Enough	253	Lines for a Bookmark	23
If He Sings It	50	Lines for a Cynic	35
If I take a stone	302	Love is	293
If you ask	426	Love Poem 1	32
If you couldn't laugh	44	Love Poem 2	33
Impellings	366	Lumber Camp Railway	27
In a strange city	37	Make some	155
In Memoriam Norman MacCaig	388	Many years	418
In Memory of George Orwell	45	Maria	199
In my dream	421	May	41

Mid February, Snow on the Wind	218	Since	475
Might a shape	410	Six Country Pieces	197
Mornese	336	Sky Lights	347
Morningside Road	350	So the heart	115
My clothes fit.	422	Socrates	26
Nansen and Johansen	29	Some Resonances and Speculations	275
National Poetry Day	469	Something So Singular	329
National Trust	385	Somewhere between	419
Near Sloc Dubh, South Uist	387	Spaces	310
Never	262	Spiritual Researches	87
New Year	308	Standing here	425
Nightpiece, Pittsburgh	39	Staples	322
No	296	Started . . .	402
No Answer	349	Sunday Afternoon	161
No Instructions	169	Sureties	445
Not only	400	Surprised in a mirror	403
Not piecework	156	Suzanne Bloch in a Billiard Room	67
Not Sand	384	T'time in the Caucasus	348
Not to Forget	476	Taken severely ill	416
Nothing	434	Takings	334
Now That April's Here	88	Tea leaves	347
Nowhere	354	Thanks	43
Observed at N.E. Corner . . .	470	The Author, to Bjarni Herjulfsson	62
On the Somme	334	The Ballad of Rillington Place	397
One Hundred Years On	343	The Borders Revisited	248
One in a Multitude	83	The Daughter of Alasdair Ruadh	354
One word	159	The dissipations	293
Or So We Are Told	442	The dog next door	44
Perhaps	357	The Drunk	48
Perhaps	412	The Elements	326
Perhaps if I begin	98	The ever presence	155
Poetics (Genesis I, v.3)	349	The Fodder	307
Post-Mortem	25	The Galvanised Dustman	285
Rain in Wales	287	The Gates of Eden	345
Reading another man's	415	The girls	426
Refractories / The efficiency of . . .	447	The going	468
Remake	263	The Great Grand-Daughter of Sine	
Remarking	430	Reisedeach Reports to her Cousin	471
Residues	222	The inscription states	404
Retarded	426	The Kid	431
Riel	181	The Last Fool: Berkeley Churchyard	251
Rightly	158	The Look	78
Scarcely	411	The Mind Turns	127
Scarcely I speak	265	The Mistake	49
Searching through	422	The Moon	45
Seven Snapshots, Northern Ontario	195	The Nicing	440
She said	413	The Octopus Ride	75
She'll come	112	The only name	423
Simply	154	The Parthenon	349

The pitch of a voice	411	Twenty Words, Twenty Days	133
The Platitudes	327	Two Jibes	157
The Poetry Reading Poem	352	Two Tunes (for Roy)	85
The Priests of Paris	162	Unimaginable	425
The Real News	396	Valgard, called the guileful	55
The Ruin	300	Victoria Regina Imperatrix	164
The Scotch Asphodel	346	Walking	424
The scratching sound	170	Walls	186
The sea	410	Wandering into	428
The seeking	294	Wandering onto a beach	412
The Sensualist	47	Watching a Burning House at Night	251
The Sierra Nevada	173	Waves on the Shingle	258
The Slater	332	We celebrate	443
The small change	263	Well . . . (for Ian)	87
The Suicide	72	Went to Hell	220
The Sun	77	What Makes the Weeds Grow Tall	288
The Unwavering Sun	294	What may be	308
The Wind	89	When I pointed out	427
The Words	50	When I Said	388
The Words	438	When I said	407
The worst	425	When I Write to You:	
There are words	359	The Diapason Closing	364
There is	399	Where	156
There is no Why	216	Where the Wind Blows	217
There's more	247	Wherever	319
These rings	304	While looking	407
These Transits / All That's Given	474	Whin	390
They are everywhere	400	Why is	399
They have taken	91	William McTaggart	431
Thighs gripping	157	With Thanks and Homage	
This craving	402	to That Critic	351
This fear	401	Witley Court Revisited	260
This Rigmarole of Going On	433	Wreaths	386
Thorir of Garth, and Asdis	56	Wulstan	290
Though I Have Met with Hardship	453	Yes (1)	337
Though we must have coals (1813)	361	Yes (2)	337
Thoughts on the 183rd Birthday		Yes, sunshine	115
of J.M.W. Turner	165	You and I	120
Time is	272	You and I	286
To all the Gods	392	You are	273
To be shaken	121	You can still see it there	430
To Tell Us	341	You Said I Should	71
To the Point for Once	24	You won't find the name	421
To the Tune of Annie Laurie	342	You're right	249
To think here	113	Your Hands, Their Touch	305
Town and City	274		
Transits: A Triptych	460		
Try Again	23		
Twentieth Century	30		

ml

MAY 2010